Genocide Perspectives V

A Global Crime, Australian Voices

Edited by
Nikki Marczak and Kirril Shields

Australian Institute for
Holocaust and Genocide Studies

UTS ePRESS

PUBLICATION INFORMATION

UTS ePRESS
University of Technology Sydney
Sydney NSW 2007
AUSTRALIA
epress.lib.uts.edu.au

Copyright Information

This book is copyright. The work is licensed under a Creative Commons
Attribution-Non Commercial-Non Derivatives License CC BY-NC-ND

http://creativecommons.org/licenses/by-nc-nd/4.0/

First Published 2017
© 2017 in the text and images, the author/s of each article
© 2017 in the original cover artwork, Torunn Higgins
© 2017 in the book design and layout, Emily Gregory and UTS ePRESS

Publication Details

DOI citation: http://dx.doi.org/10.5130/978-0-9945039-7-8
Title: Genocide Perspectives V: A Global Crime, Australian Voices
/ Nikki Marczak & Kirril Shields, editors.
ISBN: 9780994503978 (ebook) ISBN: 9780994503985 (paperback)
Subjects: Genocide. Genocide--Sociological aspects. Genocide--Political aspects.
Crimes against humanity.

Published with the systems, support and expertise of Infogrid Pacific

UTS ePRESS
Manager: Julie-Anne Marshall
Books Editor: Matthew Noble
Designer: Emily Gregory

Enquiries: utsepress@uts.edu.au

OPEN ACCESS
UTS ePRESS publishes peer reviewed books, journals and conference proceedings
and is the leading publisher of peer reviewed open access journals in Australasia. All
UTS ePRESS online content is free to access and read.

Dedicated to Professor Colin Tatz, AO

Founder of the Australian Institute for Holocaust and Genocide Studies
and the *Genocide Perspectives* series

Dedicated to Professor Colin...

CONTENTS

Acknowledgements　vii

PART 1 – TRIBUTE

Nikki Marczak and Kirril Shields
Introduction　2

Douglas Booth
Colin Tatz: "Compelled to Repair a Flawed World"　5

PART 2 – AUSTRALIA

Anna Haebich
Reflecting on the *Bringing Them Home Report*　26

John Maynard
Genocide by Any Other Name　43

Jennifer Balint
Too Near and Too Far: Australia's Reluctance to Name and Prosecute Genocide　51

PART 3 – CASE STUDIES

Michael Robertson, Edwina Light, Wendy Lipworth and Garry Walter
Psychiatry, Genocide and the National Socialist State: Lessons Learnt, Ignored and Forgotten　69

Konrad Kwiet and George Weisz

First do Harm! A Medical Experiment on Australian Prisoners of War and the Career of a Military Physician   90

Geoffrey Robertson QC

100 Year Commemoration of the Armenian Genocide, April 24, 2015 - Sydney Town Hall Speech   105

Nikki Marczak

The Early Days: Illuminating Armenian Women's Experiences   113

Annie Pohlman

Finding a Way: Women's Stories of Daily Survival after the 1965 Killings in Indonesia   131

The Honourable Michael Kirby AC CMG

North Korea: Genocide or Not?   146

PART 4 – CULTURE AND MEMORY

Tony Barta

Realities, Surrealities and the Membrane of Innocence   161

Kirril Shields

Through German Eyes: Amateur Photos and Trans-Generational Renegotiations of the Holocaust   175

Deborah Mayersen

Faith After Genocide   192

Winton Higgins

Can the American Alliance Stop Colluding in Genocide?   207

Colin Tatz

Teaching about Genocide   230

Biographies   246

Index   251

ACKNOWLEDGEMENTS

To our colleagues at the Australian Institute for Holocaust and Genocide Studies, the editing of *Genocide Perspectives V* has been an unexpected adventure for us and we thank you for the opportunity, your advice and support.

In particular, we would like to thank Winton Higgins for his work on *Genocide Perspectives V*, his insight and wit, and his (strong yet diplomatic, and always evidence-based) opinions on matters ranging from global inaction on genocide, to the metaphysical habits of thought created by inappropriately used capital letters.

To Sandra Tatz—our colleague at the Institute and Colin's lifelong partner—we recognise the indelible relationship between you and Colin. This volume is dedicated to you as much as it is to him.

Part 1
Tribute

INTRODUCTION

Nikki Marczak and Kirril Shields

As two of the newest members of the Australian Institute for Holocaust and Genocide Studies, we are humbled to have been entrusted with the editing of *Genocide Perspectives V*, the Institute's official publication. This, the fifth volume in the series, features Australian scholarship on genocide with essays written by established and well-known authors, as well as emerging scholars. The volume has also given contributors the chance to reflect on Professor Colin Tatz's significant contribution to Genocide Studies and his influence on their own paths and chosen areas of study.

In the early stages of developing this book, Tony Barta suggested *Genocide Perspectives V* be made a *Festschrift* to Colin. We felt this was perfect timing and the right volume to dedicate in his honour. Contributors agreed; Douglas Booth and Jennifer Balint had been discussing the idea of a book dedicated to Colin, and many others felt compelled to write on topics inspired by Colin's own work.

In recent years, Colin Tatz has released *The Magnitude of Genocide* (co-authored with Winton Higgins), his memoir, *Human Rights and Human Wrongs*, and his latest book, *Australia's Unthinkable Genocide* (published May 2017). At age 83, the speed at which Colin writes puts both of us, many decades his junior, to shame. His eloquence, ability to reach audiences, and original thinking remain a source of admiration for friends, family and colleagues alike. It is with a sense of the utmost respect and gratefulness shared by all contributors that we dedicate this volume of *Genocide Perspectives*, a publication he founded, to Colin.

The first essay is a piece by Douglas Booth, who has been able to fulfil his longstanding goal to write about Colin as a teacher, scholar and activist. The essay includes comments from several of Colin's colleagues. Readers who are familiar with Colin's work will see much truth in Doug's essay, and we hope it introduces Colin as a truly inspirational figure in the study of genocide and human rights to those who do not know him.

Influenced by Colin's work on Aboriginal issues, Anna Haebich, John Maynard and Jennifer Balint write on aspects of genocide in Australian history through different and complementary lenses. Anna reflects on *Bringing Them*

Home 20 years after the landmark Human Rights Commission report focused the nation's attention on the Stolen Generations and the legacy of forced removal of children. John Maynard discusses statements from journalists, government officials and other prominent people from the late 1800s and early 1900s in which the genocidal treatment of Aboriginal communities was explicitly acknowledged (though the term "genocide" had not yet been coined), and provides a personal view on the early work of Aboriginal rights activists including his own grandfather, Fred Maynard. Australia's refusal to grapple with its own history of genocide, and its poor record of prosecuting war criminals who settled in Australia, is explored by Jennifer Balint.

Essays discussing two of the "core" genocides of the twentieth century, the Holocaust and the Armenian Genocide, present new research and fresh perspectives. Michael Robertson, Edwina Light, Wendy Lipworth and Garry Walter write on psychiatry under the Nazi regime, highlighting lessons learnt and ignored, and analysing the continuing relevance of the Holocaust to medical ethics today. In a case study of the Nazis' use of medical experiments, Konrad Kwiet, a stalwart of Holocaust Studies in Australia, and his co-author George Weisz, present newly discovered evidence of medical experiments conducted on Australian prisoners of war by Nazi doctors.

Geoffrey Robertson QC has generously allowed us to publish the powerful speech he gave at Sydney's Armenian Genocide Commemoration Ceremony for the 100th Anniversary of the genocide in April 2015. Nikki Marczak, who presented at that year's commemoration event in Melbourne, sheds light on how women were affected during the early stages of the Armenian Genocide. Another case study focusing on women, by Annie Pohlman, explores women's survival after the Indonesian mass killings and arrests of 1965–1966. Parallels between women's stories emerge clearly in those two essays. Also examining a case study from Asia, The Hon. Michael Kirby AC CMG presents an insider view of the situation in North Korea and questions whether the case constitutes genocide.

Several authors have taken a theoretical approach to their essays, asking profound questions about the nature of genocide and Genocide Studies, memory, legacy and the future of genocide prevention. Tony Barta analyses the (often competing) perspectives and prejudices within studies of genocide, reflecting on his own experiences and applying his concept of *surrealities* to genocide memory. Also tackling the complexity of genocide memory, Kirril Shields looks at how our understanding of the Holocaust is influenced and shaped by postmemory, exploring the legacy of Holocaust-era amateur photographs taken from a Nazi viewpoint. Deborah Mayersen's essay examines the issue of religious faith in the aftermath of genocide and adds a new dimension to that discussion by analysing genocide through the medium of graphic novels, one dealing with the Holocaust and two set in Rwanda.

On the factors contributing to genocide and the possibility of prevention, Winton Higgins expands on ideas raised in *The Magnitude of Genocide* concerning the culpability of the West, especially the United States, in fomenting genocides around the world, or failing to prevent them. Finally, we leave readers with the words of Colin himself, on the art of teaching about the Holocaust and genocide. A broad overview of his philosophy of teaching, the essay presents his personal views, developed over three decades, on the most effective multidisciplinary approaches to teaching how and why genocides occur, who contributes to them, the factors of racism, science and governance, and that insidious final stage of genocide, denialism.

COLIN TATZ: "COMPELLED TO REPAIR A FLAWED WORLD"

Douglas Booth

Genocide Perspectives V pays tribute to Colin Tatz, the founder of the journal, and its official host, the Australian Institute for Holocaust and Genocide Studies. In this article I outline Colin's path to becoming an internationally renowned scholar of genocide; I highlight his influence as a teacher and activist, and dissect the form of his scholarship. Colin's research interests in genocide and suicide may appear, on the surface, macabre and morbid, but I will reveal him as a committed humanist with a passion for life and remarkable verve and exuberance.

My father introduced me to Colin's work. He sent me several of Colin's newspaper articles on the politics of sport.[1] Those articles constituted a landmark in sports criticism in Australia.[2] My father also paved the way for correspondence that led to Colin supervising my PhD research (1989–1993) in which I investigated apartheid in South African sport and analysed the politics of the sports boycott. Colin was the consummate supervisor: available, organised, thoroughly engaged with the subject, insightful, sharing, firm, scholarly, a master communicator and raconteur, hospitable and generous. His greatest pedagogical gift—that I now offer my students—was urging me to present my own arguments. He explains this approach in *Race Politics in Australia*. Citing Doris Lessing who deplored the education system for stifling fresh thought and creativity, Colin wrote, "She asks (and I am with her), 'why don't you read what I have written and make up your own mind about what you think. . . . Never mind . . . Professors White and Black.' "[3] Our relationship continued and grew after I graduated and we co-authored several pieces.[4] Colin and I,

---

1 Between 1980 and 1983 Colin wrote 20 feature articles on sport, 19 for the *Australian* and one for the *Sydney Morning Herald*.

2 Colin advanced the concept in his inaugural professorial lecture at Macquarie University, "Race, Politics and Sport" (1983), which was published in the first edition of *Sporting Traditions* 1, no. 1 (1984), 2–36, the journal of the Australian Society for Sport History. For a recent elaboration, see Colin Tatz, "Transient Triumphalism: Oi, Oi, Oi–The Australian Way," *Griffith Review* 53 (2016), 228–36.

3 Colin Tatz, *Race Politics in Australia: Aborigines, Politics and Law* (Armidale: University of New England, 1979), i.

4 Douglas Booth and Colin Tatz, "South Africa: A Prisoner of History?" *Current Affairs Bulletin*

and our wives, Sandra and Gaye, have now enjoyed each other's company for nearly 30 years. Like many of the contributors to this volume, Gaye and I have watched, admired, appreciated and taken pleasure in the indefatigable and complete relationship between Colin and Sandra. We are privileged that they have included us in their lives.

I met Professor Colin Tatz in 1996 while he was head of the Centre for Comparative Genocide Studies at Macquarie University. Each time I heard him lecture, I was intrigued by his in-depth knowledge of the history and politics of genocide. I was inspired to join as a volunteer for the Centre that same year. Colin became a great mentor and an inspiration for me to research and write on the Armenian Genocide. When the Genocide Centre closed at Macquarie, Colin helped form the Australian Institute for Holocaust and Genocide Studies. We did not have a permanent office to hold our meetings, but Colin and Sandra opened their hearts and home for our monthly meetings (which included a home-cooked meal). I consider it a great honour and privilege to have been associated with an historian of his calibre and integrity—VICKEN BABKENIAN

The best of teachers. Enrolling in "The Politics of Genocide" at Macquarie University set me on the path I continue on today. Sitting with Colin as he supervised me in my Honours thesis in 1991 on the definitions of genocide opened my eyes to an expansive critical engagement with the world. His other students and I were so fortunate to have him as our guide that year. Colin's unwavering demanding ethic of social justice has been a beacon in this country. He has been a pathbreaker in so many fields. I constantly meet activists and academics who sing his praises. And even now when I meet with him and Sandra in their home he opens my eyes still further—JENNIFER BALINT

The making of a genocide scholar

Colin's journey to genocide scholar began as a young boy.[5] Growing up in Jo-

---

70, no. 6 (1993), 4–11; Douglas Booth and Colin Tatz, "Swimming With the Big Boys? The Politics of Sydney's 2000 Olympic Bid," *Sporting Traditions* 1, no. 1 (1994), 3–23; Douglas Booth and Colin Tatz, *One-Eyed: A View of Australian Sport* (Sydney: Allen and Unwin, 2000).

5   Colin offers several accounts of his journey to genocide scholar. See Colin Tatz, "Breaking the Membrane," in *Pioneers of Genocide Studies*, eds. Samuel Totten and Steven Jacobs (London: Transaction Publishers, 2002), 195–216; Colin Tatz, *With Intent to Destroy: Reflecting on Genocide* (London: Verso, 2003), 1–16; "Colin Tatz Explores Life as an Outsider Through Racial Discrimination," by Richard Fidler, ABC Radio, November

hannesburg, South Africa, on the eve of and during the Second World War, he first became aware of "social injustice" and that "something was particularly amiss for Jews"—and blacks. One cue recalled by Colin was the separation of Jewish and non-Jewish students at King Edward VII high school: "We were kept truly apart . . . with no explanation or justification."[6] This embryonic awareness launched a lifelong journey into the study of politics and race. The journey began in earnest with postgraduate studies at the University of Natal (MA, Public and Native Administration) and the Australian National University (PhD in Political Science and Public Administration); it proceeded to lectureships in politics and sociology at Monash University (where he also founded and directed the Centre for Research into Aboriginal Affairs, subsequently the Monash Indigenous Centre), and continued on to professorships in politics at the University of New England and Macquarie University. Genocide was not a prominent feature of Colin's journey until the mid-1980s when, following a series of visits to Yad Vashem (Israel's official memorial site and research centre on the Holocaust), his experiences, observations and analyses of racism "merge[d] into a stream of Holocaust consciousness."[7] After Yad Vashem, Colin began teaching the politics of genocide and launched the Centre for Comparative Genocide Studies at Macquarie University, subsequently the Australian Institute for Holocaust and Genocide Studies at the Shalom Institute, University of New South Wales. In this section I look at Colin's early life experiences in South Africa to which he attributes the "accretion of values" that laid the foundations for a lifelong anti-racism project; I then turn to the 1980s and 1990s during which Colin identified genocide as the "ultimate form of racism."[8]

Colin describes his early "socialisation" in South Africa as critical to his life direction and goals. He says that his early years were "beset by wars—against . . . family, empty ritual, solitariness, school bullies, street thugs, boxing opponents, Nazi hat makers"—and locates his first encounters with "race hatred, vilification [and] humiliation" in the private realm of the home. There he saw black servants constantly "berated, demeaned or dehumanised." "Indignation arose *within*, perhaps instinctively, but certainly viscerally" and he developed a deep empathy for victims. A Rubicon moment came in the mid-1940s. After witnessing a white man plough his car into a

---

29, 2011, http://www.abc.net.au/local/stories/2011/11/29/3379167.htm; Colin Tatz, *Human Rights and Human Wrongs: A Life Confronting Racism* (Melbourne: Monash University Press, 2015).

6   Tatz, *Human Rights*, 28 and 44; Tatz, "Breaking the Membrane," 196.

7   Ibid., 204 and 205.

8   Tatz, *Human Rights*, 10; Tatz, "Breaking the Membrane," 211.

black African riding a bicycle, Colin made a statement to the police who later asked him to alter his testimony in order to cast more blame on the cyclist. He refused.[9]

During the Second World War, white South Africa swayed between support for the Allies and the Axis powers. Colin's grandparents had left Lithuania amid growing restrictions on Jews and rising antisemitism in the Tsarist Empire. The South African state classified Litvaks, who made up 90 per cent of South Africa's 120,000 Jews, as white, but neither Afrikaners nor British descendants, the dominant white tribes, were welcoming. The pro-Axis Afrikaner *Ossewabrandwag* (Ox-Wagon Guard) "attacked synagogues [and] Jewish shops . . . and printed and distributed Nazi leaflets and propaganda." Jews formed vigilante groups in response.[10] D. F. Malan, the Afrikaner nationalist who would lead the apartheid government as South African Prime Minister between 1948 and 1954, deemed Jews an "unabsorbable minority."[11]

At home, Colin followed the war through daily BBC broadcasts, which he translated for his maternal grandmother whom he called *Bobbe*. He reported the Axis forces overrunning Vilna, Kovno, Ponevezh, Shadove, Telze, and heard *Bobbe* cry, "Our family is gone." It was not until mid-1945 that the young Colin finally figured the meaning of "gone": the last clue came during a newsreel at a Saturday afternoon movie matinee showing corpses bulldozed into mass graves at Bergen-Belsen concentration camp.[12]

Collectively, these experiences planted a seed in Colin that blossomed into a mission to tackle racism. It was only much later in his career, though, that the Holocaust became part of that mission. Initially, he baulked at analysing the "appalling years" between 1941 and 1945. The turning point was Yad Vashem. It opened the door to the "death factory domain" and provided a new "analytical toolbox" in which the Holocaust connected seemingly disparate cases of racism, such as those experienced by Aboriginal Australians and Native Americans, that at first glance "have little in common with processes in the Third Reich."[13] The key to this connection is a profound definition of genocide as "the resort to biological solutions to real or confected social, political, or religious problems." The power of this definition, which underpins *The Magnitude of Genocide*, immediately reveals itself in comparative cases. For example, "Australia—while seemingly a far cry from the heaped corpses at

---

9   Tatz, *Human Rights*, 8, 28 and 42.
10 Tatz, "Breaking the Membrane," 197.
11 Milton Shain, *A Perfect Storm: Antisemitism in South Africa, 1930–1948* (Johannesburg: Jonathan Ball, 2015), 14.
12 Tatz, *Human Rights*, 10; Tatz, "Breaking the Membrane," 196.
13 Ibid., 204.

Bergen-Belsen or the death marches that Turkish authorities visited on their Armenian subjects—responded to its 'Aboriginal problem' by finding . . . a solution in biology" based on "the forcible removal of Aboriginal children from their parents, and their subsequent assimilation by intermarriage into white society."[14] The definition also launched Colin's subsequent research into youth suicide among Aboriginal Australians: "many of the suicides are either removed children or descendants of those forcibly removed" and can be linked to the "destruction of culture and language," the physical relocation of communities, "confinement to reserves and mission stations," "physical and economic abuse," "destruction of religious sites" and "solace in alcohol."[15]

Colin's journey to a scholar of comparative genocide studies commenced with experiences of racism in South Africa and culminated in a fresh comprehension and conceptualisation of genocide. This, in turn, led to a new paradigm of racism and intellectual renown. In a later section I explore the form of Colin's scholarship; first, I discuss his influence as a teacher.

Long before I knew him personally, Colin's writing had always seemed to me to stem from a deep and profound awareness of the devastating consequences of racism. He expressed something that existed inside me as well. I felt strongly the experiences of the Stolen Generations and Australia's refusal to recognise our own history of genocide. Colin embodies the relationship between the Jewish community and Aboriginal and Torres Strait Islander peoples. In my own journey from working with Indigenous communities to studying the Holocaust and Genocide, I am treading carefully in footsteps already made by Colin. Now he is there to guide me in person as well as through his writing, and he will continue to inspire new generations of scholars committed to raising awareness of history and human rights—NIKKI MARCZAK

The personal tributes in this article acknowledge, implicitly and explicitly, Colin's influence as a teacher. He recognised very early that good teachers could "promote human dignity" and "change the order of things" by using their skills of observation, inquiry, writing, talking and, where necessary, preaching.[16] Perhaps not surprisingly then, Colin chose teaching as the primary vehicle for his anti-racism mission as well as to help produce what his co-author Winton Higgins calls "socially aware and morally informed" citi-

---

14 Tatz and Higgins, *The Magnitude*, 6. See also Colin Tatz, *Australia's Unthinkable Genocide* (Bloomington: Xlibris, 2017).
15 Tatz, "Breaking the Membrane," 211–12.
16 Tatz, *Human Rights*, 347.

zens who understand those "central modern western values" of "justice, the dignity of the individual human life, and sensitivity to the suffering of others."[17] In the following section I delve further into "Colin the teacher" who one former student calls "very gifted."[18]

Teacher

The motto of Macquarie University is "And gladly teche" (adopted from Chaucer's description of the Clerk of Oxenford in the prologue to *The Canterbury Tales*). Colin taught at Macquarie for more than 17 years and as numerous voices in this volume attest, no one better embodied the University's motto. Across his teaching career Colin "triggered many career—and life-changing priorities among students."[19]

After training as a nurse I enrolled in a degree in ancient history at Macquarie. In my final year I gained special permission to enrol in "The Politics of Genocide." That course, taught by Colin, changed my life and the lives of those around me. The history was significant—the biomedical vision of race, the distortion of science and medicalised care, the role of doctors and nurses in killing—and, combined with the urgency of Colin's message, had an immense impact upon me. Today, I still share what I learned from Colin with others—doctors, nurses, students. I am indebted to him for inspiring me to be a better person, a better scholar, a better teacher, and unafraid to point out the indignity suffered by those who are marginalised and humiliated, and indeed murdered, by others' misperceptions, fabrications and machinations. This is profoundly the case when a genocidal regime inverts the "duty of care" of medicine—DARREN O'BRIEN

There are some people who come into one's life who set about a process that changes direction and creates opportunities for seeing the world anew. In 1991 I met Colin Tatz. That meeting proved pivotal: his passion for truth and justice, for making this world a better place through teaching and ensuring that the past, no matter how uncomfortable, was not lost, left a profound mark on me. As mentor, teacher, companion and friend, Colin demanded nothing less than the best I could give. The debt I owe this extraordinarily humble man

---

17 Cited in Tatz, *With Intent*, 172–73 and 182.
18 Robert Orr, review of *Human Rights and Human Wrongs*, *Indigenous Law Bulletin* 8, no. 27 (2016), 26.
19 Winton Higgins, personal correspondence, May 9, 2016.

is one I can never repay. The Talmud says there is no greater obligation for a student than to honour their teacher (Talmud Torah Chapter 5, Halachah 1). *I honour my teacher, Colin Tatz*—PAUL O'SHEA

Colleagues, too, recognise Colin's influence on their lives. John Maynard, Director at the Wollotuka Institute of Aboriginal Studies at the University of Newcastle and Chair of Indigenous History acknowledges Colin as "a source of great inspiration" throughout his career and comments that he "has always been willing to offer support, encouragement and advice."[20] Just as colleagues and students sing their praises of Colin, so is he quick to identify those who inspired him and who continue to do so. His first inspiration was a teacher at Yeoville Boys' Primary School (Johannesburg) who Colin says "changed my life":

> My first lessons in injustice, inhumanity and the width and depth of moral divides came not from family or Judaism but from Phil Green. He took us through prisoner-of-war camps, death camps, refugee camps, and South African military camps. . . . The embodiment of life learning rather than book learning, [Green delivered an invaluable] lesson: there is simply nothing better than an inspirational teacher in the flesh.[21]

Others followed Green, including Edgar Brookes and Arthur Keppel-Jones at the University of Natal, and Yehuda Bauer at Yad Vashem. In 2015 Colin still described Bauer as his "mentor and inspiration."[22]

Colin the teacher neither merely imparts knowledge nor simply assigns readings. He performs and projects his entire persona onto subject matter. At the heart of Colin's pedagogical performances lies a modulated voice with a highly controlled tempo and cadence that instantly commands the attention of those who meet and listen to him. Tony Barta and Raimond Gaita both refer to the power and presence of Colin's voice. Tony underscores a radio interview in which Colin "tells us about his early life and the way his values were formed in South Africa."[23]

Genocide Perspectives *is about different voices. Colin's writing voice is known to people concerned about genocide all round the world. Now, wherever they*

---

20   John Maynard, personal correspondence, November 16, 2016.
21   Tatz, *Human Rights*, 41–42.
22   Ibid., 257.
23   "Colin Tatz," by Richard Fidler.

are, they can hear his unforgettable speaking voice as well. It will make the same impression it immediately made on me 30 years ago, resonant and direct. His radio interventions still resonate his national importance in Australia. In this conversation he tells us about his early life and the way his values were formed in South Africa—TONY BARTA

What I most admire about Colin's work—as a writer, a "doer" (as he puts it) and as a teacher—is the way he is present in it, the way his voice informs and is informed by the content of what he says and does. To paraphrase Wallace Steven: Colin is a man whose fine character passes through him like a thread through a needle. Everything he does is stitched with its colour. To explain why a "doer by nature" should have been a teacher for much of his life, Colin refers to Elie Wiesel. Asked what anyone could do about the Holocaust Wiesel replied, "one must teach and teach again"— RAIMOND *GAITA*

Although less than enamoured with the "excruciating elocution lessons" that he endured as young boy,[24] Colin encourages his students to practise and develop their communication skills, to expel jargon, to use plain language—especially when explaining complex subjects—and to craft their writing. He leads by example on each of these fronts. Colin's alliterations inject life into his prose: "Suicide is fraught with faith, fear, folk lore, demonology, dogma, dread, mystery, secrecy, speculation and tradition."[25] He sharpens focus by juxtaposing seemingly disparate descriptions: "At Mitzpe Ramon [Negev desert] we saw some spectacular ibex goats tip-toeing on precipices. We also observed and talked to a few Russian immigrants trying to tip-toe into life in a new and very different place and culture."[26] He is creative: who else would describe a cardiac operation as "a cross between mediaeval butchery and Belgian tapestry making!"[27] He playfully exposes the follies of his opponents: Professor Goldney, a prolific writer on suicide, "embraces the real estate slogan of 'location, location, location' when he calls suicide 'depression, depression, depression.' "[28] Above all, Colin marries lucid and vivid writing with a sharp eye and ear to capture profound insights. The following account of an

---

24 Tatz, *Human Rights*, 39.
25 Colin Tatz, "Suicide and Sensibility," *Death Studies*, 2017. http://dx.doi.org/10.1080/07481187.2017.1333358
26 Tatz, *Human Rights*, 342–43.
27 Ibid., 287.
28 Tatz, "Suicide and Sensibility."

exchange in the foyer of the Moree bowling club in rural New South Wales illustrates Colin's view that sport is a "passport to respect":

> A very short, very fat Aboriginal bowler, complete with bowls case and creams, approached a very blue-rinse matron, visibly, undoubtedly a National Party conservative: "Heather, would you care to play with me in the mixed next month?" he asked. "Harold, I'd be delighted," was the unhesitating reply.[29]

Irrespective of whether they agree with Colin's arguments, peer reviewers almost universally praise his style with phrases such as "dramatic," "sharp," "enthusiastic," "passionate," "poignant and powerful," "forcefully argued," "thought provoking" and "compelling."[30] Perhaps the ultimate accolade for style and presentation comes from Israel Charny, Executive Director of the Institute on the Holocaust and Genocide (Jerusalem), who describes *The Magnitude of Genocide* as "an amazingly readable intellectual tour de force. Rarely have I seen the dread topic of genocide addressed so humanely and interestingly. Strangely, this is even a book to enjoy."[31]

Curriculum development is one area of Colin's teaching that warrants comment. He has been a prominent advocate for courses about Aboriginal Australians in contemporary society, antisemitism and the Holocaust in universities and teachers' colleges. Aboriginal activist, and Australia's first Aboriginal magistrate, Pat O'Shane, observes that in the 1960s Colin "fought a one person battle" to bring Aboriginal Australians into the curriculum beyond such traditional discussions as prehistoric and historical artefacts.[32] In the 1980s and 1990s he advocated for teaching genocide and Holocaust studies. His accounts illuminate the nature of this advocacy and, in particular, the inordinate energy expended on advancing pedagogical justifications and translating them into (typically bland and lifeless) administrative and bureaucratic goals, ob-

---

29   Colin Tatz, *Obstacle Race: Aborigines in Sport* (Sydney: University of New South Wales Press, 1995), 257.

30   Gill Cowlishaw, review of *Aborigines and Uranium and Other Essays*, Mankind 14, no. 3 (1984), 236; Bret Harris, review of *Obstacle Race*, Australian Aboriginal Studies 1 (1996), 71; Rob Hess, review of *Obstacle Race*, Victorian Bulletin of Sport and Culture 5 (1995), 17; Robert Goldney, "Is Aboriginal Suicide Different? A Commentary on the Work of Colin Tatz," Psychiatry, Psychology and Law 9, no. 2 (2002), 257; Sam Garkawe, review of *With Intent to Destroy*, Current Issues in Criminal Justice 17, no. 1 (2005), 164 and 166; Emma Kowal, review of *Aboriginal Suicide is Different*, Australian and New Zealand Journal of Public Health 30, no. 4 (2006), 394. See also Pat O'Shane, review of *Race Politics in Australia*, Australian Quarterly 51, no. 3 (1979), 114; Sally Weaver, review of *Race Politics in Australia*, Aboriginal History 4, no. 2 (1980), 223; Joseph Reser, "What Does It Mean to Say That Aboriginal Suicide Is Different?" Australian Aboriginal Studies 2 (2004), 34.

31   *The Magnitude*, back cover.

32   O'Shane, review of *Race Politics*, 110.

jectives and mission statements, lobbying peers and colleagues for support, mobilising resources, and negotiating compromises in the hotly contested and highly charged political environment of higher education.³³

I worked with Colin primarily during my tenure as Education Director at the Sydney Jewish Museum. An enduring memory I have of Colin was his absolute commitment to teaching the difficult topics of Holocaust and genocide to secondary school teachers. Despite a demanding academic schedule and many other commitments, Colin was so convinced of the importance of this work that he undertook these initiatives voluntarily. His dedication and passion for educating at all levels was palpable to all who attended these seminars. His contribution will resound as the next generation of teachers undertake their work, enriched by the knowledge conveyed so expertly and movingly by Colin—AVRIL ALBA

Curriculum changes invariably ruffle the feathers of academic conservatives. Proposals for change may be couched in the scholarly jargon of evidence and objectivity but they are no less biased and barbed. Colin constantly confronted this conservatism. In several places he tells the story of the colleague who asked him how he would balance his presentations of genocide. Never slow, Colin retorted that "there could be no such thing as a pro-genocide viewpoint" and that he would never give an ex-Nazi camp *Kommandant* the opportunity to lecture to his students.³⁴ Advocacy slides into activism in such circumstances; in the context of genocide this is particularly apt. Activism is commensurate with Colin's anti-racism project. Tony Barta puts activism at the fore of Colin's work: "Out of the dire South African environment [Colin] brought to Australia his ability, and passion, to make everything he wrote a political intervention. He made *sport* an activist concept. He made *Aboriginal Affairs* an activist site. So Lemkin's activist concept found in Colin Tatz the kind of activism that made his intellectual contribution count for so much."³⁵

Activist

Activism typically evokes discomfort in the academy where it is widely deemed incompatible with detached reflection and scholarly objectivity and

---

33 Tatz, *Human Rights*, 273–84.
34 Ibid., 277. See also Tatz, "Breaking the Membrane," 207.
35 Tony Barta, personal correspondence, May 10, 2016.

integrity. Of course, these traits are more closely associated with the positivist philosophies and methods of the hard natural sciences that conceptualise truths as independent realities that can be counted, calculated, computed, measured and weighed. By contrast, researchers in the social sciences and humanities, who opine about social phenomena, and the structural and ideological forces that bear on them as well as the overt political struggles that they entail, are more receptive to truths as the social products of contextualisation, historicisation and reason. These are Colin's primary "sources of knowledge, of discerning and perceiving." Reasoning, he explains, provides the means by which to identify "paradoxes and contradictions between stated aims and actual behaviour," to reveal "inconsistencies, why are they present, and how [to encourage] people . . . to see, even accept, the need for reasoned congruence."[36]

Reasoning is political, moral, and an element of activism. Citing the Hungarian-born scholar of politics Robert Berki, Colin declared that:

> political thought is not only descriptions and explanations in the so-called neutral sense, but also . . . evaluations and advocacies: "they are factual statements, philosophical arguments and value judgments all at the same time." Further, "they are *consequential:* their importance reaches into the realm of future alternatives. They pronounce on the morality, the rights and wrongs of actions connected with changing or maintaining the character of the state." Those are the "visions" of political (science) workers: they are also mine.[37]

By its very nature, political and moral reasoning compels researchers to insert themselves into their research, to make clear their judgements and values, and to assign responsibility. These practices resound in Colin's writings. "My bias is clear," he affirms in *Obstacle Race*, his major treatise on racism in Australian sport:

> it is pro-Aboriginal in most things and anti-racist in all things. I am not politically correct and do criticise some Aboriginal attitudes and behaviour. Every effort is made to be meticulous about matters of fact, but I cannot hide my anger or frustration at facts that by their nature embody either evil, moral turpitude or professional negligence.[38]

---

36 Colin Tatz, "Criticism of Criticism: A Reply to Thiele," *Mankind* 14, no. 5 (1984), 401.
37 Ibid.
38 Tatz, *Obstacle Race*, 8.

Such statements have brought charges of polemics. Colin does not recoil. "Yes, I am a 'polemical scientist,' " he told one critic: "[I] engage in controversial discussion or argument, attacking or refuting the opinions of others. I have spent a lifetime controverting the doctrines and belief systems of many, especially in the fields of race relations and genocide studies."[39]

Colin is unwaveringly committed to frank engagement with justice and social equity. His scholarship in race relations and genocide studies has been all the more rigorous and energetic for this commitment, which ultimately rests on a fierce fidelity to truth. While truth-seeking has won him a well-deserved international reputation as an intellectual, it has also attracted the toxic enmity of those who have a vested interest in untruth. The latter have included revisionist "historians" of Australian race relations, the Turkish government in its century-old struggle to obliterate the memory of the Armenian Genocide, and lunar-right bloggers. Colin has drawn their fire because he has not contented himself with academic publications—he has also sought to publicise his findings and arguments, thus becoming an un-ignorable public intellectual. One with the moral fibre to stand up to the inevitable thuggish hostility—WINTON HIGGINS

Colin readily assigns responsibility. In *The Magnitude of Genocide* he and Winton Higgins blame the West for the "lion's share" of genocide in the twentieth century and for "replenishing" the "swamps" in which genocide continues to "fester" in the Middle East and North Africa.[40] While many activists stop short of solutions, Colin is always alert to answers. Genocide prevention may have attracted little attention from scholars,[41] but he proposes an international agency to identify potential politicides, ethnocides and genocides. Of course, he is the first to acknowledge that any solution will require the political will to act.[42]

Colin's activism has not hinged on criticism. He also employs celebration. This is strikingly evident in his encouragement of Aboriginal Australians to celebrate their sporting successes achieved despite colossal obstacles including, *inter alia*, "geography, isolation, incarceration, prejudice, racism, alienation, exclusion, children stolen."[43] Significantly, Colin did not just en-

---

39   Colin Tatz, "Rejoinder to 'Is Aboriginal Suicide Different?' A Commentary on the Work of Colin Tatz," *Psychiatry, Psychology and Law* 9, no. 2 (2002), 260–61.
40   Tatz and Higgins, *The Magnitude*, 227.
41   Ibid.
42   Ibid., 238.

courage; he also acted, conducting research to prove these achievements *and* helping to compile the inaugural Aboriginal and Islander Sports Hall of Fame to highlight the accomplishments.[44] Colin published the research and the Hall of Fame in *Obstacle Race*; he and son Paul subsequently twice updated the Hall in *Black Diamonds* (1996) and *Black Gold* (2000).[45]

Obstacle Race articulates the three pillars of Colin's activist project: critique, celebration and scholarship. Colin is at his critical best in the opening chapters, exposing the fallacies, myths, untruths, inconsistencies and hypocrisy of Australia's anti-Aboriginal racist alliance of miners, pastoralists, big business, conservative politicians, lobbyists and policy advisers, newspaper editors, columnists and talk-back radio hosts. The final chapter, "Aboriginal and Islander Sports Hall of Fame," bestows dignity on the best Aboriginal and Torres Strait Islander athletes and helps restore confidence among victims of racism. Between these two bookends Colin showcases his research skills. Some dozen chapters describe, analyse and evaluate the circumstances of around 1,200 Aboriginal and Torres Strait Islander athletes and entire communities within the contexts of a "welfare" system and public prejudice. The historian of sport, Rob Hess, rightly calls this research, based in part on visits to 80 Aboriginal communities across Australia, "a considerable feat."[46]

Obstacle Race won the non-fiction section of the 1995 Australian Human Rights Awards and received glowing peer reviews. Hess recommended it as "essential reading for all historians" and the Australian Studies scholar Daryl Adair later acknowledged that Colin's research in this field "has been instrumental" in raising "awareness of the extent of discrimination against Aboriginal people in Australian sport, past and present."[47] Clearly, Colin has achieved his goals as an activist scholar.[48] But a scholar is judged on more than unearthing facts and raising awareness. While there is much ambiguity about

---

43 Tatz, *Human Rights*, 287.

44 For details of the selectors, see Colin Tatz and Daryl Adair, "Darkness and a Little Light: 'Race' and Sport in Australia," *Australian Aboriginal Studies* 2 (2009), 9.

45 Published by Allen & Unwin, and the Australian Institute of Aboriginal and Torres Strait Islander Studies respectively.

46 Hess, review of *Obstacle Race*, 17.

47 Ibid; Daryl Adair, "Indigenous Australians and Sport: Critical Reflections," in *Beyond C. L. R. James: Shifting Boundaries of Race and Ethnicity in Sport*, eds. John Nauright, Alan Cobley and David Wiggins (Fayetteville: University of Arkansas Press, 2014), 67. See also Richard Broome, review of *Obstacle Race*, *Sporting Traditions* 12, no. 1 (1995), 175–77; Annemarie Jutel, review of *Obstacle Race*, *Journal of Sport History* 25, no. 2 (1998), 335–57; Douglas Booth, review of *Obstacle Race*, *International Journal of the History of Sport* 12, no. 3 (1995), 202–04.

48 In 1997 Colin was awarded Officer of the Order of Australia (AO) for "service to the community through research into social and legal justice for people disadvantaged by their race, particularly the Aboriginal community, and to promoting the equal participation in community life of all Australians."

what precisely constitutes scholarship, in the following section I focus on the form of Colin's deep explanation of events and the reception of those explanations by his peers.

Scholar

Colin defines himself as a contextual historian, "an action-oriented fieldworker" with "an anthropological and sociological bent, and a particular interest in comparative analysis."[49] History is a cornerstone of Colin's political project. In his words, "if one wants to begin the very difficult journey of overcoming racism, one has to start *facing history*, looking down the tunnel of its ugliness, not dismissing it, orchestrating amnesia or sanitizing history."[50] Here, however, I am interested in the form of Colin's historical practice.

The two most prominent forms of explanation in history are argument and narrative. The latter contains a plot, a mode of organising evidence as a genre of story (for example, romance, tragedy, comedy, satire) in order to "add meaning—usually a moral meaning"—and to "wrap" the subject up "in an account . . . from which instruction can be derived."[51] Arguments often contain key elements of a narrative such as the origins of the subject and conclusions that contain moral lessons. Without a plot, however, the narrative dimensions of an argument remain "impressionistic."[52] Colin occasionally veers into narrative, particularly in his research into Aboriginal sport; mostly, he presents his history as formist and contextualist arguments. *The Magnitude of Genocide* contains both forms.

A formist explanation engages empirical evidence, rather than pre-formulated concepts, in order to emphasise the unique, distinctive and peculiar, and

---

49 Tatz, *Human Rights*, 284.
50 Tatz, *Obstacle Race*, 159.
51 Hayden White, *The Practical Past* (Evanston, Illinois: Northwestern University Press, 2014), 83. While White deems the Holocaust "the most significant event in the internal history of the West in our time" ("The Public Relevance of Historical Studies: A Reply to Dirk Moses," *History and Theory* 44, no. 3 [2005], 337), he maintains that history is not especially well suited to establishing its meaning. He suggests that the "significance" of the Holocaust—"its meaning, its relevance to us, today, tomorrow [and] for the next generation"—transcends "a discipline devoted to establishing 'the facts of the matter.' " Consistent with his views that narratives are more fundamental to representations of the past than evidence and that historians impose narratives on the past, White argues that "better narratives," "imagination and poetic insight," rather than more facts, are required if we are to "divine" the meaning of the Holocaust ("The Public Relevance," 336 and 338). White identifies Saul Friedländer's *The Years of Extermination: Nazi Germany and the Jews, 1939–1945* (New York: Harper Collins, 2007) as an exemplary ethical and intellectual representation of the Holocaust (White, *Practical Past*, 76–92).
52 Hayden White, "The Structure of Historical Narrative," *Clio* 1, no. 3 (1972), 6, 9 and 11. Arthur Danto argues that even non-narrative forms of presentation, such as statistics and economics, are typically translated into narratives. Arthur Danto, *Narration and Knowledge* (New York: Columbia University Press, 1985).

to avoid abstraction and reductionism.[53] In *The Magnitude of Genocide* Colin and Winton use comparison as a formist explanation for different grades of genocide. While acknowledging that all genocides impose "seismic calamities" on the victims, they argue that the term itself is "a single, flat word that covers a spectrum of behaviours and processes." Thus, one genocide is not the same as another and analysis demands the differentiation of events according to "type, scale, scope and intensity," and "outcome and legacy."[54] The philosophy of history is largely silent with regard to the rules of comparison other than to note that cases should be culturally appropriate and share a common context. In the end, comparison requires judgement, discernment and perspicacity on the part of the researcher who is the final arbiter of what constitutes an appropriate comparison.

Colin presents his best history as contextualist explanations, setting his subjects, whether genocide, racism or sport, within clear contexts. Contextualist explanations proceed from the assumption that " 'what happened' . . . can be accounted for by the specification of the functional interrelationships existing among the agents and agencies . . . at a given time."[55] Establishing a context is no simple task: one does not simply integrate every event and trend. Rather, the art of contextualisation involves selecting particular "threads" and joining these into "chains of provisional and restricted" explanations that constitute a "manifestly 'significant' occurrence." Advanced contextualisation also means tracing the threads outward into the surrounding social environment in which the event occurred, and both backward and forward in time. Tracing the threads backwards enables the scholar to determine the origins of the event; tracing them forwards allows them to determine the impact or influence of the event on subsequent events. Contextualisation ends when the "threads either disappear into the context of some other event or converge to cause the occurrence of some new event."[56] Like comparison, contextualisation always involves judgements and distinguishing between the significant and the insignificant.[57]

The Magnitude of Genocide contains powerful and persuasive examples of

---

53 Hayden White, *Metahistory: The Historical Imagination in Nineteenth-Century Europe* (Baltimore: Johns Hopkins University Press, 1973), 13–17.
54 Tatz and Higgins, *The Magnitude*, xiii and 7; Tatz, *Human Rights*, 261.
55 White, *Metahistory*, 18.
56 Ibid., 18–19. See also White, *Practical Past*, 90.
57 While contextualisation is primarily a matter of judgement, Arthur Marwick offers a model for a systematic approach that opens the process to the broadest possible perspectives. Marwick's model comprises four principal components: major forces and constraints, events, human agents, and convergences and contingencies. Arthur Marwick, *The Sixties: Cultural Revolution in Britain, France, Italy, and the United States, c.1958–c.1974* (Oxford: Oxford University Press, 1998), 23–25.

systematic contextualisation such as locating the Holocaust in the context of Germany's response to the forces of modernisation. This piece of contextualisation begins with a defective German state and a particularly reactionary "ethnic version of nationalism and national identity" that nurtured antisemitism. The First World War was a critical event that set the stage for the Holocaust:

> [It] exacerbated [Germany's] social breakdown and administrative dislocation; this, in turn, overwhelmed the fragile democratic republic that replaced the second Reich, and ushered in the yet more disfigured Third Reich. It pursued mass support by appealing to fanatical antisemitism.[58]

These events subsequently facilitated the rise of the key agents of the Holocaust, videlicet, the fascist movement and its Nazi elite, and provided them with "both a camouflage and a pretext for . . . genocide." The Holocaust also involved a convergence between its agents and a number of emerging forces associated with modernisation such as " bureaucratic organization," advanced "technology and infrastructure," a scientific culture built on "social engineering and the dehumanization of victims," and a mass media that pacified and lulled the broader population into "moral indifference."[59] Venturing toward the literary style of a meaningful narrative, Colin and Winton conclude that "if any event deserves the title 'a modern tragedy'—or better still, 'a tragedy of modernization'—[the Holocaust] is it."[60]

Beyond history, Colin champions multidisciplinarity. "To probe genocide," he and Winton write, "we need the analytical tools of several humanities and social science disciplines, as well as some from the natural sciences, medicine, and law."[61] A notable element of Colin's penchant for multidisciplinarity is his criticism of narrowly constituted research bogged in jargon and constricted and constricting social theory; in these regards anthropologists and medical researchers are prime targets.[62] Some scholars in turn have questioned the absence of theory in Colin's work.[63] Others, such as Tim Rowse, note that

---

58 Tatz and Higgins, *The Magnitude*, 78.
59 Ibid., 84–85.
60 Ibid., 78. White, however, argues that the Holocaust poses unique problems of historical representation. See Note 51 above.
61 Tatz and Higgins, *The Magnitude*, 8.
62 Colin Tatz, *Aborigines and Uranium and Other Essays* (Melbourne: Heinemann, 1982), 3. For example, see Colin Tatz, "Aboriginality as Civilisation," *Australian Quarterly* 52, no. 3 (1980), 362; Tatz, "Rejoinder to 'Is Aboriginal Suicide Different?' " 260–261; Tatz, *Human Rights*, 302; Colin Tatz, "Innovation Without Change: Suicide Prevention is Going Nowhere," *+61j*, March 19, 2016, www.plus61j.net.au.
63 For example, see S. J. Thiele, "Anti-intellectualism and the 'Aboriginal Problem': Colin Tatz and the 'Self

Colin's research involves "strategic evaluations" and political objectives, not theoretical positioning, while Robert Orr, Special Counsel at the Australian Government Solicitor, makes the pertinent observation that Colin wants to rise above "easy or accepted answers" and has no qualms querying "group enthusiasm for fashionable trends."[64] Colin's editorship of *Genocide Perspectives [I–IV]* offers perhaps the clearest evidence of his engagement with theory. Jurist and academic, The Honourable Michael Kirby, who launched *Genocide Perspectives IV* and whose work appears in this volume, praises the journal for its "outstanding contributions" to "both the theoretical and practical issues of genocide: past, present and potential."[65]

By any measure of assessment, Colin's scholarship is deep, rigorous, logical and systematic. It has been scrutinised and acknowledged for its impact by peers such as Michael Kirby and John Maynard; it has contributed to social knowledge and debate across a wide range of fields including the politics of race, Holocaust and genocide studies, youth suicide studies, migration studies and sport history.[66] For purely illustrative purposes, I single out four of Colin's contributions. I begin with his definition of genocide as a biological solution to social, political or religious problems. As discussed above, this definition has facilitated a new paradigm of racism that is contributing to a richer understanding of the term and its deadly consequences. The second contribution involves Colin's mediation in the international legal definition of genocide that includes a broad range of acts from physical killings, to removal of children, preventing births, and causing mental harm to a group. Responding to the breadth of these acts, Colin proposes different levels of culpability, like the laws around murder in the United States. Under this schema the law would recognise "first degree" genocide for acts such as mass murder, second degree genocide for less serious acts, and other lower degrees for even lesser acts. Thus, while removal of children from their families would still be considered genocide, such acts would be legally distinguished from the mass slaughters associated with the Holocaust and Rwanda.[67] There are two particular merits in this position. First, it intellectually disposes of comparative trivialisations

---

Determination' Approach," *Mankind* 14, no. 3 (1984), 170–72 and 177; Christopher Anderson and Ian Keen, "On the Notion of Aboriginality," *Mankind* 15, no. 1 (1985), 42, 43 and 44.

64 Ibid., 45; Orr, review of *Human Rights*, 27.

65 Michael Kirby, personal correspondence, July 1, 2016. Kirby was the Chancellor at Macquarie University between 1984 and 1993; he presented me with my PhD in 1993.

66 In early 2016 Colin's curriculum vitae included 11 sole-authored books, five co-authored books, seven edited books, 75 chapters in books and 112 journal articles.

67 Colin Tatz, *Genocide in Australia*, Canberra Australian Institute of Aboriginal and Torres Strait Islander Studies, Research Discussion Paper Number 8, 1999, 28-32; Tatz, *Unthinkable Genocide*; Tatz, *With Intent*, 146.

such as comparisons of My Lai (Vietnam) with Auschwitz (Germany). "If everything that results in the killing of more than a handful of people is genocide," Colin argues, "then nothing is genocide. There is no need for the word, the idea, the crime or its analysis."[68] Second, it offers a potential solution for dealing with some of the legal issues around genocide, including restitution for victims and their families.

Highlighting the role of the law in fostering social change is another area where Colin has contributed to social knowledge. This is no idealistic position proffered from an ivory tower. Colin fully acknowledges that the "law has been, and will continue to be, an impediment" to social change, empowerment, and access to rights and dignity. Nonetheless, he correctly identifies sets of laws that have had positive effects on social behaviour. These include laws that prohibit discrimination, allow for positive discrimination (for example, affirmative action), establish "protective legal incorporations" and provide "recourse to civil law."[69]

Finally, Colin has shown that there are different cultural values and beliefs around suicide. He argues that indigenous values warrant a "contextual anthropology" to first understand the acute sense of helplessness that fuels the problem and second, to generate targeted solutions (such as personal empowerment, literacy training, highlighting positive role models, anchoring communities in their own histories).[70] Colin's research in this area has brought him into sharp conflict with the medical profession, which insists that suicide is a medical problem grounded in depression, mental ill health, genetic tendencies and chemical imbalances.[71] But it has won him more academic plaudits. Damien Riggs, for example, believes that Colin has demonstrated "that Indigenous suicide is indeed 'different' . . . to non-Indigenous suicide," and commends his work for its "original and cutting edge approaches" with respect to "intervening in, or alleviating, suicide within Indigenous communities."[72]

Thus far I have touched on Colin the teacher, activist and scholar. What of Colin the person? In concluding this article, I draw attention to the verve, exuberance, grace and humour of a man who thinks about, teaches and finds

---

68 Ibid., 147.
69 Tatz, *Race Politics*, 49 and 52; Tatz, *Genocide in Australia*, 31. Interestingly, Sir Graham Latimer, former president of the New Zealand Māori Council, believed that the New Zealand courts had been instrumental in getting Māori and Pakeha talking to one another. Neville Glasgow, interview by Sir Graham Latimer, *Te Ahi Kaa*, Radio New Zealand, June 12, 2016, http://www.radionz.co.nz/national/programmes/teahikaa.
70 Tatz, "Suicide and Sensibility."
71 For example, Goldney, "Is Aboriginal Suicide Different?" 259.
72 Damien Riggs, review of "Aboriginal Suicide is Different," *Australian Aboriginal Studies* 2 (2005), 83.

inspiration in genocide. "Clearly," as one reviewer laconically puts it, "this is not everyone's cup of tea."[73]

Conclusion

Colin immerses himself in genocide and suicide. Yet neither subject subsumes him. On the contrary, he retains a keen sense of perspective. An insight into this dimension emerges from his comments on life in the Centre for Comparative Genocide Studies where, amid reflections on death, there was "warmth, camaraderie, even excitement" and "insider jokes" that helped relieve some of the suffering and "ever-present tears."[74] Colin is also pragmatic. While justifiably confident that his words have improved the "understanding" of genocide among "many students and members of the public," he makes no claims to having alleviated, much less prevented, the crime.[75] He disagrees with Christian notions of justice founded on "guilt, admission, absolution, expiation," that include "a prohibition on any criminal or civil action against the confessed perpetrator by the family of the deceased." Nonetheless, he concedes that the South African Truth and Reconciliation Commission, for example, is a "reasonable compromise" between those who wanted a Nuremburg-type trial and those who wanted nothing.[76] Notwithstanding the acquittal of three Australians for war crimes in the late 1990s, Colin places "more value on the evidence that emerges from trials than on conviction and punishment."[77] "Trial," he said in his inaugural Abraham Wajnryb Memorial Lecture in 1994:

> is an articulation by the state that an evil of some kind is believed to have occurred. . . . Trial is about as much of a public declaration as we can get that there are moral and ethical values which society wishes, or needs, to sustain. Trial records . . . are . . . infinitely more powerful educative tools about contemporary social and political history than the passive voice and indirect speech of history texts.[78]

---

73   Garkawe, review of *With Intent*, 166.
74   Tatz, *Human Rights*, 278.
75   Tatz, *With Intent*, 184.
76   Tatz, "Breaking the Membrane," 208.
77   Tatz, *Human Rights*, 280.
78   Colin Tatz, "Reflections on the Politics of Remembering and Forgetting: The First Abraham Wajnryb Memorial Lecture, 1994" (North Ryde, NSW: Centre for Comparative Genocide Studies, Macquarie University, 1995), 31–32.

Colin plunges to the depths of genocide and suicide but an intense and wide-ranging curiosity means that, paradoxically, he also dives head first into life.

Love of and engagement with life shines through Colin's accounts and stories of his experiences. He injects intense feelings into his descriptions of new places, sights—architecture, customs, geography—sounds and tastes.[79] Humour is a constant companion. At the 2003 Canadian Association for Suicide Prevention conference in Iqaluit (Baffin Island), the roads on the banks of Frobisher Bay were "simply frost with soil covering" and "some wag had planted a road sign in the permafrost: 'Beware of the Kangaroos.' "[80] Reflecting on his humour, Colin writes, *"to be funny, you first have to think sad. And seeing how much of my life has been about things that are sad, I do see the funny side—or at least part of it, part of the time."*[81]

In the final chapter of his memoir, Colin discusses his Jewish identity. He refers to the ethnic and intellectual traditions to which he feels strongly attached, and he highlights the concept of *tikkun olam* in which one is "compelled to try to repair a flawed world."[82] *Tikkun Olam* invokes considerable debate within Judaism but as a moral dictate to make the world a better place through your own actions, it has framed Colin's life. All of us who have been taught by Colin, worked with him, read his words, listened to him or sought his advice, and especially those who have been championed by him, have benefitted from his unyielding commitment to this commandment.

---

79 For example, see Tatz, *Human Rights*, 259, 333 and 336.
80 Ibid., 335.
81 Ibid., 346. Emphasis in original.
82 Ibid., 345.

Part 2
Australia

REFLECTING ON THE *BRINGING THEM HOME REPORT*

Anna Haebich

Introduction[1]

Bringing Them Home: Report of the National Inquiry into the Separation of Aboriginal and Torres Strait *Islander Children from their Families* (*Bringing Them Home Report*)[2] was released in 1997. It represented a crucial breakthrough in exposing the system of forced removals and placements of Aboriginal and Torres Strait Islander children from colonial times to the present, across all Australian colonies, states and territories. The report caused an unprecedented outpouring of public shock, grief and shame that was followed by counter-attacks on the veracity of the findings, igniting one of the nation's most emotional and toxic public debates. This is all well known to us, or is it? 20 years on, it is time for Australians to join with members of the Stolen Generations and their families in assessing the nation's response to the report's findings and its 54 recommendations. In this essay I reflect on the backstory and reception of the report, the remembering and forgetting of what happened, and the continued fragmenting of Aboriginal and Torres Strait Islander families in the present day.

Recalling the *Bringing Them Home Report*

The *Bringing Them Home Report* was destined for controversy on several counts. The nation was rocked by its findings of an endemic system of forced child removals and placements in institutions, foster homes, adoptive families

---

1 This essay draws on my own research, in particular: Anna Haebich, "Indigenous Child Removal and Settler Colonialism: An Historical Overview," *Australian Indigenous Law Review* 19, no. 1 (2015), 20–31; Anna Haebich, "Forgetting Indigenous Histories: Cases from Australia's Stolen Generations," *Journal of Social History* 44, no. 4 (2011), 1034–43, 1035.

2 Human Rights and Equal Opportunity Commission, *Bringing Them Home: Report of the National Inquiry into the Separation of Aboriginal and Torres Strait Islander Children from their Families* (Canberra: Human Rights and Equal Opportunity Commission, 1997).

and forced employment, and the extent of the system through time and in all states and colonies:

> Nationally we can conclude with confidence that between one in three and one in ten Indigenous children were forcibly removed from their families and communities in the period from approximately 1910 until 1970. In certain regions and in certain periods the figure was undoubtedly much greater than one in ten. In that time not one Indigenous family has escaped the effects of forcible removal (confirmed by representatives of the Queensland and WA Governments in evidence to the Inquiry). Most families have been affected, in one or more generations, by the forcible removal of one or more children.[3]

The findings revealed systematic racial discrimination, practised by targeting children of mixed descent. This system did not reflect the standards and practices legislated by state governments to protect the best interests of children. Evidence from over 500 testimonies showed forced removal and the emotional, physical and sexual abuse of children who were denied family, language, culture, country and their sense of identity and belonging. The transgenerational legacy for individuals, families and communities was presented in stories told to the Inquiry of family breakdown, ongoing medical, psychological and emotional problems, addictive behaviours, incarceration, violence, self-harm and suicide.

Sympathisers shed genuinely felt tears, made their apologies, and called for a national apology to ensure a safe future for Aboriginal and Torres Strait Islander children and families. A people's movement emerged, expressed in the advent of an annual national Sorry Day on May 26, and public signings of Sorry Books occurred, while Journeys of Healing and reconciliation marches in major cities were undertaken. Given the depth of public sorrow, it is painful to read Tony Birch's troubling observations on the passing nature of non-Aboriginal responses to the *Bringing Them Home Report*. Birch writes that:

> a reaction for and of the moment allowed "colonial listeners confronted with a narrative of their own violence . . . to simultaneously absorb and purge themselves of trauma." This outcome lacks the ethic of responsibility, reflecting Slavoj Žižek's observation that "in order to forget an event, we must first summon up the strength to remember it properly."[4]

---

3 Human Rights, *Bringing Them Home*, 30.

Meanwhile, Birch continues, Indigenous communities were left to "carry alone the burden of being left to live with the sense of injustice" and the weighty responsibility of remembering the past.[5]

Remembering "properly" became increasingly difficult in the vitriolic public debate that emerged. Media reports of attacks on the credibility of the *Bringing Them Home Report* began to eclipse accounts of public goodwill. Denialists questioned the primacy and authority given by the Inquiry to the truths of Indigenous testimony as the official voice of Stolen Generations history. They challenged the credibility of evidence not given under oath and claimed witnesses were repeating circulating variations of a "constructed Stolen Generations narrative" originating in research conducted in the 1980s by historian Peter Read.[6] The newly-elected conservative Prime Minister, John Howard, had reluctantly inherited the *Report*, introduced by the Keating Labor government in 1995. Howard allowed the critics free reign and, with his ministers, openly supported claims that children were rescued from physical and moral danger, and treated humanely by standards of the time. He rejected any generational responsibility for practices sanctioned by previous governments. Some accused Howard of playing the race card to denigrate the report and split the nation. Whatever his immediate political purpose, the lasting effect was to create a culture of denial and recrimination that irrevocably disfigured public debate on the issue.

The report's use of the language of international human rights and genocide served to further polarise public debate. United Nations instruments included in the report are the "Declaration of Human Rights" and the "International Convention on the Elimination of All Forms of Racial Discrimination"; the "Basic Principles and Guidelines on the Right to a Remedy and Reparation for Victims of Gross Violations of International Human Rights Law and Serious Violations of International Humanitarian Law" ("van Boven Principles"); and the "Convention on the Prevention and Punishment of the Crime of Genocide" (the "Genocide Convention"). The report found evidence of gross violation of human rights and systematic racial discrimination that continued after Australia had endorsed the United Nations Declarations of Human Rights

---

4   Tony Birch, " 'I Could Feel it in My Body': War on a History War," *Transforming Cultures Journal* 1, no. 1 (2006), 19.

5   Tony Birch, " 'The First White Man Born': Contesting the 'Stolen Generations' in Australia," in *Imagining Australia: Literature and Culture in the New World*, eds. Jan Ryan and Chris Wallace-Crab (Cambridge, MA: University Committee in Australian Studies, 2004), 106.

6   Bain Attwood, "Learning about the Truth: The Stolen Generations Narrative," in *Telling Stories: Indigenous History and Memory in Australia and New Zealand*, eds. Bain Attwood and Fiona Magowan (Crows Nest, NSW: Allen & Unwin, 2001), 183.

and the abolition of racial discrimination as a member of the United Nations in 1945:

> Official policy and legislation for Indigenous families and children was contrary to accepted legal principle imported into Australia as British common law and, from late 1946, constituted a crime against humanity. It offended accepted standards of the time and was the subject of dissent and resistance. The implementation of the legislation was marked by breaches of fundamental obligations on the part of officials and others to the detriment of vulnerable and dependent children whose parents were powerless to know their whereabouts and protect them from exploitation and abuse.[7]

From the "van Boven Principles" the report created a detailed road map for governments to follow in responding to the report.[8] These principles advocated a full range of reparation measures, including restitution, compensation, rehabilitation, a formal national acknowledgment of responsibility, guarantees against repetition, measures for restitution of land, culture and language, rehabilitation of those individuals, families and communities affected, monetary compensation through a national tribunal, and an apology. These recommendations panicked Prime Minister Howard, who feared a blowout of payments consuming millions of dollars of government money. He announced that there would be no apology and no compensation payouts. Six months after the report's release, the government introduced a four-year package of $63 million, principally to address family separation and its consequences through family support, parenting programmes and counselling services to be provided by government departments and community organisations that had been giving culturally appropriate expert services to members of the Stolen Generations for decades.

One of the *Bringing Them Home Report*'s most controversial conclusions was that the system of forced removal and placements of Aboriginal and Torres Strait Islander children was a form of genocide:

> Forcible removal was an act of genocide contrary to the "Convention on Genocide" ratified by Australia in 1949. The "Convention on Genocide" specifically includes "forcibly transferring children of [a] group to another group" with the intention of destroying the group.[9]

---

7   Human Rights, *Bringing Them Home*, 275.
8   Ibid., 280–314.

Genocide is not only the mass killing of a people. The essence of genocide is acting with the intention to destroy the group, not the extent to which that intention has been achieved. A major aim of the forcible removals was to "absorb," "merge" or "assimilate" Indigenous children into mainstream Australian culture. Authorities may have also believed this was in the children's best interests; however, citing debates from the drafting of the Genocide Convention, the *Bringing Them Home Report* argued that a "policy is still genocide when it is motivated by a number of objectives. To constitute an act of genocide the extermination of a group need not be solely motivated by animosity or hatred."[10] This claim of genocide was inflammatory for most Australians who were ignorant of the complexities and nuances of the convention. For them, genocide signified the engineered mass race murders of the Holocaust. The finding of genocide also coalesced with the bitter history war over British colonisation on Australia's colonial frontiers—was it peaceful and benign, or violent and genocidal?

As a leading scholar of genocide, Colin Tatz made several important observations concerning genocide in the context of the Stolen Generations. He noted Australia's hysterical rejection of any association with genocide evident in debates in Federal Parliament in 1949 that ratified the Genocide Convention. Tatz cited Labor member Leslie Haylen's assertion that "the horrible crime of genocide is unthinkable in Australia . . . [this] . . . arises from the fact that we are a moral people."[11] Tatz explained:

> As Australians see it, we can't be connected to, or with, the stereotypes of Swastika-wearing SS psychopaths, or crazed black tribal Africans. Apart from Australia's physical killing era, there *are* clear differences between what those perpetrators did and what we did in assimilating people and removing their children. But, images notwithstanding, we are connected by virtue of what Raimond Gaita calls "the inexpungable moral dimension" inherent in genocide, whatever its forms or actions.

Commenting on "genocide denialism, memory and the politics of apology," Tatz noted his concern with the politics and motives of those in power and that "exploration of what propels these people might help to develop more effective strategies to deal with, or perhaps nullify, their activities." Concerning

---

9 Human Rights and Equal Opportunity Commission, "Bringing Them Home Community Guide Update," December, 2007, http//:humanrights.gov.au.
10 Human Rights, *Bringing Them Home*, 238.
11 Colin Tatz, *With Intent to Destroy: Reflecting on Genocide* (New York: Verso, 2003), 67–68.

denialists at the highest levels of government in Australia, including "Prime Minister John Howard, two ex-state premiers, several retired senior bureaucrats, a small group of senior journalists and a quartet of academics with scholastic credentials," Tatz observed that their motives had "little in common with the Holocaust denialists but they strongly echo and parallel the Turkish denial industry."[12]

Public debate reached extremes of hostility that threatened to leave the integrity of the *Bringing Them Home Report* in tatters. Strategies of denial and character assassination supported by the Howard government (and the counter-attacks), polarised and confused public opinion causing many to avoid the issue. In this toxic environment, the Commissioners of the *Bringing Them Home* inquiry, Sir Ronald Wilson and Professor Michael Dodson, and even the highly respected national Aboriginal leader Lowitja O'Donaghue OAM, were publicly vilified. This drove many Aboriginal people back into a safe but painful silence. In this context Aboriginal and Torres Strait Islander artists turned to the potent space of visual and performing arts to reflect on stories of family separation.[13] Their works highlight the productive ways that Aboriginal people continue to recreate and take charge of the past: going beyond politics and divisive debate to use creative art and performance to elicit affective responses that are otherwise difficult to achieve.

Prime Minister Howard must have felt vindicated for his stance by the adverse court findings and media endorsement of two findings handed down by the courts over two high profile Stolen Generations cases: Lorna Cubillo and Peter Gunner suing the Commonwealth government for damages (1996–1999), and Joy Williams' compensation claim against the New South Wales government (1994–2000).[14] Howard did not escape censure by his peers, however, and in 2000 the Senate Legal and Constitutional References Committee Inquiry roundly condemned his stance in their *Healing: A Legacy of Generations Report*.[15] The Committee found that the government had failed the Inquiry and its recommendations, and that Howard should show proper leadership and supervision. They recommended the government begin by establishing a reparation tribunal, national memorial, national apology and a

---

12 Ibid., 122–23.

13 Anna Haebich, "A Potent Space: Witnessing Abuse and Violence through Visual Testimony," in *Volatile Substance: The Pressure of the Past in Ireland and Australia*, eds. Katie Holmes and Stuart Ward (Dublin: Irish Academic Press, 2012), 104–24.

14 Richard Guilliatt, "Their Day in Court," *Sydney Morning Herald*, November 20, 1999, http://www.smh.com.au/national/their-day-in-court-20130526-2n51u.html.

15 Senate Legal and Constitutional References Committee, *Healing: A Legacy of Generations Report* (Canberra: Commonwealth of Australia, 2000).

national summit. Only a memorial to the Stolen Generations was added to Reconciliation Place in Canberra in 2004.

When, after 11 years, Labor Prime Minister Kevin Rudd finally delivered a national apology to the Stolen Generations, it was stripped of the international human rights contexts that laid such heavy responsibilities on the nation. These were conveniently forgotten, allowing the luxury of expressing sorrow and remorse to the Stolen Generations without the threat of unpaid debts. The word genocide was not mentioned. Most Aboriginal people generously accepted the apology as a gesture of goodwill. No Australian government, before or since, has seriously attempted to address the moral obligations imposed by the charges of genocide and gross violation of human rights. No definitive action has been taken to stop separations. The nation has continued on, largely untroubled by the debts still owed.

Reflecting on Aboriginal remembering and activism

Here I call up some of the past that Tony Birch reminds us was left for Aboriginal people to "carry alone." The past discussed here is the many decades of activism by Aboriginal leaders and families battling to save their children. This history recounts the protesting and lobbying over many decades, a significant backstory to the Inquiry in 1995 and the *Bringing Them Home Report*. This is still relatively unknown outside of Aboriginal communities. There are important reasons to document these narratives of activism treasured by local Aboriginal communities but lost in the fog of colonial amnesia. The retelling honours the achievements of people who had to fight for their rights against insurmountable odds and at great personal cost, often without achieving their goals and being punished for their efforts instead. These stories of courage, creativity and ingenuity can inspire community pride and further action. There are lessons to learn from strategies for change that draw on Aboriginal values, knowledge, experience and ways of working together for cultural healing. These narratives may be from the past but they resonate with experiences of injustice today. It is a truism that the past is never past in the recycling of injustices to settler colonies like Australia.

Patrick Wolfe argues that settler colonialism is not a distant moment in history but is very much part of the present: ". . . settler colonialism is a structure, not an event."[16] It is a force set in motion to possess the land and its resources, to exterminate or assimilate Indigenous peoples and their cultures,

---

16 Patrick Wolfe, *Settler Colonialism and the Transformation of Anthropology: The Politics and Poetics of an Ethnographic Event* (London: Cassel, 1999), 163.

and to replace them with settler populations and colonial governance and culture. I add that Indigenous child removal is integral to both. There is some room for movement in the system: settler colonialism can fluctuate—it consolidates and then kilters off centre, opening opportunities for change, only to seek equilibrium again. Activists learn to act quickly; they can achieve incremental change but the pendulum always swings back to the rigid centre. In the meantime, they continue the groundwork for change.

Relocating entire communities to missions, settlements and reserve camps has been colonial main business for centuries and activists have resisted and protested in many ways against this intention to erase Indigenous populations from the colonial landscape. Documenting this in Nyungar country I used the term "incremental genocide" to describe governments' cumulative punitive initiatives and bungled outcomes that added to community racism and pushed officers to ever more drastic interventions, culminating in the 1930s in the genocidal policy of biological absorption to make the unwanted population disappear altogether.[17] There are many parallels with Raphael Lemkin's "techniques of genocide" that aim to destroy the "essential foundations of the life" of human groups but not as a "coordinated plan,"[18] and also with Tony Barta's account of "inevitable rather than intentional" consequences of "genocidal relations" inherent in settler colonialism that make coexistence impossible.[19] Yet the Nyungar protest continued, even in this travesty of human rights, by resisting removals, escaping from institutions, writing letters and petitions and keeping culture and memories alive in covert gatherings. At Carrolup in the late 1940s the children began creating sophisticated art works with potent new meanings and messages for settler audiences, in the manner of the artists mentioned earlier. An official report in 1949 described their living conditions as "barbarous," "most unsatisfactory," "unhygienic," "evil smelling," "wholly inadequate," and "needs immediate rectification." In these sorry circumstances the children created beauty in pastel and acrylic works that recalled their memories of life in bush camps with their families and landscapes from rambles in the bush around the settlement. They started the Carrolup art movement and left enduring symbols for the Nyungar nation and the Stolen Generations.

A consequence of assimilation policy from the 1950s was the foundation of an expanding new industry of government departments and non-government agencies working with Indigenous children and families that brought greater

---

17 Cited in Anna Haebich, " 'Clearing the Wheat Belt': Erasing the Indigenous Presence in the Southwest of Western Australia," in *Genocide and Settler Society: Frontier Violence and Stolen Indigenous Children in Australian History*, ed. Dirk Moses (New York: Berghahn Books, 2004), 267–89.
18 Ibid., 268.
19 Ibid., 270.

surveillance of family life and more interventions to remove the children to missions, foster homes and for adoption. One family's experiences of the loss and abuse of their children led to decades of trying to bring their children home. In 2013 the family finally exposed their sorrows to public scrutiny in a compensation case in Perth that showed the tenacity of official attitudes. The elderly litigants, Donald and Sylvia Collard, explained to the court how in 1959 Child Welfare officers took their baby from the local hospital without their knowledge or consent, and two years later eight more of their children were taken into state care.[20] They were seasonal rural workers living in a camp on the edge of a wheat belt town. Collards' lawyers argued that the state government had breached its obligations and duty of care to the family and in the process denied their children their biological parents, their natural familial relationships and their cultural heritage, and that the children were exposed to various forms of abuse, including isolation and trauma. The government argued it was "in the children's best interest." Mr. Collard told the court it was due to racism, not "squalor and neglect." They had lived in a racist society with no Aboriginal Legal Service or any way to plead for their rights; "they had no-one and nowhere to turn to."[21] The case was dismissed. The court ruled that the removals and wardships were reasonable by standards of the time and made for the children's welfare; that the state was not subject to the fiduciary duties alleged; that there was insufficient evidence of a policy of assimilation using the wardship of children to force Indigenous people into white Australian society; and that "all the decisions were in regard to their welfare."

The decade of the 1970s marked a turning point for activists to make Aboriginal child removals a public issue. This came about through a combination of new policies of self-determination and renewed Aboriginal activism, collaborations with non-Aboriginal supporters in positions of authority, and an interested media following the 1967 referendum, all of this culminating in 1979 in the United Nations International Year of the Child. Of several controversial cases in the media, it was events in Darwin in 1973 that exposed polarised opinion about the placement of Aboriginal children with white fos-

---

20 Gerry Georgatos, " 'Nothing to Live For,' Said Stolen Generations Father," *Stringer Independent News*, February 15, 2013, http://thestringer.com.au/nothing-to-live-for-said-stolen-generations-father-3-444#.VhdE1qSEJJM; Gerry Georgatos, "WA Supreme Court in an Unbelievable Decision Dismisses Stolen Generations Compensation Claim," *Stringer Independent News*, December 29, 2013, http://nationalunitygovernment.org/content/wa-supreme-court-unbelievable-decision-dismisses-stolen-generations-compensation-claim.

21 "WA Supreme Court Dismisses Stolen Generation Compensation Claim Launched by the Collard Family," *ABC News*, June 10, 2015, http://www.abc.net.au/news/2013-12-20/stolen-generations-test-case-dismissed-in-wa-court/5169640; "Stolen Generation Family Ordered to Pay Costs After 'Test Case' Fails in WA," *ABC News*, May 9, 2015, http://www.abc.net.au/news/2015-05-09/stolen-generation-family-must-pay-court-costs/6457256.

ter families.²² Bill Ryan, Director of the Northern Territory Legal Service and a member of the Stolen Generations, together with social worker John Tomlinson, audaciously removed an Aboriginal girl from foster care in Darwin without official permission, boarded a small plane and returned the girl to her family in a remote community. The media endorsed the department and foster parents who had detained the girl for six and a half years despite the fact that she was not a ward of the state and her parents' repeated requests for her return. Headlines exposed the depths of public ignorance, fantasising the forced return of a "civilised miss" to a "stone age world" and marriage to a middle-aged "promised husband." The then Minister for Aboriginal Affairs in the Whitlam government, Gordon Bryant, showed a refreshing new stance when he announced that he would return all Aboriginal children in foster care in the Northern Territory to their families. Nothing came of this and in the end, Bryant, Ryan and Tomlinson were punished for their actions: Bryant was dropped from the ministry, Ryan was dismissed as Director of the Aboriginal Legal Service, and Tomlinson was demoted. The girl disappeared from the newspapers but Aboriginal leaders continued to protest. In 1974 Joe McGinness, President of the Federal Council of Aboriginal and Torres Strait Islanders, called the official equating of Aboriginal family life with neglect "an absolute insult to the Aboriginal people of Australia." The new National Aboriginal Consultative Committee demanded an inquiry into fostering of Aboriginal children, but the matter was shelved.

Public memory of these sensational events may have been short but other important structural changes were happening on the ground in new Aboriginal community service organisations. They were blazing a trail of activism that would lead to the 1995 Inquiry. Legal representation by Aboriginal Legal Aid Services meant that parental rights could now be supported in court. In a landmark case in the Northern Territory Supreme Court in 1972, the judge ruled in favour of returning a two-year-old boy placed with American foster parents to the "love of his mother and extended family in which, as he grows older, he will probably feel more at home than with a white family."²³ In Melbourne, the Victorian Aboriginal Legal Service (VALS) documented high rates of breakdown in adoptions of Aboriginal children—90 per cent before 1977—and related youth incarceration.²⁴ Collaboration between Molly Dyer from VALS and the National Adoption Conference, which led opposi-

---

22 Anna Haebich, *Broken Circles: Fragmenting Indigenous Families, 1800–2000* (Fremantle WA: Fremantle Arts Centre Press, 2000), 592–600.

23 Anna Haebich and Steve Mickler, *A Boy's Short Life: The Story of Warren Braedon/Louis Johnson* (Perth: University of Western Australia Publishing, 2013), 46.

24 Haebich, *Broken Circles*, 601.

tion to forced adoption within white families, gave impetus to efforts to stop forced Aboriginal adoptions. The lead up to the 1979 International Year of the Child helped to progress the policy of indigenising child and family welfare through vital meetings held with Indigenous organisations in the United States and Canada funded by the federal Office of Child Care. By the late 1970s a range of Aboriginal organisations—Aboriginal Child Care Agencies, Link-Up and the Secretariat of National Aboriginal and Torres Strait Islander Child Care (formed in 1981)[25]—were already assisting with family reunions, placements with Indigenous families, programmes for family maintenance, and policies to sustain Aboriginal families and cultures. In 1986 the Australian Law Reform Commission recognised Aboriginal customary family law. By the 1990s the Aboriginal Child Care Placement Principle was operating in some jurisdictions.

The impetus for a government inquiry grew into a movement of lobbying and political activism during the 1990s. In 1991 the Royal Commission into Aboriginal Deaths in Custody announced causal links between child removal and deaths in custody and alarming statistics of Aboriginal and Torres Strait Islander incarceration. In the following year Prime Minister Keating acknowledged that "we took the children from their mothers" in his now iconic speech at Redfern in Sydney. A large gathering at the 1994 Going Home Conference in Darwin announced that "public ignorance of the history of forcible removal of Aboriginal children was hindering the recognition of the needs of its victims, their families and the provision of services."[26] In May 1995, the Keating Labor government appointed Sir Ronald Wilson and Professor Michael Dodson of the Human Rights Commission to lead the federal Inquiry into the Separation of Indigenous Children from their Families.

Reflecting on white Australian forgetting

Most Australians claimed to be ignorant of practices of Aboriginal child removal exposed by the *Bringing Them Home Report*. "I'm sorry I just didn't know," sobbed a woman at the 1997 National Adoption Conference in Perth.[27] Her heartfelt cry was echoed around the country. Inga Clendinnen, delivering her Boyer Lecture Series *True Stories* in 1999, confessed, "I didn't know anything about the policy."[28] The claim not to have known is puzzling. Certainly,

---

25 Ibid., 600–11.
26 Coral Dow, "Sorry: The Unfinished Business of the *Bringing Them Home Report*," Social Policy Section, Parliament of Australia, February 4, 2008, http://www.aph.gov.au/About_Parliament/Parliamentary_Departments/Parliamentary_Library/pubs/BN/0708/BringingThemHomeReport.
27 Haebich, *Broken Circles*, 563.

compelling forces operated to maintain social distance and limit the flow of information. In most states and territories segregation had been enforced by a combination of legal sanctions and informal "caste barriers." These barriers, however, were never impermeable. They were cut across by relations with employers, shopkeepers, police and bureaucrats reporting to their ministers, while the press picked up on the details. Child removals were discussed in the public domain from early times and, as we have seen, there were sometimes passionate public debates. There seemed to be a pattern of recurring surges of "waking out of [and back into] forgetfulness," to paraphrase Roland Barthes.[29]

This conundrum of otherwise informed people "not knowing" that emerged publicly in response to the report has driven my studies of institutionalised denial, national forgetting, ignorance and racism, to find out, not as Henry Reynolds asked "Why weren't we told?," but how so many people could claim not have known about the Stolen Generations. This collective Australian amnesia seems particularly cruel in the context of denialists' rebuttal and derision of Stolen Generations' remembering of their own personal experiences of trauma.

Australians' ability to forget when it comes to Indigenous history has not gone unnoticed by scholars. In his 1968 Boyer Lectures W.E.H. (Bill) Stanner described this as:

> a structural matter, a view from a window which has been carefully placed to exclude a whole quadrant of the landscape. What may have begun as a simple matter of forgetting of other possible views turned under habit and over time into something like a cult of forgetfulness practised on a national scale.[30]

More recently Tatz wrote of the "major tributary of forgetting, which claim[s] that there was nothing to remember in the first place."[31] Raimond Gaita argued that in the past colonists were "often culpably ignorant of the wrong done to Aborigines because, in racist ways, they were blind to their full humanity."[32] There are also insights from studies of bystander amnesia and denial of genocide in post-war Germany; for example, the seemingly contradic-

---

28   Inga Clendinnen, "Lecture 4: Inside the Contact Zone," *True Stories: Boyer Lectures*, ABC Radio National, December 5, 1999, http://www.abc.net.au/radionational/programs/ boyerlectures/lecture-4-inside-the-contact-zone-part-1/3562462#transcript.

29   Haebich, *Broken Circles*, 565.

30   W.E.H. (Bill) Stanner, *After the Dreaming: Black and White Australians - An Anthropologist's View* (Sydney: Australian Broadcasting Commission, 1968), 24–25.

31   Cited in Anna Haebich, " 'Between Knowing and Not Knowing': Public Knowledge of the Stolen Generations," *Aboriginal History* 25 (2002), 75.

32   Ibid., 71.

tory comments of Gordon Horwitz that "genocide cannot happen without a majority of passive bystanders" and of Jean Baudrillard that "forgetting the extermination is part of the extermination itself."[33]

In his analysis of national collective memory, Paul Connerton argues that forgetting encompasses several different functional processes. I adapted his analysis to explore how the processes might seek to erase collective memory of the Aboriginal past: the powerful master narratives that extolled white progress and denied Aboriginal humanity; the ruthless practices to force Aboriginal people to forget their own histories of activism; the pressures to forget injustices that challenged the nation's history and identity; the public's overt concern and then desire to forget injustices that seemed to be distant and yet their responsibility; and their turning away so that the issue remained forever unresolved.[34] It was, however, Nancy Tuana's discussion of the social significance of ignorance and Charles Mills' analysis of the racial contract that made the link for me between forgetting, ignorance, racism and behaviour. Tuana argues that ignorance is not a simple matter of failure or omission, an absence that we will overcome as we push out the boundaries of research and experience. Rather, it is "often constructed, maintained, and disseminated and is linked to issues of cognitive authority, doubt, trust, silencing, and uncertainty."[35] To our analyses of *why* we know we should add epistemologies of *ignorance* to account for our lack of knowledge about particular phenomena.

Looking at the Stolen Generations I could see that forgetting and ignorance are never benign: they both do things.[36] Ignorance breeds in a forgetful climate of not knowing by bestowing value on misinformation and failing to question its truthfulness. In a world of separation and suspicion of the other, hearsay and imaginings can easily become fact. Repeated by government and the media, misinformation assumes an aura of authority and authenticity. Specific groups can be defined and stereotyped on the basis of these misinformed attributes, which can then be used to rationalise and normalise discriminatory treatment of members of the group. There is an easy slippage between a mindset that promotes the distancing and dehumanising of racial groups, and the acceptance and normalising of their unequal treatment. In the process, discriminatory practices become normalised to the extent that they are rendered unremarkable and virtually invisible to the wider society, even as they may as-

---

33 Ibid., 73.
34 Anna Haebich, "Forgetting Indigenous Histories: Cases from the History of Australia's Stolen Generations," *Journal of Social History* 44, no. 4 (2011), 1035.
35 Ibid., 1035.
36 Ibid., 1036.

sume increasingly harsh forms. Large numbers of people can tacitly support these processes without fully acknowledging the meaning of what they are doing. This is not peripheral but is an integral part of the oppression of others to which they contribute directly or indirectly. This state is powerful and obstinate, persisting in the face of circulating knowledge, observable evidence, personal encounters and even public protests that might emerge. Mills argues that these steps lead to the "ironic outcome" where the perpetrators of prejudice and discrimination "fail to recognise or understand the conditions that their racism has helped to produce."[37] Tatz provides an astute link from this analysis back to racism in Australia:

> In South Africa I studied "native policy." On arrival here in 1961, I studied " Aboriginal policy." People who know of my dual interest still ask me, "Is it true to say that Apartheid was a malevolent instrument of racial oppression, whereas racism in Australia was a form of ignorant innocence, or innocent ignorance, an inability to understand or respect indigenous culture and values, albeit with some nasty consequences?" Comparisons aside, how does one categorise Australia's race relations? Much of that interracial history I call genocide.[38]

Removals keep on happening

The emotional upheaval, shock, grief, guilt and outrage about the Stolen Generations might now be part of national history, but in public memory it is once again slipping into the morass of forgetting and ignorance. For many politicians and bureaucrats the 54 recommendations of the *Bringing Them Home Report* are but a dim memory. Tragically, the breaking up of families keeps on happening. Despite ongoing activism to reclaim the children and re-indigenise child and family care, removals and placements outside of Aboriginal and Torres Strait Islander families are accelerating. The Aboriginal Child Care Placement Principle is increasingly sidelined in care arrangements. Placements such as forced adoption, rejected in the 1980s, are being reconsidered. A central Aboriginal family childcare arrangement of grandmothers caring for grandchildren is once again under scrutiny, prompting the formation of the protest group Grandmothers Against Removals (GRMAR). In a further cruelty, some newborn babies are taken from mothers who test drug

---

37   Cited in Haebich, "Forgetting Indigenous," 1036.
38   Colin Tatz, *Genocide in Australia*, Canberra: Australian Institute of Aboriginal and Torres Strait Islander Studies, Research Discussion Paper Number 8, 1999, 28–32.

positive, despite care being available within the mothers' extended family. Aboriginal mothers are also being imprisoned at unprecedented rates, leaving their children vulnerable to removal from their families. Incarceration of young people increases along with instances of their abusive treatment. A public outcry was raised by shocking images of abusive treatment of Aboriginal youths at the Don Dale Detention Centre in the Northern Territory in 2016 on ABC's *Four Corners*, now the subject of a Royal Commission into the Protection and Detention of Children in the Northern Territory. Despite public outcry about such incidents, the National Sorry Day Committee found in its *Bringing Them Home Scorecard Report 2015* that there is still "insufficient recognition of the trauma, loss and grief" experienced by members of the Stolen Generations and the "impacts on health and wellbeing."[39]

In her programme for Perth Noongar Radio that won the 2014 Human Rights Award for Radio, Yamatji radio producer and foster care mother Carol Dowling cited alarming figures from Western Australia where Aboriginal children make up 50.5 per cent of all children in out-of-home care in the state but are only five per cent of the general population.[40] Of these, 34 per cent are with non-Aboriginal carers. In an example of "bad policy economics" she claimed that expenditure to keep child protection structures in place was 50 times more than that spent on Aboriginal family support mechanisms to help keep children in their families. Dennis Eggington, Director of the Aboriginal Legal Service, insisted that funding should be relocated to holistic Aboriginal-run services to provide housing and relieve poverty, causes that lead to removal of Aboriginal children. Selena Kickett from the Dumbartung Aboriginal organisation in Perth spoke of the vital need for healing to relieve the trans-generational trauma from the ongoing break up of Aboriginal families. An unidentified mother cries out that taking the children is "killing our future." Little wonder then that Dowling named the programme "Another Stolen Generation."

How can we explain the continuing punitive agendas and policies? We know of the years of Aboriginal activism and their achievements in David and Goliath battles against the full force of the settler colonial state. Yet punitive discourses, policies, legislation and bureaucracies continue to protect and advance stakeholder interests in Indigenous land and sea, and institutions that employ thousands of people maintain control over Aboriginal people. The paradigm of Aboriginal families as sites of danger and risk for their children

---

39 John Rule and Elizabeth Rice, *Bringing Them Home Scorecard Report 2015* (Canberra: National Sorry Day Committee, 2015), 8.
40 Carol Dowling, "Another Stolen Generation," Noongar Radio, September 18, 2014, https://www.cbaa.org.au/article/another-stolen-generation-noongar-radio-perth.

continues to be rolled out to endorse ongoing removals and to raise public support for stricter levels of government intervention and management, ostensibly to improve health and wellbeing. The Federal Government used allegations that child sexual abuse was rife in Indigenous communities to validate the invasive actions of the Northern Territory Intervention. The West Australian government made similar claims in threatening to close up to 150 communities. The forced removal of Aboriginal children remains an integral process of the Australian settler colony.

The shift from principles of Aboriginal and Torres Strait Islander self-determination and pluralism represents yet another iteration of Wolfe's model of the settler colony, now fuelled by neoliberal ideologies and practice.[41] Events in today's neoliberal times represent another return to the status quo, to the familiar scenario of economic and political anxieties, antipathy to the welfare state, demands for Aboriginal lands and resources, and the use of instruments of settler colonialism to restore the balance of colonial supremacy and progress. Terri Libesman points to the accumulated consequences for Aboriginal families, of the shifts away from recognition of collective histories and rights to a more neoliberal focus on individual responsibility and compliance with mainstream measures of wellbeing.[42] This shift has been accompanied by greater prevalence of populist racist characterisations of neglect and abuse as pertaining to cultural and individual Indigenous deficits rather than founded in colonial experiences and systemic disadvantage. There has also been more anecdotal evidence about a disregard for the rule of law and more overtly discriminatory responses to Indigenous families.

We now live with escalating alarms of global terrorism, climate change, economic disaster and wars of human annihilation. Fears of so-called problem populations—Indigenous, ethnic, refugees and asylum seekers—threaten national security and peace. In this context, there is support for an encompassing state apparatus of management through surveillance, containment and banishment to institutions and/or forced assimilation into the nation state. Global terrorism generates dehumanising of "problem populations" and support for harsh solutions that hark back to carceral institutions for Indigenous populations in settler colonial states. This is the reality of accelerating incarceration of Indigenous men, women and children. For Indigenous people, the driving force of neoliberal capitalist economies for global development engages them in new struggles against global organisations to maintain their hard-won land

---

41 The following argument draws on Anna Haebich, "Neoliberalism, Settler Colonialism and the History of Indigenous Child Removal in Australia," Australian *Indigenous* Law *Review* 19, no. 8 (2015/2016), 21–22.

42 Terri Libesman, email message to author, March 12, 2015.

security and protect precious resources of water, food, minerals and energy from fast growing markets and populations. Labelled as problem populations they once again face threats of being displaced, relocated and forced to transition culturally by assimilating into the mainstream.

The model of settler colonialism presented in this essay suggests a continuing draconian settler colonial state with no end to the forced removal of Aboriginal children. As we have seen, however, there is some hope in the narratives of activism and strategies for change drawing on Aboriginal values, knowledge and experience and ways of working together for cultural healing. Freed from the strictures of government policy and bureaucracy, the Stolen Generations and their supporters can create movements of people working together with open hearts and minds to heal the past. In 2015 the National Sorry Day Committee advised that "the best sources of knowledge and understanding of the backgrounds and needs of the Stolen Generations are the Stolen Generations themselves." They are also the people best placed to drive what is needed now and into the future.

GENOCIDE BY ANY OTHER NAME

John Maynard

In this essay I step back from contemporary discussions, observations and debates around the history of Australian genocide and reveal: a) the words of policymakers and officials during the late nineteenth century about the treatment of Aboriginal people; b) the recognition of genocidal acts in newspaper coverage of the early twentieth century; and c) the assertions of prominent early Aboriginal activists, including my grandfather Fred Maynard, on the violence meted out to Aboriginal people. Neither officials nor Aboriginal activists used the term "genocide" of course, since it had not yet been coined. The terminology they used, however, aligns with a contemporary understanding of genocide. These witnesses and observers were well aware of the genocidal practices occurring during their own time.

Settler colonial societies, including Australia, continue to struggle in the twenty-first century to deal with the crimes of their forebears, crimes that impacted so devastatingly on Indigenous peoples. For the greater part of the twentieth century, Aboriginal people simply did not figure in Australia's celebratory and triumphalist history. The descent of the curtain of silence during this period, which prevented government officials or media from reporting on Australia's treatment of Aboriginal people, was described by the late anthropologist W.E.H. (Bill) Stanner as the "Great Australian Silence."[1]

Yet in the early decades of the twentieth century, Aboriginal activists, despite coming from a marginalised minority, raised their voices and protested the crimes against their communities. Their outspoken comments, echoed in the cries of their non-Aboriginal supporters, were not just confined to the atrocities committed on the frontier. They also recognised that government policy introduced at the start of the twentieth century would unquestionably lead to one result—genocide. In this paper, I recall comments made to me by Dungatti elder, Uncle Reuben Kelly, about those brave Aboriginal activists.

After that first wave of Aboriginal activism, the 1960s and 1970s saw the re-emergence of grassroots movements and a new generation of young histori-

---

1 W.E.H. Stanner, "The Boyer Lectures: After the Dreaming," *The Dreaming and Other Essays* (Melbourne: Black Inc. Agenda, 2009), 182–93.

ans who began to unpack the history of the continent post-1788 and recognise the destruction wrought upon Aboriginal Australia. Inspired by Stanner and historian Charles Rowley, others like Henry Reynolds, Noel Loos, Bob Reece, Raymond Evans and Lyndall Ryan heeded the call and lifted the veil on historical violence and massacres.[2] At the same time, Aboriginal viewpoints seeped into the public domain, from activists like Kevin Gilbert and Charlie Perkins.

As had happened earlier, this historical reality check was subsequently followed and challenged by politicians, journalists and scholars who were more inclined to support the celebratory national history of the past, one that recognised discoverers, explorers and settlers, and presented the more palatable view that Australia was peacefully settled. These debates, challenges, arguments and disputes continue to echo across this historical divide even today.

The claim of "genocide" often triggers such debate. In its landmark *Bringing Them Home Report*, the Australian Human Rights Commission argued that the forced removals of Aboriginal children over the nineteenth and twentieth centuries constituted a genocidal policy. Strongly and publicly recognising Australia's history of genocide, Colin Tatz has many times applied the terms of the UN Genocide Convention to Australia, noting that actions taken against Indigenous peoples were calculated, wanting to destroy and/or to cause serious physical and mental harm, and that the forcible removal of children conformed to the acts of genocide defined in the Convention.[3] Tatz later reflected that his disclosures upset many people who "were duly shocked, upset and bewildered by this portrait of Australia as a genocidal society."[4]

The recognised guilt in the records

Before Australia's Great Silence and subsequent rewriting of history to portray Australia as having been peacefully settled, many colonial and British government officials, legislators and politicians openly asserted Australia's role in the destruction of Aboriginal communities, and newspapers openly reported it. The Secretary of State for War and the Colonies, Lord Glenelg, between

---

2   Noel Loos, "Aboriginal-European Relations in North Queensland, 1861–1897" (PhD thesis, James Cook University, 1976); Noel Loos, "Frontier Conflict in the Bowen District, 1861–1874" (PhD thesis, James Cook University, 1970); Henry Reynolds, *The Other Side of the Frontier* (Melbourne: Penguin Books, 1982); Raymond Evans, Kay Saunders and Kathryn Cronin, *Exclusion, Exploitation and Extermination: Race Relations in Colonial Queensland* (Sydney: Australia & New Zealand Book Co., 1975); Lyndall Ryan, *The Aboriginal Tasmanians* (Sydney: Allen & Unwin, 1996); Robert Reece, *Aborigines and Colonists* (Sydney: Sydney University Press, 1974).

3   Colin Tatz, *With Intent to Destroy: Reflecting on Genocide* (London: Verso, 2003), 72.

4   Colin Tatz, *Human Rights and Human Wrongs: A Life Confronting Racism* (Melbourne: Monash University, 2015), 305.

1835 and 1839 was blunt in his assessment: "Let us not cast upon Heaven a destruction which is our own, and say the [A]boriginals are doomed by Divine Providence when the guilt lies with ourselves."[5] In official despatches, Lord John Russell—a powerful government official and twice British Prime Minister—was also forthright on where the guilt lay for the treatment of the Aboriginal population: "All too clear is the truth that from first to last the line of contact of the two races has been a red one, and the strong Caucasian has trodden the naked nomad like mire into his own soil."[6] In a later despatch, Russell would add that it was "impossible to contemplate the condition and the prospects of that unfortunate race without the deepest commiseration."[7]

Before the House of Commons Committee in 1838, Lieutenant Richard Sadlier[8] highlighted with alarm the dire situation in the Australian Colonies: "As a question of humanity nothing can be more dreadful to contemplate, or more disgraceful to a Christian and civilised nation, than the wholesale destruction going on for the last fifty years, and must continue to the end unless some plan is devised to prevent it."[9] Sadlier recognised Aboriginal people as sovereign holders of their land and his statements clearly describe colonial actions as a war of destruction with the aim of usurping the land. Contemporary scholarship of genocide often focuses on factors such as land expropriation and "cleansing" of minorities who stand in the way of colonial expansion. Sadlier was reported to have written:

> It might be presumed that the natives of any land have an incontrovertible right to their own lands, as it is a plain and sacred right which appears not to have been understood. Europeans have entered their border uninvited, and when there have not only acted as if they were the undoubted lords of the soil, but have punished the natives as aggressors if they have evinced a disposition to live in their own country. If the Australian [A]borigines have been found upon their own property, they have been hunted as thieves and robbers, driven back into the interior as if they were dogs or kangaroos.[10]

Evidence delivered to the 1838 House of Commons Committee on the Aboriginal plight horrified members. Lord Stanley wrote of his dismay: "Outrages of

---

5   Archibald Meston, "Vanishing Aboriginals," *Sydney Morning Herald*, March 25, 1922.
6   Cited in Ibid.
7   Cited in Meston, "Vanishing Aboriginals."
8   K. J. Cable, "Sadlier, Richard (1794–1889)," *Australian Dictionary of Biography* (Canberra: National Centre of Biography, Australian National University, 1967).
9   Cited in Meston, "Vanishing Aboriginals."
10 *Sydney Morning Herald*, March 25, 1922.

the most atrocious description, involving considerable loss of life are spoken of in these papers with an indifference and lightness which is very shocking."[11] A journalist for the *Newcastle Chronicle* was adamant that:

> We have not only taken possession of the lands of the [A]boriginal tribes of this colony, and driven them from their territories, but we have also kept up unrelenting hostility towards them, as if they were not worthy of being classed with human beings, but simply regarded as inferior to some of the lower animals of creation.[12]

There is no mistaking that these individuals witnessed and spoke of a war of extermination that had been unleashed against the Aboriginal population. This is only a small sample of material readily available.

Early twentieth century media observations

In the early twentieth century, journalists and commentators were forthright in their estimation of the treatment of Aboriginal people in Australia's historical past. One writer in the *Sydney Morning Herald* recognised not just the injustices of the newly federated nation's past, but also the grim future for the Aboriginal population: "Most of the white insurpers [sic] of this continent consider the blackfellow a lingering nuisance, whose inevitable demise should be hastened rather than retarded."[13] Author T.P. Bellchambers impressed the crimes of the past upon the nation's memory:

> It has been said that we acquired this country not by an act of war, but by peaceful occupation. Yes, without so much as "by your leave" we introduced ourselves as supermen and overlords; we took possession of the [A]borigines, destroyed their game and drove them from their scant water supplies . . . our "peaceful occupation" has meant many treacherous deeds. . . . We who have steeped our souls in every known sin, as judged by our laws that we have made.[14]

Aboriginal protection societies began in Britain in the nineteenth century, and similar bodies were established in Australia, gaining some momentum in

---

11 *Sydney Morning Herald*, March 25, 1922.
12 *Newcastle Chronicle*, November 18, 1869, 2.
13 *Sydney Morning Herald*, 1904.
14 *Daylight*, May 25, 1922.

the 1930s. The progress associations, sometimes called welfare leagues, campaigned strongly for the end of discriminatory laws, better living conditions and the granting of full citizenship rights. They tried hard to gain media space and attention, but were seldom heard by the press and a public that did not want to listen. After World War Two, these bodies were dismissed as "do-gooders" or worse, as Communists.

Early Aboriginal activists and their supporters

The Australian Aboriginal Progressive Association (AAPA) was formed in Sydney in 1924 and led by my grandfather, Fred Maynard (1879–1946), a Worimi Aboriginal man. Fred Maynard was an articulate and inspiring visionary. The AAPA was the first to make a pan-Aboriginal demand for a national land rights agenda, as well as advocating for self-determination. While the group itself comprised Aboriginal members, high profile non-Aboriginal people like missionary Elizabeth McKenzie-Hatton and newspaper editor John J. Moloney were active supporters.

In this section I analyse the commentary of Fred Maynard and supporters to reveal those grassroots Aboriginal movements and their understanding of a genocide being perpetrated. It is important to realise that early Aboriginal activists and their supporters were well aware of the sickening historical reality of violence perpetrated against Aboriginal populations. Their views consolidate the recognition of government officials and the media.

Fred Maynard was scathing in his assessment, not hesitating to label the British landing at Port Jackson in 1788 as an "invasion." The British had, in his estimation, decimated the Aboriginal population through "the arts of war . . . and diseases." In an interview I conducted over 20 years ago, Uncle Reuben Kelly, the respected Dungutti elder, shared his recollections of that time. Kelly was adamant that Fred Maynard was the first Aboriginal man "to speak out about the atrocities, the poisoning, the murders, and the penal system." Kelly said he revealed "the condoned and silenced massacres of the past."[15] Maynard saw parallels between the experiences of Aboriginal people in Australia and the mass killings that had taken place in the Belgian Congo.[16] While the numbers differed substantially, with the Congo witnessing a "death toll of holocaust dimensions," Maynard saw a similar genocidal intent in Australian government policy. In relation to New South Wales government policy that he

---

15   Reuben Kelly, in discussion with John Maynard, 1996.
16   Adam Hochschild, *King Leopold's Ghost: A Story of Greed, Terror and Heroism in Central Africa* (London: Pan Books, 2006), 3.

foresaw as having drastic ramifications on local Aboriginal people, he wrote: "What a horrible conception of so called legislation, Re any civilised laws, I say deliberately stinks of the Belgian Congo."[17]

The language Maynard uses to describe the government's treatment of Aboriginal people aligns with the legal definition of genocide. In his estimation, the situation facing Aboriginal peoples and their continuation as a community, was dire.

Maynard saw the government policy of separating young Aboriginal children from their families, especially the girls, as part of a genocidal policy, stating that this "objectionable practice of segregating the sexes as soon as they reach a certain age should be abolished for it meant rapid extinction."[18] He viewed the New South Wales Aborigines Protection Board and the Aborigines Act, as well as the Board's so-called apprenticeship scheme as nothing more than a thinly disguised "attempt to exterminate the race."[19] Maynard was not alone in his assessment of this callous treatment with non-Aboriginal commentators also voicing their disapproval. Richard Tomalin, manager of Mount Leonard cattle station at Windorah in Queensland, wrote to the AAPA leadership and offered his support:

> It is not necessary to give my personal experience connected with some appalling extermination methods bar the fact that their [Aboriginal] numbers were reduced not by the procedure of time, but by drastic unlawful methods adopted by the white settlers.[20]

He observed the horror of assaults upon Aboriginal family life:

> The drastic and utterly unlawful method of taking away their female children would not stand if taken direct to a British Tribunal, as under the law the freedom of a British subject cannot be taken from him, and I consider a father just as much justified in using all means he chooses to defend his children from being forcibly removed from their parental care, more so even than a banker defending his gold.[21]

Two prominent and courageous non-Aboriginal supporters of the early Abo-

---

17 Fred Maynard, private letter, NSW Premiers Department Correspondence Files, A27/915, 1927.
18 Cited in John J. Moloney, "The Aboriginals," *Voice of the North*, December 10, 1926.
19 "Aborigines: Agitation by Association," *Northern Star*, August 3, 1927.
20 Richard Tomalin, "Australian Aboriginals," *Voice of the North*, June 10, 1927, 18.
21 Ibid.

riginal political movement were the missionary Elizabeth McKenzie Hatton and John J. Moloney, the Editor of the Newcastle newspaper the *Voice of the North*. Decades ahead of their time, their words remain powerful today in challenging whitewashed Australian history. Former Prime Minister John Howard argued that, "Australians of the current generation should not be required to accept blame for past policies over which they had no control."[22] Yet McKenzie Hatton, writing in the *Daylight* in 1926, could almost be replying to Howard across the decades:

> We may claim that we are not responsible for the actions of the original British invaders who violated their homes, shot, poisoned, burned and mutilated the natives, but we cannot claim immunity from the conditions existing at the present time, and what should not be tolerated for one moment longer than it will take to rectify matters. The citizens comfortably situated on the shores of Port Jackson are, in the main, absolutely ignorant of the conditions under which the natives are existing. The moment this sore is opened up there will be a rush of apologists from the ranks of parliamentarians, parsons, priests, pedagogues, pedants, and peripatetic philosophers, but such belated excuses will be brushed aside, for the fiat has gone forth—JUSTICE TO THE NATIVES—and the people of Australia will not be satisfied until that full measure of compensation has been accorded to a much injured and sadly wronged people.[23]

This illustrates how, in the contemporary setting, the failure to accept any blame or responsibility has continued unabated, notwithstanding Paul Keating's 1992 Redfern speech and Kevin Rudd's apology to the Stolen Generations. Contemporary scholar Dirk Moses points out that the British "understood the effects of their presence in Australia" but, nevertheless, demonstrated an inability to take "responsibility for the anticipated disappearance of the Aboriginal peoples, despite the obvious connection between colonization and depopulation."[24]

---

22 John Howard, *Lazarus Rising: A Personal and Political Autobiography* (Sydney: Harper Collins, 2010), 277.

23 Elizabeth McKenzie Hatton, "The Dark Brethren," *Daylight*, October 30, 1926, 102.

24 A. Dirk Moses, ed., *Genocide and Settler Society: Frontier Violence and Stolen Indigenous Children in Australian History* (New York: Berghahn Books, 2005), 6.

Conclusion

In a letter written in 1927, J.J. Moloney, a fierce Australian nationalist, spoke out about the treatment of Aboriginal people:

> The iniquity of the position maddens me. To see these poor creatures kicked into the bush—worse than dogs—their homes built by their own hands confiscated, no compensation, no redress—their children kidnapped by the Crown and sent to work for Collins Whites at 6d a week, robbed at every turn, derided by all parties. . . . Every Church equally to blame—Priests, Bishops, Parsons—all equally guilty . . . if I were in London, I think I would try and get an audience with the King.[25]

While many historians, genocide scholars, journalists and politicians continue to debate and question the validity of whether genocide was committed in Australia, eyewitnesses had no doubt. Neither did Aboriginal people. I look back over my own family's history and that of the Worimi people of the Port Stephens region of New South Wales and realise that it is a miracle I am here today. The stark reality is that so many thousands of our people were swept away with no regard for them as human beings and, even deliberately, with genocidal intent.

If Australia is willing to accept this history and so educate our children, the evidence is here, waiting. Those who were alive at the time stated openly what they witnessed; government officials spoke honest words about the policy goal of extermination; newspapers wrote about it—the public cannot claim not to have known. Today we have a body of literature by Aboriginal and non-Aboriginal scholars that presents survivor testimony from members of the Stolen Generations and evidence of massacre and frontier warfare that resulted in large numbers of Aboriginal deaths. Aboriginal people spent decades with no legal or civil rights, no sense of belonging in Australia. In the whole menu of what constitutes "human rights," we did not have even one item. Moreover, we experienced and survived a genocide that, while clearly acknowledged at the time, remains hidden today. It is with the aim of revealing that genocide that the words of my grandfather, Fred Maynard, resonate still: the government "insulted and degraded all Aboriginal people, and it aimed to exterminate the noble and ancient race of sunny Australia."[26]

---

25 J.J. Moloney, letter to A.P. Elkin (private collection, 1927).
26 Fred Maynard, private letter (private collection, 1927).

TOO NEAR AND TOO FAR: AUSTRALIA'S RELUCTANCE TO NAME AND PROSECUTE GENOCIDE

Jennifer Balint[1]

Introduction

Another suspected war criminal found in Australia. In the Australian Capital Territory (ACT) Magistrates Court in late 2014, former Bosnian Croat soldier, Krunoslav Bonić, was the subject of an extradition hearing to face war crimes charges in Bosnia and Herzegovina. Apparently he had been living in Canberra since 1998, yet an international arrest warrant was issued by Bosnia only in 2006. This is not surprising. Australia's record on prosecuting war crimes, including genocide, is poor indeed. According to a Lowy Institute report, Australia was described in the Simon Wiesenthal Center's annual status report on Nazi war crimes investigations and prosecutions as "the only major Western country of refuge."[2] In January 2015, Bosnia dropped its extradition request and Bonić was freed. It is unclear why: serious allegations were made against Bonić by eyewitnesses in at least one case heard at the International Criminal Tribunal for the former Yugoslavia.[3]

Australia has an abysmal record in prosecuting genocide and state crime, perpetrated either here or elsewhere. There is something curious about Australia's reluctance to prosecute this crime. It is either too near (in the case of Indigenous genocide in Australia) or too far away (in the case of the Holocaust

---

1   I am grateful to Eleanor Gilbert who allowed me access to the files on the hearings in relation to the Aboriginal Embassy case, and to Evelyn Rose for her thoughtful research assistance on this chapter. My thanks to my Honours colleague at Macquarie University, Angela Jones, whose thesis, written in 1991 and supervised by Colin Tatz, provides an excellent overview of public debates at the time, something that has been lost in much subsequent analysis. Deep thanks to Colin Tatz, with whom I began this journey.

2   Fergus Hanson, *Confronting Reality: Responding to War Criminals in Australia* (Sydney: Lowy Institute for International Policy, 2009), 6.

3   International Criminal Tribunal for the Former Yugoslavia, *Kordić & Čerkez* IT-95-14/2, case transcript, September 13, 1999, see 6510. After detailing the involvement of Bonić, together with his father, in the arrest and detention of the witness, Fuad Zeco, the transcript continues: Q. Thank you. Thank you. This Krunoslav Bonić who arrested you, did you know whether he was captured by the BH army during the conflict and where he now lives? A. Yes, he was captured. After the war conflict ceased, he was arrested. I know that he was arrested and that he spent his time in prison in Travnik, and after that, after a certain amount of time spent in prison, he moved to Australia. That's what I know.

in World War Two, or genocide in Rwanda or in the former Yugoslavia). We ratified its Convention, decried in its defining into international law as an "odious scourge,"[4] yet our political leaders have almost routinely disregarded the importance of prosecuting genocide. Taskforces have been set up and abandoned, downsized, and recommendations ignored. We have failed to name or hear the crime of genocide perpetrated against Aboriginal Peoples—and it was only with the hearing of the genocide charges brought by the Aboriginal Tent Embassy in 1998 that it was made public that, despite signing the Convention on the Prevention and Punishment of the Crime of Genocide (the "Genocide Convention") in 1949, we had not in fact incorporated the crime of genocide into Australian domestic legislation.

This essay considers our record on addressing genocide and why we are so reluctant to prosecute. It suggests that in our refusal to acknowledge genocide, we maintain the charade of a country without history. We are, in many ways, a land of forgetting. This reluctance to prosecute "the past" is integral to this enterprise. That the past informs the present, however, is what is inherently risky about this apparently entrenched policy approach to an aversion to the naming and prosecuting of genocide.

Too far away: Australia's record on prosecuting World War Two crimes

In the 1980s, Australia introduced legislation to prosecute perpetrators from the Second World War who were current Australian citizens or residents. This was the first time that a domestic legislative framework was established to prosecute World War Two perpetrators who had sought refuge and asylum in post-war Australia. The Hawke Labor government amended the *War Crimes Act 1945* to allow charges to be brought against suspected war criminals living in Australia.

The *War Crimes Act* had been legislated post-war to enable the prosecution of 807 Japanese defendants, for crimes mostly perpetrated against Australian soldiers.[5] This was, it has been argued, fuelled by deep-seated racist underpinnings of Australian attitudes towards the Japanese existing prior to the Second World War with its "White Australia" policy, and by the witnessing by the Australian population of Australian prisoners of war returning home

---

4 United Nations, Convention on the Prevention and Punishment of the Crime of Genocide (1948), Preamble.
5 Helen Durham and Michael Carrel, "Lessons from the Past: Australia's Experience in War Crimes Prosecution and the Problem of the Applicable Legal Framework," *Asia-Pacific Yearbook of International Humanitarian Law* 2 (2006), 135.

after horrific experiences in Japanese camps.[6] Military trials were held in the Asia-Pacific region and in Australia, with 579 individuals convicted and 137 sentenced to death and executed.[7] The *War Crimes Act*, however, was designed to prosecute crimes solely against British citizens or subjects. It had no remit for enabling the broader prosecution of crimes perpetrated in World War Two, or in other conflicts. The witnessing of POW experiences did not extend to the experiences suffered by post-war European refugees. That harm was not visible to the broader Australian population.

There had been little public or political appetite for broader post-war prosecutions. In 1961, the Acting Minister for External Affairs, Sir Garfield Barwick announced—in response to refusing a request from the Soviet Union for extradition of an alleged war criminal, Ervin Richard Adolf Petrovich Viks—the end of war crimes prosecutions under Australian legislation. He argued that whilst there is a sense of "utter abhorrence felt by Australians for those offences against humanity to which we give the generic name of war crimes . . . there is the right of this nation, by receiving people into its country, to enable men to turn their backs on past bitterness and to make a new life for themselves and for their families in a happier community."[8] Barwick concluded in this vein: ". . . we think the time has come to close the chapter. It is, truly, the year 1961."[9] This came from someone who three years later was to become Chief Justice of the High Court of Australia. The policy of forgetting was entrenched. Even the Japanese war crimes trials had been seen to take too long. In 1950, with the announcement by the Menzies government to speed up trials, release those with insufficient evidence, and reserve the right to make a re-arrest if new material surfaced, then leader of the opposition Mr Chifley, stated: "I could not see much purpose in continuing investigations aimed at the tracing of war criminals. That sort of thing could go on for the next 20 years, and new criminals could be located almost daily."[10]

As a result of the investigative work by journalist Mark Aarons, the extent of the settlement in Australia of suspected war criminals became known.[11]

---

6 Michael Carrel, "Australia's Prosecution of Japanese War Criminals: Stimuli and Constraints," in *The Legacy of Nuremberg: Civilising Influence or Institutionalised Vengeance?*, eds. David Blumenthal and Timothy McCormack (Boston: Martinus Nijhoff Publishers, 2007), 240–42; also see Gideon Boas and Pascale Chifflet, "Suspected War Criminal in Australia: Law and Policy," *Melbourne University Law Review* 40 (2016), 48–49.

7 Carrel, Ibid., 246–47.

8 The Hon. Sir Garfield Barwick, *Press Statement on Soviet Request for Surrender of E.R.A.P. Viks* (Canberra: Commonwealth of Australia Department of External Affairs, 1961), 7.

9 Ibid.

10 Andrew Menzies, *Review of Material Relating to the Entry of Suspected War Criminals Into Australia* (Canberra: Australian Government Publishing Service, 1987), 10.

11 Mark Aarons' five-part documentary series *Nazis in Australia* was broadcast on ABC Radio National in

Much of this had begun as anecdotal—Jewish refugees sharing boats to Australia with Nazi perpetrators—and had been documented immediately postwar by the Jewish community, together with Aarons' own extensive archival work.[12] Later work demonstrated that this was a deliberate policy of excluding Jewish Displaced Persons and accepting those predominantly from the Baltic countries.[13] Early in 1986, the Executive Council of Australian Jewry had begun lobbying the Australian government for an enquiry, similar to that undertaken in Canada.[14] In June 1986 the Hawke Government appointed a retired senior public servant, Andrew Menzies, to conduct a review of material relating to the entry of suspected war criminals into Australia. Menzies found that it was "more likely than not that a significant number of persons who committed serious war crimes in World War Two entered Australia and some of these are now in Australia," and "that some action needs to be taken."[15] He recommended a special unit be established to investigate the allegations and initiate extradition, deportations or prosecutions.[16] His first recommendation to the government was that they "make a clear and positive statement to the effect that, as regards serious war crimes, it does not regard the Chapter as closed (contrary to the Barwick statement in 1961) and that it will take appropriate action under the law to bring to justice persons who have committed serious war crimes found in Australia."[17]

The government's response to that review was tabled in Parliament on February 24, 1987, by Senator Gareth Evans on behalf of the Attorney-General Lionel Bowen. It read in part:

> The Government accepts the conclusion that some persons, against whom the most serious allegations have been made, are likely to have entered Australia after the Second World War, and to be still resident here today.

1986. This was the culmination of earlier documentaries and work that had begun in 1977. He subsequently published a book detailing the allegations: Mark Aarons, *Sanctuary: Nazi Fugitives in Australia* (Melbourne: William Heinemann Australia, 1989).

12 Both Aarons and Suzanne Rutland tell how in the early 1950s, the Federal Immigration Minister, Harold Holt, threatened Jewish community leaders that if they did not stop their campaign against the migration to Australia of known Nazis, the government would block the transfer of money to Israel by the community. See Mark Aarons, "The Search For Nazi War Criminals in Australia," *Australian Journal of Jewish Studies* 26 (2012), 164–65; Suzanne Rutland, *Edge of the Diaspora: Two Centuries of Jewish Settlement in Australia* (Sydney: Collins, 1988), 334–35.

13 Leslie Caplan, *The Road to the Menzies Inquiry: Suspected War Criminals in Australia* (Darlington: Australian Jewish Historical Society, 2012), Appendix 3.

14 Ibid.

15 Menzies, *Review of Material*, 125.

16 Ibid., 168.

17 Ibid., 169.

> However, as Mr Menzies has found, their entry was achieved in the circumstances of the urgency and intensity of our post-war immigration program. Given that background, there is no value in continuing to examine the past with the idea of apportioning blame, or endeavouring to sheet home responsibility. Instead, our attention must be concentrated on the steps to be taken to ensure that suspected war criminals involved in serious crimes are brought to justice.[18]

Drawing a line under Barwick's statement, the response continued: "Where serious War crimes are concerned this Government does not regard the chapter as closed."[19] This enthusiasm was, however, short lived. Public appetite, and hence political appetite, for war crimes trials continued to be limited. The Bill took 14 months to pass both the House of Representatives and the Senate, with the *War Crimes Amendment Act* eventually becoming law on December 21, 1988, after divisive political debate.[20] The new law was still contained to World War Two era crimes and the government failed to specifically *name* genocide. Rather, war crimes were defined to include genocide as "intent to destroy":

> A serious crime is a war crime if it was: (a) committed: (i) in the course of political, racial or religious persecution; or (ii) with intent to destroy in whole or in part a national, ethnic, racial or religious group, as such; and (b) committed in the territory of a country when the country was involved in a war or when territory of the country was subject to an occupation.[21]

As a "war crime," genocide was subsumed under the category of "bad things happen in wartime" (in Europe), rather than the perpetration of the destruction of a people and of their common humanity. Like the International Military Tribunal at Nuremberg, it also continued a curtailed mandate, using September 1, 1939, as the start date, thereby omitting much of the criminal activity perpetrated prior to that date.

The *War Crimes Amendment Act 1988* led to the establishment of a Special Investigation Unit within the Department of Public Prosecutions that examined allegations of war crimes against over 800 individuals resident in

---

18   Senator Gareth Evans, *Government Response to Menzies Review* (Canberra: Parliament of Australia Senate, 1987), 496.
19   Ibid.
20   Irene Nemes, "Punishing War Criminals in Australia: Issues of Law and Morality," *Current Issues in Criminal Justice* 4, no. 2 (1992), 142–43.
21   *War Crimes Amendment Act 1988*, part 2, sec 6.1.

Australia. Evidence was found against 400 people who had arrived in Australia; of these, 200 were deceased. There was evidence for 40 prosecutable cases, and four were initially pursued.[22] There had been great hope in this new legislation, as echoed in its preamble:

> (a) concern has arisen that a significant number of <u>persons</u> who committed serious war crimes in Europe during World War II may since have entered Australia and became Australian citizens or residents;
> (b) it is appropriate that <u>persons</u> accused of such war crimes be brought to trial in the ordinary criminal courts in Australia; and
> (c) it is also essential in the interests of justice that <u>persons</u> so accused be given a fair trial with all the safeguards for accused <u>persons</u> in trials in those courts, having particular regard to matters such as the gravity of the allegations and the lapse of time since the alleged crimes.[23]

Yet, due to a combination of ill health and the advancing age of the defendants and, critically, the compounding difficulties of processing European war crimes cases in local courts in Adelaide, none were found guilty.

In the first case, Ivan Polyukhovich was charged in January 1990 with the killing of 24 Ukrainian Jews and involvement in the murder of a further 850 Ukrainian Jews between 1941 and 1943. After an appeal to the High Court on the basis of the legislation being unconstitutional (that was quashed), he was committed to trial in the Supreme Court of South Australia and, due to insufficient witness testimony, the trial ceased.[24] The second case was that of Mikolay Berezowsky. He was charged in 1991 with involvement in the murder of 102 Jews in Ukraine. Despite the hearing of 22 international witnesses, the case was dismissed in July 1992 by the magistrate during the committal hearings due to "identification difficulties."[25] In the third case of Heinrich Wagner, charges were brought in 1992 for the murder of 19 Jewish children and a railway construction worker, and involvement in the murder of 104 Ukrainian Jews in 1942 and 1943. The magistrate found sufficient evidence to commit to trial, yet prosecutors discontinued the case due to illness after Wagner suffered

---

22 *War Crimes Amendment Act 1988* (Cth), Preamble.
23 According to Graham Blewitt, Head of the Special Investigations Unit, the extent of the Australian trials was to be 12. Cited in Angela Jones, *More Than a Memory: Australia's War Crimes Trials* (Honours thesis, Macquarie University, 1991), 75.
24 For further detail, see Gillian Triggs, "Australia's War Crimes Trials: All Pity Choked," in *The Law of War Crimes: National and International Approaches*, eds. Timothy McCormack and Gerry Simpson (The Hague: Kluwer Law International, 1997), 123–49 and, in particular, 130–32.
25 For further detail, see Ibid., 132.

a heart attack.[26] There was a fourth case about to be brought; however, with the disbanding of the Special Investigation Unit by the Keating Government, this did not eventuate.

There had been little public interest in these trials. From a high point of bipartisanship when the legislation was first introduced by the Hawke Labor government in late 1987, this had deteriorated to the legislation passing in the Senate a year later by just five votes. The political atmosphere had changed. There were heated public debates around questions of money, the age of defendants (although as Angela Jones pointed out in her analysis of the trials at the time, there was no such objection raised when 80-year-old Queensland Premier Joh Bjelke-Petersen stood trial for perjury in October 1991[27]), the time that had passed, that the courts would be relying on evidence from communist countries,[28] as well as concern from particular communities who shared the same national background as the suspects. There was a sense, as expressed by Labor Senator Bernard Cooney in the Senate debate on the Bill, that "bygones be bygones."[29] What appeared to be missing, as Jones points out, was a sense of what these trials were attempting to prosecute: the crimes of the Holocaust.[30]

The unit closed in 1992. Since then, there have been only limited resources put towards the prosecution of Nazi war criminals,[31] and no prosecutions have been brought. One emerging frontier has been that of extraditions sought by other nations, mainly post-communist, for the trial of war criminals suspected to be residing in Australia. Australia has been reluctant to take this path: in a discussion of the extradition proceedings of suspected Hungarian war criminal Károly Zentai, Ruth Balint has argued that any recognition of war criminals living in Australia disrupts "the popular imaginary of the post-war period of immigration [that] has privileged a narrative of rescue of Hitler's and Stalin's victims."[32] Harbouring of perpetrators plays no role here.

It was a case outlining past and present genocide *in* Australia that brought,

---

26 For further detail, see Triggs, "Australia's War Crimes," 133–34.

27 Angela Jones, *More Than a Memory: Australia's War Crimes Trials* (Honours thesis, Macquarie University, 1991), 62.

28 For discussion of this point, see Nemes, "Punishing War Criminals," 143–45.

29 Hansard Senate War Crimes Amendment Bill 1987, 2nd reading, December 15, 1987, 4254, cited in Jones, *More Than a Memory*, 67.

30 Ibid., 56.

31 As Gideon Boas and Pascale Chifflet note, "responsibility for the investigation of such crimes has been delegated to various departments within the Australian Federal Police," and "Since the Menzies Review, there has been no large-scale or commissioned investigation into the entry of suspected war criminals into Australia."

32 Ruth Balint, "The Ties that Bind: Australia, Hungary and the Case of Károly Zentai," *Patterns of Prejudice* 44, no. 3 (2010), 284.

if not to the public but to the legislature, attention of our failure to prosecute the crime of genocide in this country.

Too near: the Aboriginal Tent Embassy genocide hearings

In the late 1990s, members of the Aboriginal Embassy tested the ability of our courts to hear genocide. The Embassy had been established in 1972 as a land rights protest on the grounds of what is now Old Parliament House, and has continued to serve as a focal point of protest.[33] On July 3, 1998, Wadjularbinna Nulyarimma, of Doomadgee Aboriginal Community in Queensland, lawyer Len Lindon, and Eleanor Gilbert who recorded much of the proceedings, went to the Canberra police station to request that charges of genocide be brought against current Members of the Australian Parliament. The amendments to the *Native Title Act* were being debated in the Australian Parliament. *The Native Title Amendment Bill 1997* was the latest iteration of the legislative regime established in 1993 to regulate Aboriginal land claims. Developed in the wake of the successful Mabo High Court decision in which the Court ruled in 1992 that Australia was not *terra nullius* ("land belonging to no-one") on settlement/invasion, it had developed into a restrictive regime of access to land known as "native title."

The claim made by the Embassy was that the imminent introduction of the revised *Native Title Act* put Aboriginal peoples at even greater risk of destruction and was part of a long history of genocidal practices.[34] In May 1997, then Prime Minister John Howard had introduced into policy a "10-point plan" in response to the High Court ruling on the Wik case.[35] The High Court in Wik found that pastoral leases did not automatically extinguish native title. Howard argued, "The fact is that the Wik decision pushed the pendulum too far in the

---

33 For more information on the Aboriginal Embassy, see Gary Foley, Andrew Schaap and Edwina Howell, eds., *The Aboriginal Tent Embassy. Sovereignty, Black Power, Land Rights and the State* (Abingdon: Routledge, 2014).

34 Damien Short has argued that genocide is a "continuing process in an Australia that has failed to decolonise and continues to assimilate," is "predicated on a victim's understanding of the culturally genocidal dimensions of settler colonialism and the central importance of land to the survival of many indigenous peoples *as peoples*." See Damien Short, "Australia: A Continuing Genocide?" *Journal of Genocide Research* 12, no. 2 (2010), 46. For further relevant discussion, see Colin Tatz, "Genocide in Australia," *Journal of Genocide Research* 1, no. 3 (1999), 315–52; Colin Tatz, "Confronting Australian Genocide," *Aboriginal History* 25, no. 1 (2001), 16–36; Katherine Bischoping, and Natalie Fingerhut, "Border Lines: Indigenous People in Genocide Studies," *Canadian Review of Sociology* 33, no. 4 (1996), 481–506; Larissa Behrendt, "Genocide: The Distance Between Law and Life," *Aboriginal History* 25 (2001), 132–47; Patrick Wolfe, "Nation and Miscegenation: Discursive Continuity in the Post-Mabo Era," *Social Analysis* 36 (1994), 93–131; Patrick Wolfe, "Settler Colonialism and the Elimination of the Native," *Journal of Genocide Research* 8, no. 4 (2006), 387–409.

35 *Wik Peoples* v *Queensland* (1996–187 CLR 1). This was a successful native title claim on land on the Cape York Peninsula brought by the Wik and Thayorre People.

Aboriginal direction. The 10-point plan will return the pendulum to the centre."[36] The subsequent *Native Title Amendment Act 1998* had at its core the extinguishment of native title (as outlined in its originating Bill):

> States and Territories would be able to confirm that "exclusive" tenures such as freehold, residential, commercial and public works in existence on or before 1 January 1994 extinguish native title. Agricultural leases would also be covered to the extent that it can reasonably be said that by reason of the grant or the nature of the permitted use of the land, exclusive possession must have been intended. Any current or former pastoral lease conferring exclusive possession would also be included.[37]

The United Nations Committee on the Elimination of All Forms of Racial Discrimination was to call this a racially discriminatory piece of legislation on the basis that, as Damien Short points out, it "detail[s] a host of white property interests that would automatically extinguish native title."[38] It was put to the Court that the native title legislation demonstrated "intent to destroy" as required by the Genocide Convention that Australia had ratified, although not implemented. On July 6, 1998, papers and an affidavit by central claimant Wadjularbinna Nulyarimma were presented to the Registrar of the ACT Magistrate's Court, asking that John Howard and Tim Fischer (as Prime Minister and Deputy Prime Minister) be charged with attempt, conspiracy and complicity in genocide (in their formulation of the "10-point plan" and enactment into legislation), Brian Harradine (Independent Member of the Senate) be charged with complicity in genocide (in his agreeing to the Native Title Amendment Bill), and Pauline Hanson (MP and leader of the One Nation party) be charged with public incitement to commit genocide (that over the past two years she had deliberately and publicly incited genocide). The Registrar of the ACT Magistrate's Court replied to the Embassy claimants: "I have come to the conclusion that the offences alleged [genocide, attempted genocide, aid and abet genocide, conspiracy to commit acts of genocide] in those informations are unknown to the law of the ACT."[39]

The hearing took place over seven days from July to September 1998, including one morning "around the fire" at the Embassy where Justice Crispin

---

36   John Howard, "Amended Wik 10-Point Plan," media statement, May 8, 1997, http://australianpolitics.com/1997/05/08/howard-amended-wik-10-point-plan.html.

37   *Native Title Amendment Bill 1997 Explanatory Memorandum*, Parliament of the Commonwealth of Australia, http://www.austlii.edu.au/au/legis/cth/ bill_em/ntab1997237/memo2.html, chap. 2.2.

38   Short, "Australia," 55.

39   Letter from PR Thompson, Registrar ACT Magistrates Court, to Mrs W. Nulyarimma, July 7, 1998.

heard testimony.[40] Affidavits were gathered and presented to the court from communities around Australia. The case was joined by Tom Trevorrow, Irene Watson, Kevin Buzzacott and Michael Anderson, Alice Hoolihan, Daisy Brown, Albert Hayes, Alister Thorpe, Yaluritja Clarrie Isaacs and Mingli Wanjurri Nungala. The claimants spoke to the reality that Australia had not recognised the genocide perpetrated here. They gave testimony that detailed their own and their community's experiences of genocide, both past and continuing. Wadjularbinna stated in an affidavit:

> The applicants' main concern is that the genocide against our people all Aboriginal peoples be stopped and prevented. We invoke your criminal law primarily to get your people to stop the genocide [par. 10]. . . . We see the Parliamentarians failure to prevent genocide against us by legislation or otherwise as another act of genocide [par.17]. . . . We have had enough of this genocide. This is a crisis situation and irreparable damage is being done [par. 35].[41]

There was a clear sense in the claims put forward in the case that there was continuing intent to perpetrate genocide in Australia, illustrated by the failure to integrate the Genocide Convention into domestic legislation and the use of law in fact to perpetuate genocide.[42] Wadjularbinna testified:

> Australia has ratified the Convention but they have not backed it up by making laws to prevent further genocide . . . speaks volumes . . . there is an ongoing intent . . . to continue the genocide.[43]

Justice Crispin did not find for the applicants from the Tent Embassy. He argued that members of Parliament could not be liable for criminal prosecution in the carrying out of their duties and in the formulation of policy. He also argued that he could not find within the common law any recognition of the offence of genocide, stating that "no offence of genocide is known to the

---

[40] For a detailed discussion of the case, see Jennifer Balint, "Stating Genocide in Law: The Aboriginal Embassy and the ACT Supreme Court," in *The Aboriginal Tent Embassy: Sovereignty, Black Power, Land Rights and the State*, eds. Gary Foley, Andrew Schaap and Edwina Howell (Abingdon: Routledge, 2014), 235–50.

[41] Affidavit of Wadjularbinna Nulyarimma, July 8, 1998.

[42] For a broader discussion of the use of law in the perpetration of genocide and how law can make genocide 'allowable', see Jennifer Balint, *Genocide, State Crime and the Law: In the Name of the State* (London: Routledge-Cavendish, 2012), in particular Chapter Two.

[43] Wadjularbinna, Tent Embassy case transcript, 77.

domestic law of Australia."[44] But he did find that genocide had occurred. Following a discussion of the Genocide Convention, he stated:

> There can be little doubt that the shameful chronicle of abuse suffered by aboriginal peoples in Australia since 1788 included many acts of the kind described in this definition. Given the passage of time, the paucity of contemporary records and the inevitable tendency for people to indulge in self justification it is not easy to determine whether particular atrocities were committed with the requisite intent. Nonetheless, the nature, scope and frequency of such acts suggests at least a strong probability that some at least were so motivated. In 1983 Murphy J referred to the Aboriginal people of Australia as having been the subject of "attempted genocide." However, the concept of genocide contained in Article 2 of the Convention does not require that the relevant "national, ethnical, racial or religious group" be destroyed, but only that one or more of the specified acts be committed with the intention of destroying the group "in whole or in part." Many of the atrocities plainly satisfied this description. In 1989 J.H.Wootten QC expressed the view that assimilation in its crudest forms, and particularly the removal of aboriginal children, fell within this definition. For present purposes, it is unnecessary for me to determine whether the particular conduct to which he referred would have been sufficient to sustain charges of genocide if such an offence formed part of the domestic law of Australia. *There is ample evidence to satisfy me that acts of genocide were committed during the colonisation of Australia.*[45]

This was a significant statement as it was the first time in Australian law that genocide against Indigenous Peoples had been so clearly recognised. Further, the case and its appeal prompted realisation that while Australia had signed the Genocide Convention, it had failed to integrate it into domestic legislation. While Australia was amongst the first to sign the Genocide Convention (on the day it was opened for signature, December 11, 1948), and ratified it in 1949, it subsequently failed to introduce legislation that would enable its domestic prosecution. On the one hand, this was not surprising. Those debating the ratification of the Convention in 1949 were convinced that it could never happen here. As Colin Tatz relates, in some 19 pages of the June 1949 parliamentary debate on Australia's ratification of the Convention, Aborigines were not mentioned.[46] Archie Cameron, Liberal Member for Barker argued in Parliament:

---

44 Supreme Court of the ACT 1998, no. 457, par. 73.
45 Ibid. (author's italics)

No one in his right senses believes that the Commonwealth of Australia will be called before the bar of public opinion, if there is such a thing, and asked to answer for any of the things which are enumerated in this convention.[47]

That Australia and Australians could be capable of genocide, past or present, was unthinkable. Little has changed, although the academic consensus now acknowledges that genocide is an apt descriptor for the Australian Aboriginal experience, and that the "intent to destroy" required to establish the crime of genocide need not be *malevolent*—that the effect of destruction remains the same.[48] Yet Australia had failed to introduce legislation to enable genocide to be prosecuted in Australia.

There had been no space in law previously to hear these claims of genocide. In his 2008 apology, then Prime Minister Kevin Rudd spoke of indignity, degradation, mistreatment, but not genocide.[49] The *Bringing Them Home Report* named genocide, but its recommendations, including a national compensation mechanism, failed to be implemented.[50] Cases have unsuccessfully been brought attempting to have genocide put on record—at least indirectly.[51] There had been fleeting recognition of genocide earlier, where in *Coe v Commonwealth* 1979 in the Australian High Court, Justice Murphy noted: "the

---

46 Colin Tatz, *With Intent to Destroy: Reflecting on Genocide* (New York: Verso, 2003), 69.

47 Archie Cameron, cited in Ibid., 67.

48 Tatz, *With Intent*, 98–99.

49 Kevin Rudd, "Apology to Australia's Indigenous Peoples," *Parliamentary Debates* (Canberra: House of Representatives, Parliament of Australia, 2008), 167–77.

50 See Andrea Durbach, "Repairing the Damage: Achieving Reparations for the Stolen Generations," *Alternative Law Journal* 27, no. 6 (2002), 262–66.

51 See Chris Cunneen and Julia Grix, *The Limitations of Litigation in Stolen Generations Cases* (Canberra: Australian Institute of Aboriginal and Torres Strait Islander Studies, 2004); also see Ann Curthoys, Ann Genovese and Alex Reilly, *Rights and Redemption: History, Law and Indigenous People* (Sydney: University of New South Wales Press, 2008). Most of the cases have been based on breaches of duty of care, wrongful imprisonment, and the consequences of child removal. Where genocide has been put to the courts, it has been on the whole rejected. For example, in *Kruger v The Commonwealth of Australia* (1997–190 CLR 1), the judges expressly noted that the Aboriginals Ordinance 1918, which authorised the removal (between 1925 and 1944) of the nine children who brought the case, did not authorise acts of "genocide" as defined in the Genocide Convention. As Chris Cunneen and Julia Grix note on page 27: "Government records are likely to paint a picture in which the removal and subsequent treatment of Indigenous children complied with 'their best interests' and met the standards of the time. Protection laws are characterised as benign in their intent, as 'beneficial' laws – even if discriminatory. Under these circumstances, the likelihood that the forced removal of Indigenous children will be considered by the courts as constituting genocide is remote." One case that has been successful is that of Bruce Trevorrow, taken from his family at the age of 13 months from hospital by the Aboriginal Protection Board and placed in a non-Indigenous foster family for the next 10 years. In *Trevorrow v State of South Australia* (No. 5) (2007–SASC 285), his removal was found to be unlawful and he was awarded $525,000 in compensation. South Australia, alongside Tasmania and most recently NSW, has now instituted a Stolen Generations reparations scheme.

aborigines did not give up their lands peacefully; they were killed or removed forcibly from the lands by United Kingdom forces or the European colonists in what amounted to attempted (and in Tasmania almost complete) genocide."[52] These are rare moments. No justice space has been created of acknowledgement, recognition and redress; rather a policy of " reconciliation" has been the policy approach taken by successive governments.

The case and its appeal prompted the bringing of a Private Senator's Bill, the Anti-Genocide Bill 1999 (Cth) by Australian Democrat Senator Brian Greig, who, in his second reading speech "referred to the prevention and punishment of the crime of genocide as 'unfinished business' of the Commonwealth Parliament."[53] The Bill was referred by the Senate to the Legal and Constitutional Affairs References Committee, whose June 2000 report found that "anti-genocide legislation in Australia was both necessary and timely, and recommended that the Bill be referred to the Attorney General for consideration of the matters identified by the Committee in respect of its contents."[54]

The Bill was overtaken by the ratification of the International Criminal Court Statute by Australia. In 2002, as a result of pressure from other signatories to the International Criminal Court, Australia introduced the *International Criminal Court (Consequential Amendments) Act 2002*. A key principle of the Statute of the new International Criminal Court, which holds jurisdiction to hear crimes of genocide, war crimes, and crimes against humanity, was that it would not usurp genuine national attempts to try these crimes. The "principle of complementarity" means that the Court will only take the case if the state where the crime was perpetrated is unwilling or genuinely unable to do so.[55] This meant that Australia is obliged to implement legislation to enable prosecution even if, as Gillian Triggs has noted, "The existence of such laws by no means indicates the extent of their enforcement. Indeed, Australian practice suggests that war crimes prosecutions have ultimately depended upon political will."[56] This is reflected in the "Declaration" that Australia included in its last-minute signature, reinforcing "the primacy of its criminal jurisdiction" and that the Attorney-General must authorise any arrest or extradition to the

---

52 *Coe v Commonwealth 1979 HCA 68*, par. 8.

53 Shirley Scott, "Why Wasn't Genocide a Crime in Australia? Accounting For the Half-century Delay in Australia Implementing the Genocide Convention," *Australian Journal of Human Rights* 10, no. 2 (2004): article 22, n.p.

54 Senate Legal and Constitutional Committee 2000 cited in Ibid., n.p.

55 The Preamble notes that "the International Criminal Court established under this Statute shall be complementary to national criminal jurisdictions" and this is reiterated in Article 17 of the Rome Statute.

56 Gillian Triggs, "Implementation of the Rome Statute for the International Criminal Court: A Quiet Revolution in Australian Law," *Sydney Law Review* 25, no. 4 (2003), 518.

Court.[57] Much of this was for Australian public consumption rather than for the purposes of operation of the Court.[58]

The approach taken, as Triggs has outlined, was to amend the Australian *Criminal Code Act 2005* by creating a new Chapter 8—"Offences Against Humanity and Related Offences."[59] In relation to genocide, five new offences of genocide were added to the *Criminal Code*, that incorporate the definition of genocide in the ICC's *Elements of Crimes* that had been drafted by the Preparatory Commission of the Court (and are taken from the Genocide Convention). These are: 268.3 Genocide by killing; 268.4 Genocide by causing serious bodily or mental harm; 268.5 Genocide by deliberately inflicting conditions of life calculated to bring about physical destruction; 268.6 Genocide by imposing measures intended to prevent births; 268.7 Genocide by forcibly transferring children.[60]

Yet while genocide has become a criminal offence in Australia, and is now prosecutable—and indeed, *named*—it is up to the Attorney General to bring prosecutions, with the decision final and no challenges allowed. This has had the effect of Australia continuing to fail to prosecute genocide.

"Closing the chapter" again?

In his foreword to the *Review of Material Relating to the Entry of Suspected War Criminals into Australia*, Andrew Menzies wrote that "In the case of such crimes, the argument that the culprits, by coming to this country, have turned their back on such events has, in my view, no validity."[61] Yet in Australian policy and practice today, we see a selective application of this approach. While "foreign fighters" legislation gets rushed through, we have no such equivalent scrutiny of the crimes perpetrated in genocide and other state crime internationally—or nationally. The provision of the Attorney-General to veto any prosecutions, means that it is in the hands of the government to determine prosecution of genocide.

This was evident with the halting of the investigation by the Melbourne Magistrates' Court into the indictment filed by Arunachalam Jegatheeswaran,

---

57 Much of the declaration is concerned with Australia having primary jurisdiction over crimes, which is reflected in any case in the core principle of the Court of "complementarity." See https://treaties.un.org/doc/source/training/regional/2009/13-17October-2009/reservations-declarations-questions.pdf.

58 Alex Bellamy and Marianne Hanson, "Justice Beyond Borders? Australia and the International Criminal Court," *Australian Journal of International Affairs* 56, no. 3 (2002), 417–33.

59 Triggs, "Implementation," 520.

60 *International Criminal Court (Consequential Amendments) Act 2002* (Commonwealth of Australia), https://www.legislation.gov.au/Details/C2004A00993.

61 Menzies, *Review of Material*, 12.

an Australian citizen, against Sri Lankan President Mahinda Rajapaska (who was about to visit Perth to attend the Commonwealth Heads of Government Meeting) on charges of war crimes and crimes against humanity. In a media conference, Jegatheeswaran stated: "He's [Rajapaksa] the commander-in-chief and nothing would have happened without his knowledge or his directions, and ultimately, he should be answerable to what was happening."[62] Slated for hearing on November 29, after having been filed late October 2011 under Division 268 of the *Criminal Code Act 1995*, the then Attorney-General Robert McClelland refused to support the matter, thus effectively ending the investigation.

Two years later, then Prime Minister Tony Abbott, in speaking on the issue of alleged war crimes committed during Sri Lanka's civil war and on persistent human rights concerns under the Rajapaksa government, stated that while his government "deplores the use of torture we accept that sometimes in difficult circumstances difficult things happen."[63] Meanwhile, countries such as Canada and the Netherlands have routinely been hearing charges of genocide, most recently in relation to the genocide in Rwanda. Yet in Australia, our response is that we must "move on." On the appointment of Indonesia's new security minister Wiranto, a former general who was indicted for crimes against humanity by the United Nations-established Serious Crimes Unit in Timor-Leste, the Australian Federal Justice Minister Michael Keenan responded that "we in government need to pursue what is in Australia's national interest in 2016."[64] In 1993, with the recognition of at least one former Khmer Rouge official living in Australia who was identified as responsible for the torture and killing of Cambodians in "Democratic Kampuchea," the Cambodian Advisory Council of Australia requested amendments to the *War Crimes Act* so that prosecution could occur here. As Mark Aarons relates, nothing was done.[65]

---

62 Arunachalam Jegatheeswaran, cited in "Rajapaksa Indicated for War Crimes in Australian Court," *Tamil Guardian*, October 23, 2011, http://www.tamilguardian.com/content/rajapaksa-indicted-war-crimes-australian-court?articleid=3754.

63 Tony Abbott cited in Amanda Hodge, " 'Difficult Things Happen': Tony Abbott Defends Sri Lanka," *Australian*, November 16, 2013, http://www.theaustralian.com.au/national-affairs/difficult-things-happen-tony-abbott-defends-sri-lanka/news-story/e1bac24a820d0b817bacd250eb18cd73.

64 Michael Keenan cited in Jewel Topsfield, "Alleged Timor War Crimes Forgotten as Ministers Fly in for Bali Terror Summit," *Sydney Morning Herald*, August 10, 2016, http://www.smh.com.au/world/alleged-timor-war-crimes-forgotten-as-ministers-fly-in-for-bali-terror-summit-20160809-gqokk8.html. Wiranto had been the Defence Minister and Commander of Indonesian Armed Forces and was charged with "command responsibility for murder, deportation and persecution committed in the context of a widespread and systematic attack on the civilian population in East Timor." See "Timor-Leste Court Issues Warrant for Former Indonesian Defence Minister," *UN News Centre*, May 10, 2004, http://www.un.org/apps/news/story.asp?NewsID=10677.

65 Mark Aarons, *War Criminals Welcome: Australia, A Sanctuary or Fugitive War Criminals since 1945* (Melbourne: Black Inc., 2001), 40.

Aarons' investigative work, alongside others, has shown, as he notes, that "it is a statistical certainty that Australia has war criminals, torturers and mass killers from almost every major killing field of the past half-century."[66] There have been allegations made by members of the Chilean, Cambodian, Afghani, Bosnian, and Rwandan communities, among others, about perpetrators who now live here.[67] Victims have run into perpetrators at community centres, after years of refuge.[68] Most recently, the issue has been raised of returning ISIS fighters being held responsible for the genocide against the Yazidi people in Northern Iraq.[69]

Genocide is not seen as worthy of trial in Australia. We can understand the three war crimes hearings held in the early 1990s as an anomaly. Barwick's claims, that Australia must be "history-less," are a more accurate reflection of where Australia stands. Tony Barta has argued that as beneficiaries of genocide, Australians cannot address it—as to do so is to acknowledge what we have gained.[70] We can understand this is a form of denial, which Tatz and Winton Higgins identify as integral to genocide.[71] As a "history-less" country that does not acknowledge its own history, we cannot acknowledge others. In denying our own history as settler-colonial, based on genocide, we also must deny others their history—as victims or perpetrators or bystanders—of conflicts elsewhere.

Irene Nemes, in her commentary on the closure of the Special Investigations Unit in the early 1990s, noted that "By abandoning the investigations, the government is allowing Nazi war criminals to remain complacent and protected from their past."[72] We could add to this, that Australia remains protected

---

66 Ibid., 47.
67 Ibid. See chapters One and Two for an account of allegations and sightings of various perpetrators.
68 Ibid., chap. Two.
69 Nikki Marczak, "Comment: Seeking Justice For an Ongoing Genocide," *SBS News*, August 22, 2016, http://www.sbs.com.au/news/article/2016/08/22/comment-seeking-justice-ongoing-genocide.
70 Tony Barta, "After the Holocaust: Consciousness of Genocide in Australia," *Australian Journal of Politics and History* 31, no. 1 (1985), 154-61, see 160. "In Australia, where all of us are the beneficiaries of crimes against the Aborigines, the question can't seriously penetrate our ideological defences. Anyone interested in the continued hegemony of our social values—property acquisition at the very centre of them—has a kind of functional incredulousness: how could our kind of society be criminal?" Barta continues: "Consciousness of genocide will have political implications, too. Anyone who knows what took place in this country must surely know what has to happen now." While I disagree with Barta's assessment of Germany's citizens not having "gained" from the removal of the Jewish population, his assessment of Australia, and why we have failed to recognise the genocidal foundations of this society, is spot on. In Colin Tatz and Winton Higgins, *The Magnitude of Genocide* (California: Praeger, 2016), the authors also note how "beneficiaries" can be understood as integral to the paradigm of genocidal actors, comprising "perpetrators, bystanders, victims, rescuers, and beneficiaries," and also post-settler-colonial nations as "straightforward beneficiaries of genocide" (see 85 and 194).
71 Tatz and Higgins, *The Magnitude*, in particular Chapter Nine.
72 Nemes, 156.

both from its collective past and its current present. In a climate in which Australia shows no compassion for those fleeing conflict and seeking better lives elsewhere, it would seem necessary to demonstrate to the Australian population what it is that asylum seekers and refugees flee from. The domestic prosecution of perpetrators of genocide and other state crime, including war crimes, would seem to serve this purpose. If a reason is needed beyond that criminal behaviour will be punished, across the globe, no matter where it was perpetrated, no matter to whom, and no matter how long ago, then I suggest we put this one forward. It may also help us face up to our genocidal past, and present.

Part 3
Case Studies

PSYCHIATRY, GENOCIDE AND THE NATIONAL SOCIALIST STATE: LESSONS LEARNT, IGNORED AND FORGOTTEN

Michael Robertson, Edwina Light, Wendy Lipworth and Garry Walter

Introduction

The attempted genocide of European Jews perpetrated by the National Socialist regime in Germany and its collaborators was a distinctly modern event. The bureaucratised and industrialised nature of the Nazi plan (the *Endlösung* or Final Solution) is generally considered the defining characteristic of the Holocaust. Prior to the establishment of extermination camps in Poland, the Nazi regime had perpetrated or fomented both sporadic massacres and a militarised programme of executions in Eastern Europe, in what has been termed "Holocaust by bullets."[1] Yet despite the murder of 1.5 million Jews by SS and police mobile killing squads (*Einsatzgruppen*), the defining symbol of the Holocaust was the industrialised killing centre at Auschwitz-Birkenau. Importantly, the gas chambers of the Reinhard camps (Belzec, Sobibor, and Treblinka II) and Auschwitz-Birkenau did not appear *de novo* for the purposes of killing Europe's Jews.[2] The medical profession, in collusion with Adolf Hitler's Chancellery (*KdF*), had earlier developed and refined a large-scale, state-financed and well-concealed program of victim selection and mass transportation to dedicated killing centres with effective techniques of gassing and disposal of victims' remains. The template for the *Endlösung* evolved as a medical procedure, developed primarily by psychiatrists.[3]

It is argued that the Holocaust may be conceptualised as not a "moment in history" but rather as the "hidden face" of the culture that persists.[4] The involvement of psychiatrists in this highly organised programme thus raises questions relevant to the contemporary psychiatric profession. While facile comparisons of present-day ethical dilemmas in psychiatry with extreme acts

---

1 Patrick Desbois, *The Holocaust by Bullets: A Priest's Journey to Uncover the Truth Behind the Murder of 1.5 Million Jews* (New York: Palgrave Macmillan, 2008).
2 Henry Friedlander, *The Origins of Nazi Genocide: From Euthanasia to the Final Solution* (Chapel Hill: University of Noth Carolina Press, 1995).
3 Michael Burleigh, *Death and Deliverance: "Euthanasia" in Germany 1900–1945* (London: Pan, 2002).
4 Zygmunt Bauman, *Modernity and the Holocaust* (Ithaca: Cornell University Press, 1989).

of certain psychiatrists in the Nazi regime do little to enlighten psychiatric ethics and likely lead the discourse away from the contemporary significance of the period, some formulations of the Holocaust have utilised the concept of "biopower,"[5] which along with the notion of a "dual role dilemma,"[6] provides a means to better understand current challenges in psychiatric ethics.

Biopower represents a means of governmental or state control of individual or population biology and is a modern progression from the coercive power of the sovereign to control life. The mass sterilisation or destruction of the sick and disabled under Nazism was a distinct application of biopower. Our argument is that through this particular programme of persecution of the sick and disabled, largely executed by the psychiatric profession, the Nazi regime created a biological "crisis" situated initially in the discourse of eugenics and later, racial hygiene. The regime used this as a pretext for a large-scale exercise of biopower over the *Volk* (population). This raised a specific crisis in psychiatric ethics: in the setting of a totalitarian state, the psychiatric profession was made responsible to the state and the health of the *Volk*, at the extreme expense of many individual patients. This, in turn, created a form of the dual-role dilemma.

The "dual role dilemma" was originally a construct from ethical discourse in forensic psychiatry, highlighting tension between the conflicting obligations of the psychiatrist to the patient and a third party, in that instance, the court system. Many dilemmas in psychiatric ethics can be reduced to manifestations of the dual role dilemma and, as we will argue, the situation of the psychiatric profession in the Nazi regime was one of history's greatest dual role dilemmas in that it placed the psychiatric profession in a tension between obligations to patients and to the regime and the *Volk*.

Most present-day psychiatrists acknowledge the role their profession played in the Nazi period (1933–1945).[7] Much attention in this regard has been paid to human rights violations perpetrated against people with psychiatric, intellectual and physical disabilities. Both these abuses and the broader history of the German psychiatric profession in the Nazi regime offer many lessons for contemporary psychiatric ethics. In the first part of this essay, we provide a broad survey of the main themes in the history of the psychiatric

---

5   Michel Foucault, *The Birth of Biopolitics: Lectures at the Collége de France, 1978–1979* (New York: Picador, 2004); Paul Rabinow and Nikolas Rose, "Biopower Today," *BioSocieties* 1 (2006), 195–217; Giogio Agamben, *Homo Sacer: Sovereign Power and Bare Life* (Stanford: Stanford Univeristy Press, 1988).

6   Michael Robertson and Garry Walter, "Many Faces of the Dual-role Dilemma in Psychiatric Ethics," *Australian and New Zealand Journal of Psychiatry* 42, no. 3 (2008), 228–35.

7   Rael D. Strous, "Psychiatry During the Nazi Era: Ethical Lessons for the Modern Professional," *Annals of General Psychiatry* 6, no. 8 (2007); Michael von-Cranach, "Ethics in Psychiatry: The Lessons We Learn from Nazi Psychiatry," *Eur Arch Psychiatry Clin Neurosci* 260 (2010), 152–56.

profession in the Nazi regime. In the second part, we provide a deeper analysis of the significance of this period for contemporary psychiatric ethics.

Part 1—A historical survey

Psychiatry before National Socialism

Two iconic figures and two divergent views on mental illness characterised German psychiatry during the late nineteenth and early twentieth centuries. The work of Emil Kraepelin and Sigmund Freud left momentous clinical and cultural legacies to the present day.[8] The differences between the two psychiatrists' projects broadly represented the split in the German psychiatric profession's views of mental illness at the time, regarding such illness as either a biological phenomenon (*Somatiker*) or a disease of the soul (*Psychiker*).[9] Freud's ideas were rejected and demonised by both the German psychiatric profession and Nazi regime as the foundation of the "Jewish Science" of psychoanalysis.[10] This void enabled Kraepelin's legacy to profoundly influence German psychiatry. Kraepelin's project included, *inter alia*, classification of psychiatric disorders and establishment of the paradigm of biological psychiatry, culminating in his founding the German Institute for Psychiatric Research.[11] Kraepelin was drawn ultimately to the tenets of Social Darwinism, eugenics and racial hygiene, and the idea that society had countered natural selection and allowed dysfunctional genetic traits to flourish. He was concerned about "the number of idiots, epileptics, psychopaths, criminals, prostitutes, and tramps who descend from alcoholic and syphilitic parents, and who transfer their inferiority to their offspring," and argued that "our highly developed social welfare has the sad side-effect that it operates against the natural self-cleansing of our people."[12] These ideas were developed further by devotees (including psychiatrist, eugenicist and Nazi, Ernst Rüdin), which ensured this

---

8   Hannah S. Decker, "How Kraepelinian was Kraepelin? How Kraepelinian are the Neo-Kraepelinians?—From Emil Kraepelin to DSM-III," *History of Psychiatry* 18, no. 3 (2007), 337–60.

9   Albrecht Hirschmueller, trans. by Magda Whitrow, "The Development of Psychiatry and Neurology in the Nineteenth Century," *History of Psychiatry* x (1999), 395–423.

10   Geoffrey Cocks, *Psychotherapy in the Third Reich: The Göring Institute* (New York: Oxford University Press, 1985); James Goggin and Eileen Brockman-Goggin, *Death of a Jewish Science: Psychoanalysis in the Third Reich* (West Lafayette: Purdue University Press, 2001).

11   This institute would later become part of the main German academic body of the twentieth century, the Kaiser Wilhelm Society.

12   Martin Brüne, "On Human Self-Domestication, Psychiatry, and Eugenics," *Philosophy, Ethics and Humanities in Medicine* 2, no. 1 (2007), 21.

aspect of Kraepelin's work dominated interwar German psychiatry[13] and was at the service of the National Socialists in their justification for genocide.[14]

In the early 1900s, a growing anti-psychiatry sentiment in Germany fostered debate over asylum care versus family care for the "insane,"[15] although the systems of asylum (*Irrenanstlaten*) persisted as the locale of psychiatric practice.[16] Asylums became the focal point of psychiatric clinical practice in the period leading up to the Nazi regime and consisted of *Heilanstalten* (sanatoria) and *Pflegeanstalten* (nursing homes or care institutions). From 1880 to 1920, the number of asylum inmates in Germany increased by nearly 500 per cent.[17] Patients in these asylums had always fared badly—nearly 70,000 German psychiatric patients died of starvation and other consequences of deprivation during World War One,[18] and the high cost of maintaining these institutions was a constant concern for state treasuries.[19]

During the same period, psychiatrists began to expand their approaches to asylum patient care and treatment, including patient engagement in "work therapy" (*Arbeitstherapie*), akin to what many would recognise as occupational therapy today.[20] The large numbers of psychiatric casualties from the 1914–1918 war had also prompted German psychiatrists to experiment with more radical therapies[21] such as malaria therapy,[22] aversion therapy[23] and insulin coma therapy.[24] This enabled a "reform" movement in German psychi-

---

13 Matthias Weber, "Ernst Rüdin, 1874–1952: A German Psychiatrist and Geneticist," *American Journal of Medical Genetics* 67, no. 4 (1996), 323–31.

14 Eric Engstrom, Matthais Weber and Wolfgang Burgmair, "Emil Wilhelm Magnus Georg Kraepelin (1856–1926)," *American Journal of Psychiatry* 163, no. 10 (2006), 1710.

15 Heinz-Peter Schmiedebach, "Zerquälte Ergebnisse einer Dichterseele?–Literarische Kritik, Psychiatrie und Öffentlichkeit um 1900," in *Moderne Anstaltspsychiatrie im 19. und 20. Jahrhundert–Legitimation und Kritik*, eds. Heiner Fangerau and Karen Nolte (Stuttgart: Franz Steiner, 2006).

16 Andreas Pernice and N.J.R. Evans, "Family Care and Asylum Psychiatry in the Nineteenth Century: The Controversy in the *Allgemeine Zeitschrift fur Psychiatrie* Between 1844 and 1902," *History of Psychiatry* 6, no. 21 (1995), 55–68.

17 Dirk Blasius, *Einfache Seelenstörung: Geschichte der deutschen Psychiatrie 1800–1945* (Frankfurt am Main: Fischer, 1994).

18 Heinz Faulstich, *Hungersterben in der Psychiatrie 1914–1949: mit einer Topographie der NS-Psychiatrie* (Freiburg im Breisgau: Lambertus, 1998).

19 Michael Burleigh, "The Legacy of Nazi Medicine in Context," in *Medicine and Medical Ethics in Nazi Germany: Origins, Practices, Legacies*, eds. Francis Nicosia and Jonathan Huener (New York: Berghahn Books, 2002).

20 Heinz-Peter Schmiedebach and Stefan Priebe, "Social Psychiatry in Germany in the Twentieth Century: Ideas and Models," *Medical History* 48 (2004), 449–72.

21 Heinz-Peter Schmiedebach, "Psychiatry in Germany in the early 20th Century," *Neurology, Psychiatry and Brain Research* 22, no. 2 (2016), 29–3.

22 Cynthia Tsay, "Julius Wagner-Jauregg and the Legacy of Malarial Therapy for the Treatment of General Paresis of the Insane," *Yale Journal of Biology and Medicine* 86, no. 2 (2013), 245–54.

23 F. Kaufmann, "Die planmäßige Heilung komplizierter psychogener Bewegungsstörungen bei Soldaten in einer Sitzung," *Feldärtz Beilage Münch Med Wochenschr* 63 (1916), 802ff.

atric asylums.[25] Despite the introduction of such treatments, there remained a group of patients whose illness and disability proved intractable. This group's failure to respond to new treatment methods strengthened views about the financial costs and the perceived futility of their lives.

The psychiatric profession and the Nazi regime

After the National Socialists took power, the professions were subject to a process of alignment to the values of the Nazi regime.[26] The *Gleichschaltung* (alignment) of the medical profession was positioned around notions of public health and hygiene.[27] As part of the *Gleichschaltung*, Jewish physicians were subjected to restrictions to their medical practice, were forced out of their university posts or imprisoned. Around 50 per cent of German physicians joined either the Nazi party or associated bodies,[28] and psychiatrists were enthusiastic participants in the regime. Motivations for participation in the NSDAP were variably political or ideological, or inspired by opportunism and institutional loyalty.[29] The transcripts of criminal trials in West Germany of perpetrators of the Nazi "euthanasia" programme provide some insight into such motivations for participation in the murder of patients, including ideological affinity with Nazi doctrine, vanity and ambition, a distorted sense of obedience, "inertia" of the will, careerism and personality vulnerability.[30] Other justifications include seemingly self-serving variations of the concept of empathy in that many of the killers sought to reframe the murder of the sick and disabled patients as

---

24 I. Murray Rossman and William B. Cline "The Pharmacological 'Shock' Treatment of Chronic Schizophrenia," *American Journal of Psychiatry* 94, no. 6 (1938), 1323–36.

25 Edward Shorter, *A History of Psychiatry: From the Era of the Asylum to the Age of Prozac* (New York: Wiley, 1997).

26 Claudia Koonz, *The Nazi Conscience* (Cambridge, Mass: Bellknap, 2003).

27 Robert Jay Lifton, *The Nazi Doctors: Medical Killing and the Psychology of Genocide* (New York: Basic Books, 2000).

28 Omar Haque, Julian De Freitas, Ivana Viani, Bradley Niederschulte and Harold Bursztajn, "Why Did So Many German Doctors Join the Nazi Party Early?" *International Journal of Law and Psychiatry* 35, no. 5–6 (2012), 473–79.

29 Henry Friedlander, "Physicians as Killers in Nazi Germany: Hadamar, Treblinka, and Auschwitz," in *Medicine and Medical Ethics in Nazi Germany: Origins, Practices, Legacies*, eds. Francis Nicosia and Jonathan Huener (New York: Berghahn Books, 2002); Michael Dudley and Fran Gale, "Psychiatrists As a Moral Community? Psychiatry Under the Nazis and its Contemporary Relevance," *Australian and New Zealand Journal of Psychiatry* 36, no. 5 (2002), 585–94.

30 Michael Bryant, *Confronting the "Good Death": Nazi Euthanasia on Trial, 1945–1953* (Boulder: University Press of Colorado, 2005).

acts of mercy or benevolence.[31] Some authors, however, define the motivation purely in terms of economic necessity.[32]

The primary theoretical underpinning of the *Gleichschaltung* in the case of German psychiatry was eugenics.[33] The term "eugenics" usually refers to the improvement of the health of a population by the promotion of desirable heritable characteristics through the elimination of "inferior" genetic stock from the breeding pool. Although the concept dates to Plato, the modern term is attributed to British polymath Francis Galton.[34] Despite its clear link to Kraepelin's ideas, eugenics was by no means solely a German phenomenon. In the early twentieth century, eugenic societies existed in numerous countries and grew in popularity in the face of the massive social change that followed World War One.[35] This legitimated racist immigration policy, particularly in the US and Australia in the 1930s.[36] Well before it was used for genocidal purposes, the conflation of genetics and race offered by eugenics enabled the Nazi regime to sanction its programme of social exclusion through "medical science" and establish a collaborative relationship with the German medical profession. Many influential psychiatrists were enthusiastic eugenicists, including the co-founder of the German Society for Racial Hygiene, Kraepelin's acolyte Ernst Rüdin.[37]

Krankenmorde and the Holocaust

Psychiatrists were not only keen advocates of the principles of eugenics; they also put these principles into action—and, indeed, extended them—by taking a central role in the Nazi regime's so-called "euthanasia program."[38] Contemporary memorial sites in Germany and Austria now refer to this part of the Holocaust as *"Krankenmorde"* (the murder of the sick). Like eugenics, "euthanasia" of the mentally ill was publicly debated in the US at the same time

---

31 David Deutsch, "Immer mit Liebe: Empathic Violence in Nazi Euthanasia," *Holocaust Studies: A Journal of Culture and History* 22, no. 1 (2016), 1–20.

32 Gerrit Hohendorf, *Der Tod als Erlösung vom Leiden: Geschichte und Ethik der Sterbehilfe seit dem Ende des 19. Jarhunderts in Deustchland* (Göttingen: Wallstein, 2013).

33 Friedlander, *The Origins*.

34 Francis Galton, *Hereditary Genius: An Inquiry Into Its Laws and Consequences* (London: Macmillan, 1869).

35 Burleigh, *Death and Deliverance*.

36 Robert Proctor, *Racial Hygiene: Medicine Under the Nazis* (Cambridge, Mass: Harvard University Press, 1990).

37 Lifton, *The Nazi Doctors*.

38 Ernst Klee, *"Euthanasie" im NS-Staat: Die "Vernichtung lebensunwerten Lebens"* (Frankfurt-am-Main: Fischer, 1983); Friedlander, *The Origins*.

as it rose in popularity in Germany, with prominent US neurologist Foster Kennedy[39] arguing that the "feeble minded" should be killed.[40] In July 1933, the German Reichstag passed the "Law for Prevention of Hereditary Diseased Offspring" following which "Hereditary Health Courts" mandated sterilisation of several hundred thousand adults of child-rearing age deemed by their doctors as having hereditary diseases. There followed the sporadic murder of disabled children by deliberate overdoses of barbiturates, or combinations of morphine and scopolamine. Following successful experiments with carbon monoxide gas chambers, a centralised process of mass murder of those deemed "life unworthy of life" was organised from *Tiergartenstraße* 4 in Berlin. The secret operation—*Aktion T4*—coordinated the identification of victims in institutions in Germany and Austria, their mass transportation to six dedicated killing centres equipped with gas chambers, the disposal of remains, and a process of deception about the manner of death of the victims. Jewish patients were among the first to be killed, regardless of their clinical status or work capacity.[41] By late summer 1941, growing community awareness of the programme led to public protest, prompting Hitler to order the gassings to halt. Undeterred, many German psychiatrists continued to murder patients—mostly by deliberate overdose or starvation—in a process termed *Wilde Euthanasie* (decentralised euthanasia).[42] Many senior psychiatrists participated in *Aktion T4*, with a number of doctors later participating in coordinated killing of sick prisoners in the concentration camp system under *Aktion14f13*.[43] Accounting for the sporadic murders of asylum patients in Nazi occupied Europe, around 300,000 disabled people were killed in the period 1933–1945.[44] It is noteworthy that after the T4 programme was disbanded, more than 90 per cent of those who worked in it later participated in the extermination camps of *Aktion Reinhard*, the process of eliminating Poland's Jewish population.[45]

Psychotherapy in the Nazi regime

The immediate effect of National Socialism on the practice of psychotherapy

---

39 Foster Kennedy, "The Problem of Social Control of the Congenital Defective: Education, Sterilization, Euthanasia," *American Journal of Psychiatry* 99, no. 1 (1942), 13–16.

40 Jay Joseph, "The 1942 'Euthanasia' Debate in the *American Journal of Psychiatry*," *History of Psychiatry* 16, no. 2 (2005), 171–79.

41 Rael Strous, "Extermination of the Jewish Mentally-ill During the Nazi Era—The 'Doubly Cursed,' " *Israel Journal of Psychiatry Related Sciences* 45, no. 4 (2008), 247–56.

42 Gerhard Schmidt, *Selektion in der Heilanstalt, 1939–1945* (Berlin: Springer, 2011).

43 Friedlander, "Physicians as Killers."

44 This estimate is provided by the official memorial to the victims of Nazi euthanasia in Berlin.

45 Klee, *"Euthanasie" im NS-Staat*.

was evident in the expulsion of Jewish therapists from practice as part of the *Gleichschaltung*. The Berlin Psychoanalytic Institute existed within the tradition of Freud and many of its esteemed alumni were Jews. The changes to psychotherapy in the Nazi regime have been documented.[46] Central to these accounts is the establishment of the so-called Göring Institutes. The exclusion of Jewish therapists and the denouncement of the "Jewish science" of psychoanalysis created an opportunity for Mathias Göring (first cousin of Hermann Göring) to establish a series of psychotherapeutic institutes that practised brief and focal therapies (*Kleintherapie*), including biofeedback, behavioural modification and some forms of family therapy. In keeping with the instrumental goals of the Nazi regime, the critical shift in psychotherapy was away from the patient growth and introspection sought by psychoanalysis, toward the improvement and enhancement of the health and function of the population.

Psychiatrists in the military

German psychiatrists were well integrated into the armed forces, particularly the Wehrmacht. The main concern of psychiatrists working in the military under the Nazi regime was war neurosis (*Kriegsneurosen*), or what would be now considered post-traumatic stress disorder. Each army district had an advisory psychiatrist (*Beratender Psychiater*) who provided data to the central authorities, including the incidence of different forms of psychological disturbance and problematic behaviours such as self-inflicted wounds, desertion and insubordination. Most psychiatrists working in the Wehrmacht refused to acknowledge *Kriegsneurosen* as a legitimate clinical concern.[47] The commonly held assumption was that such problems did not occur in the Wehrmacht due its superior command structure and morale, and successful recruitment and replacement policies.[48] As part of recruitment processes, psychiatrists advised the Wehrmacht how to exclude unsuitable recruits.[49] The likelihood is that the comparatively low reported rate of war neurosis was attributable to the success of the Wehrmacht in the first years of the war.[50] After 1942 and the failures of campaigns in North Africa and the Soviet Union, the rates of psychiatric casualties increased exponentially.

---

46   Cocks, *Psychotherapy*; Goggin and Brockman-Goggin, *Death of a Jewish*.
47   Robert Schneider, "Stress Breakdown in the Wehrmacht: Implications for Today's Army," in *Contemporary Studies in Combat Psychiatry*, ed. Gregory Belenky (Santa Barbara: Praeger, 1987), 87–101.
48   R. Valentin, *Kankenbatallione* (Dusseldorf: Droste, 1981).
49   Peter Reidesser and Axel Verderber, *Maschinengewehre hinter der Front. Zur Geschichte der deutschen Militärpsychiatrie* (Frankfurt am Main: Fischer, 1996).
50   Schneider, "Stress Breakdown."

Some personnel with war neurosis were diagnosed with organic conditions such as encephalitis and treated in military hospitals as medically ill. Others were either deemed "psychopaths" or malingerers and subject to hard labour in specific units or, in some circumstances, imprisoned or sent to concentration camps.[51] In cases where a diagnosis of war neurosis was accepted, management derived from the approach of "forward treatment" (immediacy, proximity, expectancy, simplicity, and centrality) developed by American psychiatrist Thomas W. Salmon during World War One. An additional carryover of the treatment of "shell shock" from World War One was the use of the so-called "Kaufmann cure" that involved the administration of electric shocks to traumatised soldiers in order to facilitate a desire to return to the front.[52] In the Nazi regime, this approach became the specialty of psychiatrist Frederich Panse at the Ensen Hospital near Weimar—the treatment was renamed *Pansen*.[53] Panse had a long-standing interest in military psychiatry and had published on themes of compensation neurosis and malingering in soldiers.[54] *Pansen* was initially opposed by many in the Wehrmacht and in the health bureaucracy; however, with the escalation of psychiatric casualties in the latter part of the war, this resistance softened.

Part 2—Lessons learnt, ignored and forgotten

The meaning and understanding of "Holocaust"

In order to understand the lessons of psychiatry in the Nazi period, it is necessary to consider not only psychiatrists' participation in the Nazi regime, but also the fact that they played a critical role in the "Holocaust." Our approach to the Holocaust as "the seminal ethical event of modernity"[55] or the "paradigm of genocide" necessitating a "new categorical imperative"[56] and contemporary reflection, extends from the analysis of Zygmunt Bauman. Bauman argues that the Holocaust represents both a central moment in Jewish history and the "hid-

---

51 Ibid.

52 Kaufmann, "Die planmäßige Heilung."

53 Ralf Forsbach, "Friedrich Panse—Etabliert in Allen Systemen: Psychiater in der Weimarer Republik, im 'Dritten Reich' und in der Bundesrepublik," *Nervenarzt* 83 (2012), 329–36.

54 Friedrich Panse, "Das Schicksal von Renten—und Kriegsneurotikern nach Erlangung ihrer Ansprüche," *Archiv für Psychiatrie* 77 (1926), 61–92.

55 Shmuel Reis and Tomi Chelouche, "Medicine and the Holocaust—Lessons For Present and Future Physicians," *Medicine and Law: The World Association for Medical Law* 27, no. 4 (2008), 787–804; Colin Tatz and Winton Higgins, *The Magnitude of Genocide* (Santa Barbara: Praeger, 2016).

56 Theodor Adorno, *Negative Dialectics* (New York: Seabury Press, 1973).

den face" of modernity.⁵⁷ Key features of Bauman's definition of modernity are the removal of unknowns and uncertainties through control over biology, creation of bureaucracy, enforced rules and regulations, and control and categorisation of individuals leading to a process of exclusion.⁵⁸ The latter is significant in that the origins of the Holocaust exist within the culture—in this case, one characterised by modernist beliefs and values—and therefore can recur under similar cultural circumstances. Along similar lines, Colin Tatz and Winton Higgins describe the Holocaust as the coalescence of the different components of the modern state—infrastructure, bureaucratic hierarchies, and a culture of scientism that legitimated the process.⁵⁹

Bureaucracy in the Holocaust

Of the various features of modernity, bureaucratisation seems to have been particular important. Max Weber's formulation of the modern bureaucracy in the most recognised. Weberian bureaucracy is characterised by a hierarchical organisation, with delineated lines of authority and fixed areas of activity.⁶⁰ In a bureaucracy, action is taken by neutral officials or functionaries working under specific rules within a hierarchic structure.⁶¹

For Bauman, one of the critical preconditions of the Holocaust was bureaucratic and industrialised organisation.⁶² This meant that antisemitism and modernity, while necessary, were not sufficient conditions in themselves for the Holocaust. What was needed beyond political will was a rational bureaucracy, as rationalisation was the critical process in enacting genocide. Indeed, the organisational aspects of the Holocaust for Bauman were its defining characteristic. It is evident that the organisational aspects of the Holocaust flourished in the Nazi regime's "euthanasia" programme. *Aktion T4* provided the definitive template of the Holocaust—a centrally controlled bureaucratic process of identification, exclusion and collection of victims, mass transporta-

---

57 Bauman, *Modernity and the Holocaust*.
58 This is Bauman's concept of "solid modernity," as against his subsequent development of "late" or "liquid" modernity.
59 Tatz and Higgins, *The Magnitude*.
60 For Weber, the bureaucratisation of government and society is characterised by a process of "rationalisation" in which traditional values, such as filial or community bonds, are replaced by "outcomes" such as markers of efficiency or economy. Weber did not demonise bureaucracy; indeed, he saw it as an inevitable part of large government. He did, however, describe how it created "technically ordered, rigid, dehumanized society," with profound influences on self-concept and community relationships. For Weber, the modern world was shaped by bureaucratic rationalisation, which creates what he famously proclaimed as the *Stahlhartes Gehäuse* (iron cage). See Max Weber, *The Protestant Ethic and the Spirit of Capitalism* (1905; London; Penguin, 2002).
61 Max Weber, *Economy and Society* (Berkeley: University of California Press, 1922).
62 Bauman, *Modernity and the Holocaust*.

tion to dedicated industrialised killing centres arranged in a network, efficient killing and disposal methods, and elaborate deception. The association of bureaucracy and the Holocaust is also at the core of Hannah Arendt's formulation of the criminality of Adolf Eichmann, the prototypic *"Schriebtischtäter"* (desk criminal).[63] Arendt's observation was that Eichmann's involvement in the programme of genocide emerged through him operating thoughtlessly and following orders efficiently (even proclaiming his Kantian ethics),[64] without consideration of the victims.[65]

German medicine and bureaucracy

It is argued that German modernity, including its relationship to Nazism, was characterised by the persistence of aristocratic power structures and under-developed liberal democratic institutions.[66] The series of revolutions in Europe in 1848, in which liberalism became a political reality, failed in Germany. This meant that the authoritarianism of aristocracy and Prussian militarism were preserved, and that modern German social institutions and professions evolved with a particular relationship to the authority of the state. Most notably, loyalty to the state was placed above all else in any professional ethics. Kühne argued that the Nazi state had achieved an even more material manifestation of the *Volksgemeinschaft* (people's community) through exclusion of non-Aryans (and genetic inferiors) and that this enabled such ethical inversions in the professions as well as the community.[67]

The 1946–1947 Doctors' Trial in Nuremberg,[68] and a number of later prosecutions in West Germany, provide some insight into the individual and collective motivations of the German medical profession and its relationship

---

63   Hannah Arendt, *Eichmann in Jerusalem: A Report on the Banality of Evil* (London: Faber & Faber, 1963).

64   In Arendt's *Eichmann in Jerusalem*, she notes his justifications for devotion to duty by his stating he had been schooled in Kant's categorical imperative.

65   Not everyone accepts this portrait of Eichmann, which is challenged by the account of Benjamin Murmelstein, an elder of the Jewish leadership (*Judenrat*) in the Theresienstadt concentration camp, who claimed he witnessed Eichmann's extreme antisemitism during Kristallnacht in Vienna in November 1938, proclaiming to filmmaker Claude Lanzmann: "Eichmann was not banal, he was a demon." Later analysis of Eichmann's correspondence while in Argentina, and in particular his scheming and his endorsement of his crimes to fellow émigré Nazis in South America, also challenge Arendt's argument. See Bettina Stangneth, *Eichmann Before Jerusalem* (New York: Vintage, 2011). Stangneth does not reject specifically Arendt's concept of the banality of evil—she argues that Eichmann was not a good example of it. His particular evil was anything but banal.

66   Barrington Moore Jr., *Social Origins of Dictatorship and Democracy: Lord and Peasant in the Making of the Modern World* (Boston: Beacon Press, 1966).

67   Thomas Kühne, *Belonging and Genocide: Hitler's Community, 1918–1945* (New Haven: Yale University Press, 2010).

68   Nuremberg Military Tribunal 1: *USA v Karl Brandt et al.* (the trial of 23 alleged perpetrators of unconsented and cruel experiments and the "euthanasia" programme).

to the Nazi regime and its genocidal programme. The special advisor to the Nuremberg Tribunal, Austrian-born émigré psychiatrist Leo Alexander, reflected later on his observations of the trial, arguing that there were two critical moral failings underlying the crimes of the "Nazi doctors."[69] First, the process began with the subtle shift of attitudes of physicians about a relative value of life. Second, Alexander argued that the physicians working in the Nazi regime drifted from an approach of an "essentially maternal and religious idea" of care, to an assumption of responsibility for cure or restoration of function. This, in turn, emerged as a shift in emphasis of medical practice from serving the individual to serving the state. This was the ultimately malignant influence of bureaucracy and Bauman's modernity on the medical profession.

In the German medical profession, there existed two traditions of *Sorge* (care). *Fürsorge* was the clinical care of the individual, as against *Vorsorge*, meaning public health and preventive care. Under *Gleichschaltung*, the focus of German medicine aligned with the bio-political aims of the Nazi regime and a duty of *Vorsorge* became the moral obligation of the profession.[70] In keeping with Lifton's notion of National Socialism as a form of "applied biology," the medical profession was tasked with the health of the *Volk* (the homogenous Aryan population). Under National Socialism, illness and health became a critical part of the *Volkskörper* metaphor (the body of the German people), considered "a bodily metaphor or an expression of the organic creed characteristic of fascist ideology."[71] Health and illness became a "focal point for the myriad larger social, economic, and psychological concerns of the era."[72] Such metaphors enabled racist and other exclusionary discourses to flourish. This legitimated the Nazi regime's later programmes of persecution of the weak or undesirable, and the eliminative genocide of the Holocaust. The emphasis on the metaphors of health and illness allowed Jewish people to be defined as "cancer" or "bacillus" and their elimination as a form of medical cure. This process also placed the medical profession and its bureaucratic structures as a critical actor in the Nazi regime's programmes of persecution and genocide.

The transition in German medicine from *Fürsorge* to *Vorsorge* began during the chancellorship of Bismarck (1871–1890). Medicine gradually became a state-controlled and state-sponsored enterprise. Oncologist Erwin Leik de-

---

69   Leo Alexander, "Medical Science Under Dictatorship," *New England Journal of Medicine* 241, no. 2 (1949), 39–47.
70   Warren T. Reich, "The Care-Based Ethic of Nazi Medicine and the Moral Importance of What We Care About," *American Journal of Bioethics* 1, no. 1 (2001), 74–84.
71   Boaz Neumann, "The Phenomenology of the German People's Body (*Volkskörper*) and the Extermination of the Jewish Body," *New German Critique* 36, no. 1 (2009), 149–81.
72   Geoffrey Cocks, *The State of Health: Illness in Nazi Germany* (New York: Oxford University Press, 2012).

spaired of the advent of socialised medicine in Germany, supervised by the state and also by the market, believing that it had compromised individual care and created a generation of *Kässenartze* (cashier doctors).[73] He described how doctors were compelled by social insurance systems into a mechanised and overly scientifically focused practice that endorsed cost constraint and community and economic perspectives at the expense of patient care.[74] Under the Nazi regime, the German medical profession was enjoined in a social and economic transformation of the population through the valorisation of *Vorsorge* and the privileging of medical science in public policy-making.[75] In the first instance, this manifested in the persecution of the weak through involuntary sterilisation and later *Krankenmorde*, although, as the groundbreaking work of Robert Proctor demonstrates, this also involved revolutionary change in public health.[76] Beyond the metaphoric surgical excision of Jews, the disabled and other "undesirables," the Nazi regime sought to eliminate cancer in the population through a raft of initiatives aimed at reducing smoking, alcohol and environmental pollutants, and encouraging healthier plant-based diets. Proctor sees this as a historical first; the implementation at the individual level of initiatives aimed at enhancing the productivity and, ultimately, war-making capacity of the *Volk*. This form of modern public health was not "in spite of fascism, but in consequence of fascism."[77]

This focus on the care of the population represented a particular version of "German modernity"—one that was at odds with the liberal prioritisation of the individual self, and instead linked the entitlement to health care to the capacity for productivity in service of the greater German people's community or *Volksgemeinschaft*.[78]

None of this is to suggest that individual motivations were irrelevant in driving the actions of psychiatrists under the Nazi regime. As mentioned previously, participation in the regime was driven by myriad factors including ideology, obedience, ambition, fear and opprobrium. However, German modernity—with its particular form of bureaucracy—clearly played an important role.

---

73 Mary Seeman, "Psychiatry in the Nazi Era," *Canadian Journal of Psychiatry* 50, no. 4 (2005), 218–25.
74 Ibid.
75 Jennifer Leaning, "War Crimes and Medical Science," *British Medical Journal* 313 (1996), 1413–15.
76 Robert N. Proctor, *The Nazi War on Cancer* (Princeton: Princeton University Press, 1999).
77 Ibid., 249.
78 Cocks, *The State*.

"Biopower" and the State

As we noted earlier, one component of modernity for Bauman was control over nature and biology. This recruits biological and biomedical disciplines as executors of, or at least part of, modernity. Our thesis is that the significance of the Holocaust to contemporary medical ethics, and in particular psychiatric ethics, is usefully framed through the concept of "biopower"—a concept that, for reasons we will explain later, is particularly salient in forms of modernity that are characterised by the bureaucratisation of medicine.

The term *"biopouvoir"* (biopower) appeared initially in Michel Foucault's work, *History of Sexuality* (1976), and was later developed in a series of lectures he gave at the *College de France*. The core idea in Foucault's construct of biopower is the integration of sovereign power with biological science and the reformulation of politics as, ultimately, control over life. Foucault introduced the term "governmentality" to provide a critique and modification of the pre-modern notion of power being the exercise of coercion by a sovereign power or ruling class and, in particular, the means by which this power is exercised. In essence, governmentality through biopower seeks to either "make live" or "let die"—an inversion of the ancient legal apparatus of Roman law of *Pater familias* that would be "let live and make die."[79] Related to this, Foucault described a shift from "sovereign" power to "discursive" power—in this formulation power is generated by a particular discourse (evident in a "discursive formation") in the absence of a particular "ruling class."[80] Foucault considered a "discourse" as an institutionalised way of speaking or writing about reality that defines what can be intelligibly thought and said about the world and what cannot. A discourse creates a form of truth, rather than discovering it as it is.

Within modernist societies, bureaucracies create contexts that are particularly ripe for the exercise of biopower because a critical component of modernity is the control of biology, inevitably co-opted into a bureaucratised medical profession. According to Foucault, biopolitical power emerges with particular force and efficiency in the context of the modern capitalist nation state where it is exercised in, for example, interventions to effect control over fertility, vaccination, screening and treatment of disease, diet or pharmaceutical manipulation. Biopolitical power is exercised at both the level of the

---

79 Michel Foucault, *The History of Sexuality, Volume One: An Introduction* (London: Penguin, 1981), 137.
80 This is a manifestation of Foucault's formulation of the indistinguishability of power from knowledge. Foucault considers knowledge is always an exercise of power and power always a function of knowledge. See Michel Foucault, *The Archaeology of Knowledge*, trans. A.M. Sheridan Smith (New York: Pantheon Books, 1969).

individual and the population (what he terms the "massification" of individuals into a population).

The modern state's scientifically inspired "disciplinary institutions" replaced the pre-modern power of the sovereign over both the individual and groups in the population, through a technologically driven process of behaviour control.[81] The dissonant observations of the Nazi "war on cancer,"[82] juxtaposed with the persecution of the disabled, can be reconciled within the framework of biopower. In both instances, the medical profession acts as the executive in the process aimed to improve the economic situation (or in the case of the Nazi regime, the war-making capacity) of the population.

It has been argued that Foucault's notion of *Dispositif* (loosely translated as an "urgent need") provides a pretext to the exercise of biopower by the state.[83] *Dispositif* can be conceptualised as a network of different discourses, institutional responses or laws in response to a defined or perceived crisis.[84] An obvious example includes quarantine or regional isolation in the case of infectious disease. In a contemporary example of biopower and the *Dispositif*, the problem of the obesity "epidemic" arises from construction of ideal biological parameters consistent with a notion of "health," as defined in this case by weight, adiposity or other biochemical markers.[85] The application of biopower by the state facilitates urgent interventions in public and individual health, arguably targeting the financial burden posed by the phenomenon and its threat to the state's finances. Our argument is that the 1930s' constructs of racial hygiene or eugenics represent equally apposite examples of *Dispositif*—the perceived threat to the population posed by purportedly inferior racial and genetic stock initiated a state-directed programme of registration, exclusion, sterilisation and mass murder, unprecedented in terms of scale and technological sophistication. The Nazi regime utilised eugenics and racial hygiene to legitimate its use of extreme forms of biopower through its "euthanasia" programme and subsequent racially based eliminative genocides in Europe.[86]

---

81   Michel Foucault, *Security, Territory, Population: Lectures at the Collège De France, 1977–1978* (New York: Palgrave, 2007).
82   Proctor, *The Nazi War*, 249.
83   Christopher Mayes, *The Biopolitics of Lifestyle: Foucault, Ethics and Healthy Choices* (New York: Routledge, 2016).
84   Ibid.
85   Mayes, *The Biopolitics*.
86   The concept of "biopower" as a means of formulating the behaviour of nurses in the *T4* programme has been explored by Thomas Foth, whose work also situates "Dispositif" in the asylum setting. See Thomas Foth, "Analyzing Nursing as a Dispositif Healing and Devastation in the Name of Biopower." PhD thesis, University of Ottawa, 2011; Thomas Foth, "Understanding 'Caring' Through Biopolitics: The Case of Nurses Under the Nazi Regime," *Nursing Philosophy* 14, no. 4 (2013), 284–94.

As stated earlier, eugenics had a long history in Germany and other democratic societies. It was popular across the political spectrum in the Weimar parliament in Germany (1919–1933). There was also enthusiasm for eugenic ideas in the middle and professional classes, part of a so-called "techno-bureaucratic intelligentsia."[87] Eugenic societies were influential in numerous other countries, most conspicuously the USA. The state of Indiana had passed the first compulsory sterilisation law in 1907. Until the 1960s, 29 other US states enacted similar laws. German and American eugenic institutions collaborated closely until the outbreak of the war. American eugenicists were profoundly influential in the formulation of the 1924 US federal *Immigration Act*.[88] Prominent American physicians advocated the "euthanasia" of "feeble-minded" patients,[89] and it was only when the mass murder of the disabled under Nazism became apparent that German and other western eugenic movements parted company.[90] The attempted "psychiatric genocide" of people with schizophrenia in Germany during the Nazi period failed: the prevalence of the disorder actually increased after the war.

Eugenic notions have served as the basis of state policy in a number of countries in the post-war era and represent continuations of this form of biopower. In China, for example, the 1995 *Maternal and Infant Health Law* forbade people carrying heritable mental or physical disorders from marrying, and promoted mass prenatal ultrasound testing for birth defects. Then Chinese Premier, Deng Xiao Ping, also encouraged social and economic policies to ensure educated and successful young Chinese would meet and procreate. The since revised "one child policy" was another manifestation of the process. In Singapore, the Family Planning and Population Board (FPPB) advocated population control. In the 1970s, Singaporean social and economic policies sought to increase the reproduction rate of educated and successful women and reduce that of low-paid, uneducated women. In most post-industrial liberal democratic societies, tacit forms of eugenic-based biopower are found in state-funded and professionally-endorsed routine prenatal screening for foetal abnormality. As a result of these programmes, for example, numerous studies indicate that the vast majority of pregnancies with Down Syndrome are terminated at the point of pre-natal diagnosis.[91] It has also been averred that

---

87 Burleigh, "The Legacy."
88 Adam Cohen, *Imbeciles: The Supreme Court, American Eugenics, and the Sterilization of Carrie Buck* (New York: Penguin, 2016).
89 M. Louis Offen, "Dealing With 'Defectives': Foster Kennedy and William Lennox On Eugenics," *Historical Neurology* 61, no. 5 (2003), 668–73.
90 Edwin Black, *War Against the Weak: Eugenics and America's Campaign to Create a Master Race* (New York: Basic Books, 2003).

legitimating termination of pregnancies on the basis of specific evaluative "criteria" enables discrimination against those who live with Down Syndrome or other disabilities.[92]

"Thanatopolitics"

As shown in the Nazi regime, in extreme authoritarian settings biopower becomes the literal question of life and death. This is what Foucault and later writers termed "Thanatopolitics." Foucault considered genocide as the logical extension of biopower through the revisitation of the right of the sovereign to kill, an exercise of coercive power at the level of life, species, race and population.[93] Foucault saw that genocide was the ultimate expression of this.

Despite the traditional definition of genocide interrogating the deliberate elimination of a national, ethnical, racial or religious group, many in the field of disability studies have argued that "disability" is as much a social category as race.[94] Moreover, any reading of the history of the first part of the twentieth century in the United States or Europe sees the categories of "disability" and "race" as manifestations of biological inferiority and therefore the pretext for exclusion and ultimately annihilation. The firm nexus between eugenics and racism in the United States and Europe in the first part of the twentieth century is a core premise of what has been dubbed the "eugenic Atlantic."[95] The genetic and racially inferior fall into the same category and so therefore does their elimination. The *Krankenmorde* is therefore arguably as much a genocidal act as the Shoah. It is important to recognise that of the German victims of the Nazi regime, the more than 200,000 people with disabilities who were murdered represent the group with the highest mortality.[96]

Thanatopolitics is at the core of the work of philosopher Giorgio Agamben. Agamben defined the threshold of biological modernity as the point where the species and the individual as living bodies becomes the focus of politics—the state and, by extension, the focus of the state bureaucracy, becomes a "biomass" of population, or, as in the case of the Nazi regime, the *Volk*. Agamben

---

91   Brian Skotko, "With New Prenatal Testing, Will Babies With Down Syndrome Slowly Disappear?" *Archives of Disease in Childhood* 94, no. 11 (2009), 823–26.

92   Alicia Ouellette, "Selection Against Disability: Abortion, ART, and Access," *Journal of Law, Medicine and Ethics* 43, no. 2 (2015), 211–23.

93   Foucault, *The History*.

94   Catherine Kudlick, "Disability History: Why We Need Another Other," *American Historical Review* 108, no. 3 (2003), 763–93.

95   David Mitchell and Sharon Snyder. "The Eugenic Atlantic: Race, Disability, and the Making of an International Eugenic Science, 1800–1945," *Disability and Society* 18, no. 7 (2003), 843–64.

96   According to the US Holocaust Memorial Museum, the death toll for German Jews was around 180,000.

makes use of the ancient figure of *"Homo Sacer"*[97] as a metaphor for those excluded from society and its protections: living within the law but not protected by law. This creates a situation redolent of the ancient concept of "bare life"—life without the privileges or rights of citizenship.[98]

For Agamben, the Holocaust was the fullest realisation of biopower and the concentration camp its ultimate manifestation. Agamben argued that when the state shifts into an authoritarian mode, in circumstances of perceived or manufactured threat, it creates what he terms "states of exception."[99] This is a state of virtual war on certain parts of the population and a means of elimination—social exclusion and starvation were forms of biopower used against "undesirables" and enemies of the Nazi regime. The particular obsession of the Nazi regime with food, and the use of starvation as a means of control and murder, demonstrates a particular manifestation of a form of biopower expressed through thanatopolitics.[100] The *Musselmänner* of the concentration camps, the diseased and starved figures of the Polish ghettos, or the inmates of starvation houses in "de-centralised euthanasia" centres are reduced to bare life in a biologically-driven state of exception. Agamben sees this phenomenon in the present day in Guantanamo Bay or the refugee camps and detention centres of Europe (and, we would argue, the Pacific).

The psychiatric profession and the state

To eschew a Hippocratic tradition and then be enjoined in an exercise of biopower, the medical profession and its specialties must realise a form of professional ethic. The complex relationship between the psychiatric profession in Germany and the Nazi regime has been analysed from multiple perspectives.[101] A critical dimension to the analysis of this period is that of professional ethics in psychiatry.[102] "Professional ethics," as contrasted with particular normative theories of ethics such as utilitarianism or virtue ethics, situates the psychiatrist as moral agent within the context of a complex network of relationships, laws and obligations with the community.

---

97 Agamben's use of *Homo Sacer* (or the "sacred man") refers to the status of being outside protection of the law or excluded from society. It is a complex concept with multiple examples throughout history.
98 Giorgio Agamben, *State of Exception*, trans. Kevin Attell (Chicago: University of Chicago Press, 2005).
99 Ibid.
100 Gesine Gerhard, *Nazi Hunger Politics: A History of Food in the Third Reich* (New York: Rowman and Littlefield, 2015).
101 Lifton, *The Nazi Doctors*; Klee, *"Euthanasie" im NS-Staat*.
102 Michael Robertson and Garry Walter, "Overview of Psychiatric Ethics I: Professional Ethics and Psychiatry," *Australasian Psychiatry* 15, no. 3 (2007), 201–06.

A "profession" is a group possessed of a certain expertise, knowledge and set of skills that applies these in service of the "greater good," usually of the community.[103] In exchange, the professional group is afforded status, material reward and autonomy. This arrangement is a form of "social contract" that, through laws, negotiated binding arrangements or policy applications, effectively trumps other approaches to moral deliberation and action by the professional group.[104] It is in the nature of such arrangements to privilege the interests of the community over the individual, which frequently places the professional's obligations to the individual patient in conflict with obligations to the community under the professional social contract. In such a situation, the Hippocratic injunction to do no harm may need to be abandoned.[105]

This creates a situation of a "dual role dilemma."[106] The concept of dual role dilemma originates from the perceived conflict of obligations forensic psychiatrists have to both impartiality to the court and the Hippocratic obligations to the individual patient.[107] It can be argued that most dilemmas in psychiatric ethics may be framed as variants of the dual role dilemma, many of which arise from conflicting obligations between the psychiatrist's obligations under the professional social contract and duties towards the individual patient.

Leo Alexander highlighted in his analysis of the Doctor's Trial in Nuremberg 1946–1947 that the critical step in the pathway to the crimes perpetrated by psychiatrists under the Nazi regime was a shift from individual care to that of productive capacity or economic utility.[108] The "useless eaters" destined for death in the T4 programme were thus defined by the cost of their existence, rather than their individual value as human beings. Karl Brandt, Hitler's physician, coordinator of the T4 programme and lead defendant in the doctor's trial, highlighted this dual role dilemma in the seemingly conflicted statements he made in his defence. On the one hand he proclaimed: "Any per-

---

103   "Medical Professionalism in the New Millennium: A Physician Charter," *Annals of Internal Medicine* 136, no. 3 (2002), 243–46.
104   Robertson and Walter, "Overview of Psychiatric."
105   Allen R. Dyer, *Ethics and Psychiatry: Toward Professional Definition* (New York: American Psychiatric Press, 1987).
106   Michael Robertson and Garry Walter, "Psychiatric Ethics and the 'New Professionalism.' " in *Psychiatry's Contract With Society: Concepts, Controversies, and Consequences*, eds. Dinesh Bhugra, Amit Malik and George Ikkos (London: Oxford University Press, 2010), 221–39.
107   Philip Candilis, Richard Martinez and Christina Dording, "Principles and Narrative in Forensic Psychiatry: Toward a Robust View of Professional Role," *Journal of the American Academy of Psychiatry and the Law* 29, no. 2 (2001), 167–73.
108   Alexander, "Medical Science."

sonal code of ethics must give way to the total character of the war."[109] On the other, he provided rationalisations about his actions being motivated by the relief of suffering:

> Would you believe that it was a pleasure to me to receive the order to start euthanasia? For fifteen years I had labored at the sick-bed and every patient was to me like a brother, every sick child I worried about as if it had been my own. . . . And thus I affirmed euthanasia. I realize the problem is as old as man, but it is not a crime against man nor against humanity. Here I cannot believe like a clergyman or think as a Jurist. I am a doctor and I see the law of nature as being the law of reason. For that grew in my heart the love of man and it stands before my conscience.[110]

Conclusion

Throughout this essay, we have reflected upon how the German psychiatric profession was enrolled in an enterprise on behalf of the state and the health of the *Volk*, in exchange for unprecedented power and status in the Nazi regime. As an instance of professional ethics, the obligation to the collective (as we have argued, a malignant application of biopower in the origin of genocide) creates a situation of doctors becoming "healer killers" and instruments of genocide.[111] A similar dual role dilemma born of professional ethics emerged in the Soviet Union several decades later through the persecution of political dissidents by psychiatric diagnosis and restraint,[112] and subsequently in China through the persecution of Falun Gong practitioners in forensic psychiatric hospitals.[113] In all three instances, the obligations of the profession to the community, represented by an authoritarian or totalitarian state, creates a diabolical dual role dilemma.

The moral analysis of the history of the Nazi regime needs to move beyond normative comparisons with an "outlier" period in the history of psychiatry, that is, "what the Nazis did." The conceptualisation of the Holocaust as an enduring possibility in Western culture is an important precondition of any ex-

---

109 Charles Hamilton, *Leaders and Personalities of the Third Reich: Their Biographies, Portaits, Autographs, Volume One* (San Jose: James Bender Publishing, 1984).

110 Ulf Schmidt, *Karl Brandt: The Nazi Doctor: Medicine and Power in the Third Reich* (London: Continuum Books, 2007).

111 Lifton, *The Nazi Doctors*.

112 Sidney Bloch and Peter Reddaway, *Soviet Psychiatric Abuse: The Shadow Over World Psychiatry* (London: Gollancz, 1983).

113 Sunny Lu and Viviana Galli, "Psychiatric Abuse of Falun Gong Practitioners in China," *Journal of the American Academy of Psychiatry and Law* 30 (2002), 126–30.

ploration of the period. As Paul Rabinow and Nikolas Rose have argued, the Holocaust is not "an exceptional moment of throwback to a singular barbarianism, but an enduring possibility intrinsic to the very project of civilization and the law."[114] If we accept that the culture that produced the Holocaust remains the context of the practice of psychiatry, then the contemporary significance of the period requires deeper analysis. Eugenics and euthanasia must be reconceptualised and, in our analysis, the prism of biopower and thanatopolitics are among the most valid ways to do so. The proclamations of international medical groups and the public atonement of those professionals implicated in these crimes are important historical events, but on their own do not enlighten fully the true significance of this period to psychiatry. If one accepts that what happened under the Nazi regime was an extreme form of dual role dilemma—for example, the application of a highly malignant process of the exercise of biopower—then current dilemmas in psychiatric ethics need to be constructed along similar lines. Whether this concerns debates around mental health policy, medicalisation of problems of life, or contemporary biologically based conceptualisations of disability and mental illness, the dual role dilemma remains a function of the empowerment of the psychiatric profession by the community and the expectations that arise from it. If the key participants of this exceptional period in history remain framed as evil doers, indifferent bystanders and heroic resisters, such lessons are lost, forgotten or unlearnt.

---

114 Rabinow and Rose, "Biopower Today."

FIRST DO HARM! A MEDICAL EXPERIMENT ON AUSTRALIAN PRISONERS OF WAR AND THE CAREER OF A MILITARY PHYSICIAN

Konrad Kwiet and George Weisz

Introduction

On May 20, 1941, the Wehrmacht launched Operation *Merkur*—the large-scale airborne invasion of the Greek island of Crete.[1] It was the first of its kind in the history of warfare. The fierce battle between German parachutists and glider-borne infantry, and the Allied "Creforce," lasted 12 days, each side suffering severe losses. Thousands of soldiers were killed, injured or went missing in action: Germans and Austrians, Britons, Australians and New Zealanders, Greeks and Cypriots, Palestinians and Indians. More than 16,000 Empire troops were taken prisoner, among them 3,109 Australians, almost half the Australians deployed on Crete,[2] and more than one-third of those captured by the Axis powers in Europe during World War Two.[3] The defeat at Crete was Australia's "largest single catastrophe of the war, surpassed only by the fall of Singapore in February 1942."[4] Despite extensive research on the military campaign, one incident on the sidelines has, to date, evaded notice: five Australian prisoners of war (POWs) on Crete who were exposed in the summer of 1941 to a hepatitis experiment,[5] presumably the first recorded case in

---

1 Peter Monteath, *P.O.W.: Australian Prisoners of War in Hitler's Reich* (Sydney: Pan Macmillan Australia, 2001), 75.

2 Ibid., 78.

3 *Australian War Memorial Encyclopedia*, https://www.awm.gov.au/encyclopedia/pow/ww2.

4 Joan Beaumont, "Introduction," in *Australia's War 1939–1945*, ed. Joan Beaumont (Sydney: Allen & Unwin, 1996), 12.

5 George Weisz was the first to access and evaluate the personal open files of the Australian POWs housed at the National Archives of Australia. He published his findings in a short article, George Weisz, "Nazi Medical Experiments on Australian Prisoners of War: Commentary on the Testimony of an Australian Soldier," *Journal of Law and Medicine* 23, no. 2 (2015), 457–59. The article attracted considerable media attention in Australia and abroad. Konrad Kwiet joined the project, searching for records in German archival depositories on the career of the military physician who conducted the medical experiment. Weisz, a surgeon, dealt with the medical dimension. Kwiet, a historian, constructed the historical narrative. We would like to sincerely thank friends and colleagues who assisted us in researching this case study: Clement Boughton, Klaus Toyka, Paul J. Weindling, Giles Bennett, Astrid Ley, Rüdiger Overmans, Jürgen Förster, Sarah Haid, Joachim Schneeweiss, Beate Winzer and Jane Sydenham-Kwiet.

Australian history. They belong to the forgotten victims and survivors of murderous Nazi medicine.[6]

At the core of this contribution stands a review of the life history of Friedrich Meythaler, and a critical assessment of a hepatitis experiment he conducted during the Second World War. Meythaler was an eminent physician whose career illustrates the easy transition, indeed the continuity, from Nazi medicine to medicine in post-war Germany.

Our research is ongoing as there are still many gaps in the known history to be filled. One key question that remains is whether Meythaler's medical experimentation had long-term effects on the health of the POWs who served as his test subjects. Privacy regulations restrict access to patient records that may be held at hospitals, insurance companies and clinics. In addition, more research needs to be conducted to shed light on the medical and institutional networks of the Nazi regimes within which Meythaler was operating.[7] Furthermore, there is evidence to suggest that Meythaler's experiment represents only the tip of the iceberg. Many more POWs from Australia and other Allied countries, held in custody of the German Wehrmacht, might have been selected for human experiments conducted by Nazi doctors.

For the Cretan population, Nazi rule and terror commenced in May 1941. From the outset, the occupying military authorities implemented examples of their extermination policies. Instructed by Hermann Göring, Commander-in-Chief of the Luftwaffe, General Kurt Student, commander of the XI *Fliegerkorps*, issued an order to his men to "annihilate" civilians in retaliation for local resistance—immediately and without any judicial proceedings.[8] On June 2, parachutists arrived in Kondomari to slaughter 50 men. The following day a firing squad perpetrated another horrific war crime known as the " Holocaust of Kandano." 180 civilians were massacred and all buildings were dynamited or torched and the village razed to the ground. The murder site was declared a "dead zone." War crimes committed by the Wehrmacht continued unabated in the course of "pacifying" the conquered island.[9] The fate of the small, ancient

---

6   Paul J. Weindling, *Victims and Survivors of Human Experiments: Science and Suffering in the Holocaust* (London: Bloomsbury Academic, 2015).

7   Beate Winzer's PhD explores the history of the *Luftmedizinische Forschungsinstitut der Luftwaffe, 1934–1945*, to be submitted at the University Berlin Charité. We thank her for bringing this military research centre to our attention, and providing us with details of the military and medical networks.

8   Detlef Vogel, "Das Eingreifen Deutschlands auf dem Balkan," in *Das Deutsche Reich und der Zweite Weltkrieg, Bd.3 Der Mittelmeerraum und Südosteuropa*, ed. Militärgeschichtliches Forschungamt (Stuttgart: Deutsche Verlags-Anstalt, 1984), 508.

9   Norman Paech, "Wehrmachtsverbrechen in Griechenland," *Kritische Justiz* 3 (1999), 380–97; Christian Hartmann, Johannes Hürter, Ulrike Jureit, Jan Philipp Reemtsma and Horst Möller, *Verbrechen der Wehrmacht: Bilanz einer Debatte* (München: C.H. Beck, 2005).

Jewish community of Crete was sealed three years later. On May 29, 1944, about 300 Jews were rounded up, destined for Auschwitz. They were transported under appalling conditions to the port city of Heraklion and forced to embark the ill-fated Tanais, together with 400 Greek hostages and 800 Italian POWs. The boat was torpedoed by a British submarine and sank within minutes. There were no survivors. Accused of war crimes, General Student was sentenced in 1947 to five years in prison. One year later he was set free. Members of the killing units were never tried.

Friedrich Meythaler also escaped criminal prosecution after the war. He held the rank of *Oberstabsarzt* (Surgeon Major) and headed a sanitation company. He also served as consulting physician to the 12th German army that operated in the Balkans; such positions were reserved for Germany and Austria's medical elite. Much has been written about the crimes perpetrated by Nazi doctors in concentration camps, about the forced sterilisation of more than 400,000 people and of the murder of more than 300,000 psychiatric inmates in mental institutions as part of the so-called " Euthanasia" programme, code-named *Aktion T4*.

Little is known about the recruitment and activities of consulting physicians.[10] With the beginning of the Second World War, university professors, *Privatdozenten* (post-doctoral university fellows) and other specialists were called up for military service. Recruitment and deployment, arrangements and monitoring were in hands of the Berlin-based Army Medical Inspectorate, its affiliated Military Medical Academy, and the Research Institute of the Airforce for Aviation Medicine, set up in Göring's Reich Ministry of Aviation.[11] Consulting physicians were not only deployed at home in the military districts but were also assigned to army groups, offering their services in all war-relevant areas of medicine. Later, they examined the ever-increasing cases of shell shock, bedwetting, self-harm and suicide attempts among soldiers, and referred patients to the brutal military justice systems.[12] They continued medical research behind front lines, prescribed cures and treat-

---

10 Karl Philipp Behrendt, Die Kriegschirurgie von 1939–1945 aus der Sicht der Behandelnden Chirugen des Heeres im Zweiten Weltkrieg (PhD thesis, Albert-Ludwig University, Freiburg, 2003). See also Jürgen Förster, "Ideological Warfare in Germany, 1919 to 1949," in *Germany and the Second World War: Volume IX/I: German Wartime Society 1939–1945: Politicization, Disintegration, and the Struggle for Survival* (Oxford: Oxford University Press, 2008), 487–88.

11 See Alexander Neumann, *Arzttum ist immer Kämpfertum: Die Heeressanitätsinspektion und das Amt "Chef des Wehrmachtssanitätswesen" im Zweiten Weltkrtieg (1939–1945)* (Düsseldorf: Droste, 2005). See also Wolfgang Uwe Eckart, and Alexander Neumann Eckhart, eds., *Medizin im Zweiten Weltkrieg: Militärmedizinische Praxis und medizinische Wissenschaft im "Totalen Krieg"* (Paderborn: Schöningh, 2006).

12 See Gine Elsner and Gerhard Stuby, *Wehrmachtsmedizin und Militärjustiz, Sachverständige im Zweiten Weltkrieg: Beratende Ärzte und Gutachter für die Kriegsgerichte der Wehrmacht* (Hamburg: VSA, 2012).

ments, and presented their findings at conferences. Medical experiments, in particular human experiments, were an integral part of their role. A directive for consulting physicians authorised the experiments: "In time of war unique opportunities for medical research present themselves. These opportunities must not be missed."[13]

Upon his arrival on Crete, Meythaler selected five healthy Australian POWs in the port city of Rethymno, located on the central north coast of the island, for a hepatitis experiment. Declared "sick," they were admitted to the local hospital where they were examined and x-rayed. Blood and urine tests were performed. They were then injected with the blood of highly suspected hepatitis-affected German soldiers, some with, others without jaundice. This non-consensual human-to-human blood injection for diagnostic purposes did not only constitute a war crime but a clear violation of the 1907 Hague and the 1929 Geneva Conventions on the treatment of POWs. It also contravened the spirit of the ancient Hippocratic Oath that imposes on doctors the duty, to use the popular phrase, "First do no harm!" or also described as: "Practice two things in your dealings with disease: either help or do not harm the patient!"[14] Meythaler's experiment was harmful and painful. It was, of course, totally unacceptable, both professionally and ethically. Australian records, recently digitised in the National Archives, identify the Australian POWs and trace their military service. The personal dossiers comprising the Service and Casualty Forms, the Attestation Sheets, letters and reports, POW files and the Proceedings of Discharge provided the biographical data.

The victims were young, born between 1907 and 1920. They came from Sydney, Melbourne and Hobart, and grew up in a lower socio-economic environment, earning their living as labourers, a cook and grocery assistant. One was a Catholic, the others Anglicans. Two were married. They enlisted after the outbreak of the war and joined in the ranks of the 2nd and 5th Australian Infantry Battalions that fought with the 16th Brigade Composite Battalion on Crete. After being discharged from the Rethymno hospital, they returned to military captivity. One of them managed to escape—like so many Allied soldiers—and sought refuge in the Cretan hills sheltered by locals. The others had to wait some time before they were shipped to Thessaloniki and incarcerated

---

13 Behrendt, *Die Kriegschirurgie*, 19.
14 Geoffrey Lloyd, ed., *Hippocratic Writings* (London: Penguin Books, 1989), 94.

in a transit camp.[15] From there they embarked on a long and harrowing journey to Germany.

In March 1942, they arrived in the small city of Lamsdorf to be incarcerated in nearby Stalag VIII B, one of the largest POW camps that administered more than 100,000 prisoners of Allied nationalities. Subjected to harsh forced labour in mining, factories and railway construction, they were transferred to *Arbeitskommandos*, labour detachments, living and working outside the main camp. One test subject, WJL, belonged to the 242 Australian POWs who did not survive Hitler's Reich.[16] The Germans informed the Australian military of his death on May 30, 1942, and dispatched his German POW card. It was marked with the red death symbol and the handwritten entry: "*Auf der Flucht erschossen*" ("shot while attempting to escape"). It was the standard phrase to disguise murder. WJL was buried by the Germans in the Krakow military cemetery—Row 8, Grave 13—and posthumously awarded with an Australian war service medal. The other three POWs returned to Australia and were discharged in 1945–1946 "on compassionate grounds." None of them informed the authorities about their treatment at the Rethymno hospital, nor lodged a claim for compensation for long-term damages caused by the experiment. The grocery assistant applied in the early 1950s to the POW Memorial Trust for a grant on the basis of his "nervous disabilities" and "suffering from nervous strain."[17]

It was left to the Australian POW who had managed to escape from Crete in November 1941 to inform the Australian military about the medical experiments and the damage these had caused. Arriving in Melbourne in early August 1942, he experienced several symptom-free weeks, alternating with one or two weeks of fever. The attacks gradually became less frequent, but were accompanied by muscle pain and lower back pain. In September 1942 he was admitted to a military hospital in Melbourne and examined by military physicians. They were unable to confirm the initial suspected diagnosis of "typhus," "malaria" and "pyrexia of unknown origin," but several doctors commented on the back pain and blood test results found abnormalities.[18] After several examinations and interrogations, the classified findings and clinical

---

15 The OKW (Supreme Command of the Armed Forces) did not raise any objections to transporting British, Australian and New Zealand POWs to Germany. However, the OKW did not favour transporting Jews to Germany, instead suggesting that "they could remain on the Balkans and perhaps be deployed in war relevant work." R 40.741. Letter OKW to Foreign Affairs, June 11, 1941.

16 Monteath, *P.O.W.*, 414.

17 Research has yet to be conducted as to whether the test subjects applied in 1986 for compensation for harsh treatment in German camps. The scheme was set up by the Australian government in the wake of Nazi war crimes investigations and public debates.

18 A high reading of 10% Eosinophilia (normal 1-3%).

notes were submitted to higher military authorities. A Colonel of the Australian Military Forces who saw the report stated: "If true, and there seems no reasons to doubt the veracity, (the case) is one which merits any protest which can be lodged by Dep. Prisoner War."[19] No protest was lodged. Instead, the Australian Army staff in London were instructed to take up "the matter ... with the United Kingdom authorities."[20] A report was dispatched; however, no record of any British response has yet been found.[21] In Australia, the case was closed. Appearing before a Medical Board, the psychiatric examiner concluded: "Apart from the fact that he was rather underweight and mildly anxious about himself, he did not appear to be permanently invalidated by his alleged experiences."[22] Discharged on "mild psychiatric grounds" the patient left behind a lengthy testimony of the events in Crete.[23] Having lost a lot of weight, he described the hunger rations as minimal, one meal per day of "a handful of cooked beans and one slice of Greek bread" and a pint of water twice a day. He remembered in detail the arrival of a doctor who "approached me and turned up my upper eyelid." The doctor returned the next day and conducted an examination, x-ray of the chest, and blood and urine tests. "He then stated I was sick, conducted me to a ward, in which there were a number of German patients, and ordered me into one of the five beds that had been set apart in the ward. ... The same day the four other Australians ... were brought in."[24]

He continued with his recollection of the experiment, and his testimony is worth quoting here at length:

On the following day we were again examined, temperature, pulse, and blood and urine tests. Later that day the doctor returned and withdrew half a syringeful of blood ... from the arm of the German patient in the room and immediately injected it into a vein of my arm, after first applying a tourniquet in my upper arm. The blood went into my arm without clotting. The other Australians received similar injections, but I do not know from whom the blood was taken, as I was not paying attention to them at that time. The following day the doctor returned and after the customary examinations, temperature, pulse, blood and urine he injected into the vein at the same

---

19 (G.A.S) Chronological Record of Movements; Medical case sheet, October 19, 1942; Letter AMF-Southern Command to DDMS Victoria, April 2, 1943.
20 Ibid., Department of the Army, minute paper, April 14, 1943.
21 Ibid., letter to Australian Army Staff in London, May 5, 1943.
22 (G.A.S), letter AMF-Southern Command to DDMS Victoria, April 2, 1943.
23 Ibid., statement, April 10, 1943.
24 Ibid.

place in my arm a clear fluid. The others were similarly treated. Following this injection we all became, within the space of 24 hours, feverish with high pulses, and felt very sick. We were not provided with any medicine as relief, but every morning thereafter until the 10th day the doctor examined us—eyes, temperature, pulse, blood, urine, and prodded us and tested us for pains in various parts of our bodies. It seemed to me that he appeared to be disappointed on observing the colour of my urine. By the 10th day the fever and body pains had gradually subsided, and we were given a second injection of blood, on this occasion in the buttocks. . . . Two hours later we were all very ill, suffering all the discomfiture of the first attack, but to a greater degree. . . . On the 11th day a clear fluid was injected into each of us and thereafter until the 18th day the procedure was the same . . . except that several of my friends had a tube inserted into their stomach through their throats.[25]

Importantly, he also stated that the Germans from whom the blood had been taken were all very sick and receiving medical treatment: "Several of them had a very yellow complexion, and one particularly was yellow in the eyes."

After three weeks the Australians started to recover. They knew they had been "used for experimental purposes." They protested their treatment both in hospital and to the military authorities upon their return to the POW camp. The escaped POW suffered for months with high fevers and pains, especially in the back, and cramps in the legs.

German records, accessed in several archival depositories,[26] and the literature consulted, shed light on the career of Friedrich Meythaler.[27] They document his deployment in Crete, the human experimentation, and support the validity and plausibility of the Australian POW's testimonial accounts. The clinical notes taken during the examinations and experiments have not come to light as yet. The findings, however, were made public in a lecture presented

---

25 (G.A.S), letter AMF-Southern Command to DDMS Victoria, April 10, 1943.

26 The archival studies were conducted in the Freiburg-based Military Archives of the Federal Archives, the Federal Archives in Berlin, the Political Archives of Foreign Affairs in Berlin, and in the State Archives Nuremberg.

27 Michael Buddrus and Sigrid Fritzlar, eds., *Die Professoren der Universität Rostok im Dritten Reich: Ein biographishes Lexikon* (Berlin: Walter de Gruyter, 2007), 277; Paul J. Weindling, *Nazi Medicine and the Nuremberg Trials: From Medical War Crimes to Informed Consent* (London: Palgrave Macmillan, 2006), 38; Paul J. Weindling, *Victims and Survivors*, 64–66; Brigitte Leyendecker and Burghard F. Klapp, "Deutsche Hepatitisforschung im Zweiten Weltkrieg," in *Der Wert des Menschen: Medizin in Deutschland 1918–1945*, eds. Christian Pross and Götz Aly (Berlin: Edition Hentrich, 1989), 261–93; also Brigitte Leyendecker and Burghard F. Klapp, "Hepatitis-Humanexperimente im Zweiten Weltkrieg," *Zeitschrift für die gesamte Hygiene* 35, no. 12 (1989), 756–60.

at a conference of military physicians,[28] and in an article published in a medical journal in 1942.

Friedrich Meythaler came from a well-established middle-class family in which Christian values were cultivated. Born in 1898 in Offenburg, he attended high school at a *Gymnasium* in the final years of the Wilhelmine Empire. He then joined the army in World War One, fighting at the Western Front as a platoon leader. Decorated and discharged as Lieutenant in early 1919, he undertook his studies in medicine at the top universities of Heidelberg and Munich, graduating in record time in 1923 with distinction. His doctoral dissertation explored a special case of bleeding of the kidney. Meythaler embarked on a career within the university hospital's system, treating patients, teaching and researching, gradually climbing the hierarchical ladder from intern to registrar, station doctor to senior doctor, and finally to chief physician and medical superintendent. Specialising in internal medicine, he attained a post-doctoral qualification in 1933. Three years later he was awarded a special teaching assignment to lecture in the field of aviation medicine. This teaching position secured his integration into Göring's Research Institute for Aviation Medicine, paving the way for his later deployment to Crete and recruitment as consultant physician. Moreover, the Medical Faculty of Rostok University had emerged as one of the key centres for liver research. In 1939, on the eve of World War Two, Meythaler was awarded a professorial title.

Since the National Socialist seizure of power, Meythaler had witnessed the systematic expulsion of Jewish doctors, first from universities and hospitals, then from private practices.[29] About 8,000 lost their positions; many found refuge in exile, but those who remained trapped in Nazi Germany fell victim to the programme of the "Final Solution." Non-Jewish physicians profited from the removal of Jewish doctors. After the war, facing a denazification tribunal, Meythaler recalled the names of Jewish doctors under whose guidance he had worked in the years of the Weimar Republic.

His affiliation with National Socialism was determined less by ideological convictions than by professional interests; joining Nazi organisations assisted him in cementing and enhancing his academic career. In November 1933 he joined the SA, Hitler's Stormtroopers, offering his services within the SA

---

28   Frederick Taylor, *Exorcising Hitler: The Occupation and Denazification of Germany* (London: Bloomsbury, 2011); Norbert Frei, *Vergangenheitspolitik: Die Anfänge der Bundesrepublik Deutschland und die NS-Vergangenheit* (Munich: C.H. Beck, 2012).

29   Avraham Barkai, *From Boycott to Annihilation: The Economic Struggle of German Jews 1933–1939* (Hanover: University Press of New England, 1989); Marianne Kaplan, *Between Dignity and Despair: Jewish Life in Nazi Germany* (New York: Oxford University Press, 1998), 26; Günter Plum, "Wirtschaft und Erwerbsleben," in *Die Juden in Deutschland 1933–1945*, ed. Wolfgang Benz (Munich: C.H. Beck, 1983), 268–313.

Medical Corps. He then joined other organisations affiliated with the Nazi Party but it was only in May 1937 that he joined the NSDAP. The high party number (4,403,603) allocated to him attests to his late entry. Unlike the infamous SS doctors engaged in barbaric medical experiments, he saw no need to apply for membership in Heinrich Himmler's SS.

On the eve of World War Two, Meythaler was called up for military service. As *Internist* of a *Feldlazarett* (Field Hospital) he participated in the German conquest of Poland. He might have been aware of the atrocities and murderous campaigns unleashed by SS and police units alongside ethnic Germans against Jews and "saboteurs," politicians, intellectuals and priests. By the end of 1939, the death toll amounted to more than 60,000.[30] In May 1940 the Wehrmacht launched its *Blitzkrieg* (Lightning War) against countries in Western Europe. Meythaler took up a position at the Field Hospital of a newly established *Waffen-SS* Division—the infamous 3rd Panzer Division *Totenkopf* (Death's Head).

By the time Meythaler was selected to go to Crete he had developed a reputation as an authoritative figure in the fields of liver dysfunction and infectious diseases. He could point to an impressive list of 66 publications; at the end of the war the number had risen to 73, documenting ongoing research on hepatitis and diabetes and his new pioneering studies on malaria. The supervision of 25 doctoral dissertations and papers, submitted by his students and interns in the pre-war years, was equally remarkable.[31] Undoubtedly, these academic credentials led to the assignment in Greece, where "*Hepatitis sine Icterus*," that is, hepatitis without but mostly in conjunction with jaundice, was rampant. German and Allied soldiers alike were severely affected by jaundice. On Crete they were admitted to field and local hospitals. Meythaler hastened to carry out research on the differential diagnosis of the Mediterranean diseases amongst the German soldiers, and their causes and prevention.

The findings were submitted to the Berlin-based Army Medical Inspectorate,[32] along with all the other reports from consulting physicians. As the hepatitis epidemic spread across Europe, causing a major problem for the army, at many places efforts were undertaken to identify the agent of the infectious hepatitis via animal trials and person-to-person experiments. Kurt

---

30 Jürgen Matthäus, Jochen Böhler and Klaus-Michael Mallmann, eds., *War, Pacification and Mass Murder, 1939: The Einsatzgruppen in Poland* (Lanham MD: Rowman & Littlefield 2014); Jochen Böhler, *Auftakt zum Vernichtungskrieg: Die Wehrmacht in Poland 1939* (Frankfurt am Main: Fischer, 2006); Alexander B. Rossino, *Hitler Strikes Poland: Blitzkrieg, Ideology and Atrocity* (Lawrence: University Press of Kansas, 2003).

31 Friedrich Meythaler, "Die wissenschaftlichen Arbeiten von Prof. Dr. Meythaler und Liste der wissenschaftlichen Arbeiten der Assistenten und Liste der Dissertationen," compiled on January 14, 1944.

32 Neumann, *Arzttum ist Kämpfertum*.

Gutzeit played a vital role in this research. A member of the SS since 1933, he served as Consultant Internist at the Army Medical Inspectorate and ran a department of internal medicine at the Military Medical Academy. Initially he conducted an experiment on himself. Two assistants carried out non-consensual experiments. Hans Voigt infected psychiatric patients from a mental hospital in Breslau. Arnold Dohmen had permission from Heinrich Himmler to select 11 Jewish juveniles from Auschwitz and to expose them to a barbaric hepatitis experiment in the Sachsenhausen concentration camp.[33]

This hepatitis research illustrates that university-based Nazi doctors often took the initiative and determined the scope of the experiments. They competed against each other to be the first to discover the infectious nature of the rampant disease. They used all available sites for their experiments: POW camps and field hospitals, universities and research institutions, psychiatric wards and concentration camps. The International Committee of the Red Cross, entrusted with the task of monitoring experiments in POW camps and concentrations camps, "was a catastrophic failure" in this regard.[34]

Meythaler's findings were quickly published. In August 1942 his article appeared in the medical journal *Klinische Wochenschrift*.[35] The timing and scope of the research were mentioned: "In summer and autumn of 1941 I had the opportunity to personally see on the Balkan, in Greece and Africa, a large number—around 2,500—cases of *hepatitis infectiosa* and to observe the course of the disease."[36] Outlining the results of his examinations, he then admitted the blood injection from hepatitis-infected soldiers. The central sentence reads in English as follows:

> As the causative agent is unknown, I carried out on Crete transmission experiments through transfer of blood from person to person in a pre-ikterian condition. The result in three of the test persons was an elevation of the sedimentation, a decreased body reaction with initial increase in the body temperature and a distinct liver enlargement over an observation period of 8 days, but no appearance of jaundice.[37]

Meythaler repeated this statement when he gave the keynote address at a sci-

---

33 Astrid Ley and Günther Morsch, eds., *Medical Care and Crime: The Infirmary at the Sachsenhausen Concentration Camp, 1936-45* (Berlin: Metropol, 2008).

34 Weindling, *Victims and Survivors*, 65.

35 Friedrich Meythaler, "Zur Pathophysolologie des Ikterus," *Klinische Wochenschrift* 21, no. 32 (1942), 701–06.

36 Ibid., 701.

37 Meythaler, "Zur Pathophysolologie," 703.

entific symposium in Athens on October 28, 1942.[38] A newly established research centre was entrusted with the task of carrying out clinical examinations and medical experiments to combat the hepatitis epidemic. Research teams were sent from the Army Medical Inspectorate in Berlin, recruited by its consulting internist, Professor Gutzeit. Meythaler reiterated his findings:

> There exists also a contagious infectious syndrome, a hepatitis *infectiosa sine iktero*. It can be assumed that it (hepatitis) is transmittable from human to human as well via experiments on animals. All hypotheses from clinical or experimental research point to a virus infection, whose agent has not been identified.

Meythaler's experiment can be evaluated as follows: he observed a febrile condition in a geographic region with numerous bacterial and parasitic infections. The illness appeared to result from a blood inoculation taken from sick German soldiers. Without documented blood group analyses in donors and recipients, the consequent illness could be either a transfusion reaction with blood group incompatibility or a rapid infection by a pathological agent. The rather short interval between blood transfer and the reactions of the recipients would imply an infectious illness with virtually no incubation period. This would be very unlikely with a viral infection like hepatitis A. The time interval would rather favour the interpretation of a transfusion reaction as indicated by hepatomegaly without jaundice. This led Meythaler to suggest blood-borne transmissibility of infectious hepatitis. That result had not yet been confirmed in laboratory tests. Other endemic infections ought to be taken into account:

> a) The most likely alternative diagnosis was thought to be Malta Fever caused by the bacterium *brucella mellitensis,* which causes undulant fever attacks, lasting 10–14 days, of decreasing frequency and with persistent low-grade lumbar and muscular pain, corresponding to spondylitis (osteochondritis of the lumbar spine).
> b) Malaria was excluded a year later in the Heidelberg Military Hospital.
> c) Jaundice from either a viral infection, leptospirosis or spirochaetosis was not observed.

The five Australian POWs were seemingly used in a non-consensual, enforced experiment, probably in an ad hoc, ill-prepared attempt to diagnose the Ger-

---

38 Friedrich Meythaler, "Zur Pathogenese und Klinik der Hepatitis infektiosa (epidemica contagiosa)."

man soldiers' infection. The experiments were unscientific and inconclusive, a surprisingly poor quality experiment for an academic physician.

In December 1942 Meythaler returned to Germany to take up a professorship in internal medicine and a directorship of the outpatient clinic at the University of Erlangen, located in close proximity to Nuremberg. A link with the military was maintained. He was assigned to a sanitation unit and held in great esteem. In July 1944 the Medical Faculty of the University Halle ranked him first in line for a professorship. The Dean praised his academic credentials and emphasised his achievements as a military physician, saying "he excelled in this position, above all in the fight against malaria."[39]

Professorial candidates required the approval of the Nazi Party. Wolfgang Wagner, in charge of the political surveillance of the academic staff, did not raise any objections against his Party colleague.[40] Meythaler remained in Erlangen. At the end of his Nazi career he was again called up as consulting physician against the background of the drastic shortage of doctors to look after female patients from Poland. They were incarcerated in a small forced labour camp at the outskirts of Erlangen, presumably providing slave labour for a Siemens plant.[41] On April 16, 1945, Erlangen was liberated by American troops.

Like most Germans, Meythaler experienced the liberation as the "German Catastrophe." The downfall of the National Socialist state meant for him immediate dismissal from the University, decreed by the American Military Government. Banned from teaching, researching and practicing medicine, facing the loss of a professorial salary and status, he was offered a job in a toy factory as an unskilled labourer.

While struggling with his dismissal, he learnt about the International Military Tribunal convened to hold captured Nazi leaders accountable for their crimes. Conducted in the Nuremberg Palace of Justice, 21 top officials were tried and sentenced on charges of "crimes against peace," "war crimes" and "crimes against humanity," legal codes regarded as milestones in the history of International Law. The Nuremberg Doctors' Trial followed.[42] Twenty-three defendants were accused of "war crimes" and "crimes against humanity" perpetrated in concentration camps, research institutions and mental hospitals. Seven death sentences were handed down, five life imprisonments,

---

39 Friedrich Meythaler, letter to Reich Ministry of Science, Education and Popular Education, July 7, 1944.
40 Ibid., letter Wolfgang Wagner to Eckart Moebius, August 7, 1944.
41 The files only contain a brief reference to this forced labour camp. Our research is ongoing to trace archival material.
42 Angela Ebbinghaus and Klaus Dörner, eds., *Der Nürnberger Ärzteprozess und seine Folgen* (Berlin, Aufbau, 2001).

four long-term imprisonments and seven acquittals. The hepatitis experiments, including Meythaler's research, were discussed at the Doctors' Trial.[43] Moreover, the defence lawyer for Karl Brandt, Adolf Hitler's "escort" physician and Reich Commissioner for Sanitation and Health, considered calling Meythaler as an expert witness to testify that hepatitis experiments were neither painful nor lethal. Meythaler declined to appear citing medical reasons.[44] In addition, he was caught up in his own judicial procedure; that is, with the process of denazification.

The ambitious denazification programme was designed by the Allied powers to remove the vast army of over 8 million National Socialists from office and to impose sanctions upon those inculcated in Nazi beliefs. A series of Allied directives was issued to initiate and secure the path to a stable and peaceable democracy.[45] Hugely unpopular, the different Allied strategies, and the rapid emergence of the Cold War, limited and finally aborted the efforts. From early 1946 civilian tribunals were set up in each zone of occupation and in each major town, commissioned with the task of examining the comprehensive, often ridiculed *Fragebögen* (questionnaires) completed by the accused and the documentary evidence submitted. A verdict was then handed down, classifying the status of the accused. They ranged from "Exonerated" and "Followers" to "Lesser Offenders" and then to "Offenders" and "Major Offenders."

Meythaler's denazification in Erlangen lasted several months. Maintaining ignorance and innocence he declared, as did so many Germans after the war, that he was neither an antisemite nor a participant in the persecution of the Jews. Self-defence and lies followed the pattern of an entire generation: "I was shocked to hear of the annihilation of the Jews and the horrific crimes perpetrated in concentration camps after the Allies marched in."[46] He admitted that he knew of the killing of mental patients, adding immediately that as a devout Christian and member of the Catholic Church he had rejected the " euthanasia" programme. As far as his medical services were concerned, he saw no reason to reveal the experiments conducted on the Australian POWs on Crete. Instead he proclaimed, "Wherever my services as a doctor were required, I was only concerned with medical considerations. I never allowed myself to be dictated by Party or State authorities."[47]

---

43 Nürnberg Dokument NO 922, 42.
44 Nürnberg Dokument NO 922, 2.2137.
45 Frederick Taylor, *Exorcising Hitler: The Occupation and Denazification of Germany* (London: Bloomsbury, 2011); Norbert Frei, *Vergangenheitspolitik: Die Anfänge der Bundesrepublik Deutschland und die NS-Vergangenheit* (Munich: C.H. Beck, 2012).
46 Letter Meythaler to Spruchkammer, January 25, 1947.

Several statements and affidavits were submitted praising the character and credentials of the accused. Most fell into the category of *Persil-Scheine*. This term was borrowed from the advertisement of the well-known laundry product Persil, propagating its whiteness and cleanliness. All denazification tribunals were flooded with such whitewashing certificates. Meythaler could rely on this classic example:

> In his professional capacity as doctor, Meythaler always took pains to show tolerance and to follow the letter of the human principles of the Geneva Convention. His deep Christian convictions were manifest in his care for sick prisoners of war, regardless of nationality. A thousand times over, Meythaler demonstrated his unflinching professional ethics as a physician.[48]

On June 26, 1947, the tribunal handed down its verdict. Referring only to his membership of the NSDAP and other Nazi organisations, Meythaler was classified as "Follower," a mere "*Mitläufer*" of National Socialism. "Exonerated" persons and "Followers" represented the bulk of the denazified Germans. They were the first granted the privilege of resuming their positions. The rapid reintegration of doctors and lawyers, judges and academics, teachers and policemen, artists and industrialists in the western zones of occupation secured the continuity of the social conservative elites. It provided a decisive impulse for the restoration process that characterised the emergence of the Federal Republic of Germany.

Meythaler's case is a classic example of the ease of transition from murderous Nazi medicine to post-war medicine in Germany. He was not among the ranks of the most brutal and infamous Nazi doctors who, with the permission of Heinrich Himmler, selected inmates in concentration camps and prisons. The victims of such doctors were subjected to terrible experiments without restraint and most were eventually murdered. Those who survived remained traumatised, suffering from lifelong symptoms. Rather, Meythaler typifies the "ordinary" Nazi doctor. He was one of a vast army of physicians who used the circumstances prevailing in Nazi Germany to further their research and careers. Nazi doctrines, policies and warfare escalated into a "Total War" in which legal barriers, medical constraints and moral concerns were abandoned. In this context, doctors were encouraged and instructed to select test subjects from POW camps and other institutions. Nazi doctors, especially the elite of

---

47 Ibid.
48 *Spruchkammer Erlangen-Stadt*, January 1, 1947, Affidavit K.E.S.

the medical profession, grasped the opportunity to continue and intensify their research, without being held accountable for the suffering they inflicted or the crimes they committed.

After his denazification in 1947 Meythaler was appointed Director at the Second Medical Clinic of the city hospital in Nuremberg. One year later he was re-installed as Professor for Internal Medicine at the University of Erlangen. Over the next two decades he distinguished himself again as physician, teacher and researcher, leaving behind a plethora of books, book chapters, edited and co-edited volumes, journal articles and papers.[49] After pioneering wartime research on malaria,[50] he moved into a new field—cancer research.[51] In the early 1950s he founded the Scientific Doctors' Conference, which emerged as a key centre of medical training and education. Later he joined, again as devout Catholic, the chorus of German physicians protesting against the distribution of the "Anti-Baby Pill." He loved and cared for his children, some of whom followed in the footsteps of their father, embarking on medical careers. Aged 69, Friedrich Meythaler died in 1967 in Erlangen. Obituaries paid homage to his life and achievements without mentioning the experiment on Crete or his links to National Socialism. One oration—"In Memoriam Friedrich Meythaler"—published in the medical journal *Bayerisches Ärzteblatt*, summed up his personality in this way:

> It would be difficult to characterize his personality in a few words. He was a man of contradictions. Outwardly he appeared to be a tough guy ("*harter Typ*") with fast but sound judgement; his inward response was one of help and care, whenever the sick were in need.[52]

---

49 To name a few of Meythaler's publications, several of which were co-authored: *The Viruspneunomie des Menschen* (1952); *Prophylaxe. Früherkennung und vorbeugende Therapie innerer Erkrankungen* (1950); *Die Erkrankungen der Leber-und Gallenwege: Ein Grundriss für Ärzte und Studierende* (1957); *Die Indikation zur Splenektomie. Mit besonderer Berücksichtigung der splenomegalen Leberzirrhose* (1960).

50 Friedrich Meythaler, *Differentialdiagnose und Therapie der Malariagruppe im Kriege* (Stuttgart: Hippocrates, 1944).

51 Friedrich Meythaler and H. Truckenbrodt, "Körpereigene Abwehr und Krebs," *Ärztliche Praxis* 1, no. 2 (1963); Friedrich Meythaler, E. Holder and R. du Mesnil de Rochemont, eds., *Therapie maligner Tumore, Hämoblastome and Hämoblastosen, Bd.1: Die operative Behandlung der Geschwülste. Bd.2: Pathologie and Chemotherapie* (Stuttgart: Enke, 1968).

52 *Bayerisches Ärzteblatt* 23, no. 1 (1968), 16.

100 YEAR COMMEMORATION OF THE ARMENIAN GENOCIDE, APRIL 24, 2015 – SYDNEY TOWN HALL SPEECH

Geoffrey Robertson QC

On August 22, 1939, Adolf Hitler summoned his generals to a villa in Salzburg and in a shockingly brutal speech, urged them to show no mercy towards local women and children when invading Poland—there would be no retribution, because, he said, "after all, who now remembers the annihilation of the Armenians?" The *blitzkrieg* crimes and the annihilation of Jews and Roma, and other minorities, were committed by Nazis who believed they would have the same impunity that 20 years before had been granted those who oversaw the extermination of over half the Armenian population. In 1915, Armenians were rounded up and community leaders killed; the perpetrators executed able-bodied men and then sent women, children and old men on marches into the Syrian desert, knowing that hundreds of thousands would die. The Ottoman Turks may not have used gas ovens, but they used death squads, starvation, typhus, and concentration camps in places we have only heard of today because they are now being overrun by ISIS. Their intention was to destroy Armenians as a Christian people, killing them to cries of *"Allah Akbar"* whilst passing laws to seize their homes, lands and churches, because they were not coming back to those homes and lands and churches, which have never been restored to them.

Historically, there is an interesting link between the Armenian Genocide and Australia that has gone largely unnoticed. It began, as genocides often do, with the arrest and murder of the intelligentsia: Armenian scholars, writers and community leaders, rounded up in Constantinople (now Istanbul) on April 24, 1915, the night before the dawn landing at Gallipoli. That was no coincidence. As the Turkish army prepared to repulse the Gallipoli landing, the Young Turk Government took the opportunity to begin the physical extermination of those it termed "the enemy within." This was a people of 2 million who had lived there since before the birth of Christ, and were the first to convert to Christianity in 301 AD, a century before it became the religion of the Roman Empire. They had lived on in the Ottoman Empire under the Muslim caliphate of the Sultan, but as a despised minority, and the Gallipoli landing was used as an excuse to begin a genocide that took over a million civilian lives.

What now do we owe to those lives, people butchered and starved as the result of internal state planning during a world war that the Ottomans had opportunistically entered on the side of Germany? The Armenians were not killed *in* war, they were killed *under the cover of war*. I compare their deaths with that of my own grand-uncle on the beach at Gallipoli on 24 April. William Robertson, or "Piper Bill" as he was known (he played the bagpipes in the Leichhardt Town Band), pretty quickly copped a load of bullets in "Sniper's Alley." He had volunteered to fight and was killed, lawfully, by Turkish soldiers defending their own land. Piper Bill is owed no special mourning a century on, other than sadness at the futility of this war, and anger perhaps at the stiff-necked and stupid political leaders who took their nations to war and refused, for over four years, to contemplate a peace agreement. The million or so Armenians who died because of massacres and deportations were, by contrast, victims of a crime against humanity. Should they be remembered a century on, merely as victims of war, like Piper Bill? I believe they have a special claim on our memory, and on our thinking about how to avoid such atrocities now and in the future.

There is, of course, an international debate about whether Armenian massacres and deportations amount to genocide. Turkey denies it and insists that all Armenian deaths following the decrees of the Young Turk government were justified. Most democracies in Europe, however, have recognised this as genocide, and some have even made it a crime to deny it. The debate even touched Australia when the speaker of the Turkish parliament threatened politicians from New South Wales with exclusion from ANZAC Day ceremonies at Gallipoli because in 2013 they had voted to recognise the genocide.

Former Prime Minister Tony Abbott followed in the footsteps of Barack Obama, who proclaimed during his first presidential campaign in 2008 that, "The Armenian genocide is a widely documented fact supported by an overwhelming body of historical evidence. The facts are undeniable—as President, I will recognise the Armenian genocide." But Obama reneged and dropped any use of the g-word, preferring instead *Meds Yeghern*, an Armenian word that means nothing to Americans. Obama does call it "one of the worst atrocities of the 20th century" in which, he says, 1.5 million Armenians were brutally massacred. He goes on to say elliptically, "I've already said what my opinion is on what happened in 1915. It has not changed." If you want his opinion on what happened to the Armenians you have to Google his 2008 speech to find that he believes it *was* genocide. It is a word he does not utter for fear of Turkish reprisals: the closing of spy bases or airfields currently used to pummel ISIS.

The truth is too inconvenient to utter. Turkey is simply too important to NATO for governments to speak the truth. 43 state legislatures in America have recognised the genocide, but not the US. In Britain, where Scottish and

Welsh parliaments have recognised the crime, the UK government will say anything to avoid expressing the inconvenient truth. It disingenuously claimed that the evidence for genocide is "not sufficiently unequivocal." The reason for this I discovered in some secret memoranda obtained under the Freedom of Information Act—Turkey is "neuralgic" on the subject. "We are unethical," the Foreign Office secretly admitted, "but given the importance of our political, strategic and commercial relations with Turkey, UK equivocation was the only convenient option."

Because of all this genocide equivocation, I have attempted to settle the issue in my book, *An Inconvenient Genocide: Who Now Remembers the Armenians?* by applying the law to the facts agreed upon by historians. My conclusion, beyond any doubt, is that the Armenian people were victims of genocide as defined by the Genocide Convention and by the Statute of the International Criminal Court. I will not weary you with the evidence, and I will not describe in detail the massacres, the Euphrates River so swollen with dead bodies that it changed its course, the beheading of boys and the selling into sexual slavery of girls, the forced conversions to Islam, and so on.

The Armenian minority in the Ottoman Empire had always been denied civil rights and been allocated the title of an inferior status. In 1894–1896, the period of the first massacres, 200,000 were killed, which was warning enough to the Young Turk Government that took power in 1909, of underlying racial and religious tensions. That government increased these tensions by a "Turkification" programme that stressed racial superiority and demeaned the Armenians, referring to them as tubercular microbes on the body politic. The government even changed the names of streets and towns, from Christian to Muslim. They banned the use of the name "Armenian" from companies and associations, and refused to teach the Armenian language in schools. At the outset of the war, their tame Imam declared a *Jihad* against Christians, although he had to, somewhat embarrassingly, exempt Germans as they were Ottoman allies.

In April 1915 came the roundup of the intellectuals, the call-up of Armenian men to be placed in army labour battalions and then massacred, and the deportation law that required all Armenians without exception to be deported. This meant relocation to the Syrian desert where most died either from starvation on the long march, or from typhus and dysentery in camps beyond Aleppo. Then came the laws that expropriated their property as "abandoned," a euphemism for confiscation. It is interesting to compare the euphemisms used to cover up genocide: Adolf Eichmann's Wannsee Conference minutes talk of "evacuation" of Jews to the east, because of wartime necessity. The Young Turk Government similarly spoke of "relocating" the Armenians because of wartime necessity. Both governments knew they were transporting people (the Armenians mainly on foot) to their deaths.

Evidence of the Ottoman Turkish government's genocidal intentions comes from many sources, most compellingly from their allies, the Germans, whose consuls reported to Berlin that the Turks were bent on extinguishing the Armenians as a group. They were very worried that Germany would be held complicit in what the British, French and Russians denounced as "a crime against humanity," and they urged Chancellor Theobald von Bethmann-Hollweg, and the Kaiser, to take action. They refused. "It's unheard of to criticise your ally in the middle of a war," replied the Chancellor. The American diplomats, neutrals at this stage, were appalled by the destruction. Talaat Pasha, the Turkish Interior Minister, made no bones about his determination to destroy the community: "We are solving the Armenian question by eliminating the Armenians," he told Henry Morgenthau, the US ambassador. There is telling evidence from German and American missionaries, from Austrian and Italian diplomats, from captured Australian diggers (themselves treated decently enough by the Turks), who reported with some horror how their captors would massacre Armenians and send them off to starve. At the end of the war, an extensive enquiry led by American General James Harbord described this as "the most colossal crime of all the ages . . . this wholesale attempt on a race."

Well, that is genocide in my book and by definition of Raphael Lemkin, the brilliant Polish law professor who coined the word and the concept. Lemkin was bothered by the fact that there was no international criminal law that would punish the perpetrators of state-sponsored racist massacres outside of their own country. The British had rounded up 68 of the main Turkish officials, taken them for trial in Malta, but discovered they had no jurisdiction to try political or military leaders for killing their own people. In 1919, there was no international criminal law. The main perpetrators were given refuge by Germany, and in 1922 Talaat Pasha was assassinated by a vigilante whose family had died in the deportations. The jury heard defence evidence from German generals and missionaries, and acquitted the assassin.

Lemkin thought you could not leave genocide to the justice of the vigilante. It was a peculiar and horrific event that should be made an international crime, with the states of the world obliged to punish it. He examined its history, from the destruction of Carthage to the latest twentieth century example that he gave as the destruction of the Armenians. It was this event that inspired his campaign throughout the 1930s, and it gained momentum with the Nazi genocide. Lemkin lobbied all the embassies of the war. He was a pain in the neck and the Canadians, to get rid of him, palmed him off on the Australian, Dr Herbert Evatt, who could also be a pain in the neck. These two legal geniuses hit it off and Evatt was the statesman who supported Lemkin and who introduced the Genocide Convention at the UN in 1948 as President of the General Assembly.

So the whole concept of an international law against genocide was inspired by the Armenian experience, which was not, as the Australian Government now says, a tragedy. It was a crime, and is now the worst crime of all, with a Convention that obliges the world to act against its perpetrators.

It is important to understand that genocide does not mean that the target group is extinguished. It is sufficient if part of the group is intended for destruction. There was genocide, the International Court of Justice has ruled, in Srebrenica, when 7,000 Muslim men and boys were killed, and 18,000 women deported. Nor does it mean killing or injuring. Genocide includes, by Convention definition: "deliberately inflicting on the group conditions of life calculated to bring about its physical destruction in whole or part." There can be no doubt, therefore, that what happened to the Armenians in 1915 was genocide. It is true that no court has yet held this to be the case, and all books about it have been written by historians. Mine is the first, I think, by an international lawyer.

But the evidence is overwhelming. Why, then, does Turkey dispute it? First, it states that there were only 1.1 million Armenians in the country at the time, so 1.5 million could not have died. It estimates the death toll at "only" 600,000 and I put "only" in inverted commas, because 600,000 is over half of 1.1 million. In any event, the Armenian Church records, far more likely to be accurate, count 2.1 million. So "only 600,000" is hardly a sensible objection. Then the Turkish Government says that the "relocations," as they put them, were for "military necessity." That does not excuse the massacres, which they put down to a few "unruly officials." "Unruly" is another of genocide's euphemisms, intended to cloak barbarism ordered by the government. As for the "relocations," what was the military necessity in killing children, women and old men? Necessity in war can never justify the deliberate murder of civilians: if suspected of treason or loyalty to the enemy they may be detained or interned or prosecuted, but not sent on death marches from which they are not expected to return.

This Turkish argument, promoted by a massive propaganda exercise in the run-up to the genocide's centenary, is very dangerous. Deliberately killing civilians can never be justifiable in order to gain a military advantage. There were, admittedly, dangers on the Russian front, and there were some Armenians who defected to the Russian army, and there were some outbreaks of violence from Armenians, generally in self-defence. Only in one town, Van, did they succeed in driving out the Turkish army and then only for two months.

The danger of giving legal credence to the Turkish argument is that it would apply to all genocides where there is civil resistance. It would justify Rajapaksa in Sri Lanka, killing up to 70,000 civilians in order to eliminate the Tamil Tigers. It could be used by the Pakistani army to justify the killing of 3 million Bengalis back in 1971, because they harboured a small number of freedom fighters. It is during war that the law of genocide is most necessary to protect minority groups, and it is ironic that the Turkish government denies genocide of the Armenians on the pretext that they were "the enemy within" during a war, the very circumstances in which special obligations on a state to protect racial or religious groups are essential.

That is why genocide trials continue today in The Hague for those perpetrators of Srebrenica: five Bosnian Serb generals have been convicted, and it is only a matter of time before General Mladić joins them. Srebrenica, a Muslim enclave surrounded by a predominantly Serb-populated countryside, in the racially jumbled geography of Bosnia, was attacked by Bosnian Serb commanders who did not, merely by taking the town, commit genocide. That happened shortly afterwards when Mladić ordered the deportation of all Muslim women, children and old men, whilst at the same time about 7,000 able-bodied men and boys were separated and detained, ostensibly to "screen" them for war crimes, but in fact to be carted off, killed and buried in mass graves that later yielded corpses with hands tied behind backs, shot from behind. Remember the incriminating footage that came from a private camcorder, with grainy images of Muslim men and boys huddled in fields, surrounded by soldiers who wait impatiently to be blessed by Serb Orthodox priests so they can, with easy consciences, shoot their prisoners before nightfall. The International Criminal Tribunal for the Former Yugoslavia (ICTY) and the International Court of Justice have concluded that the operations—the deportations and the massacre—prove that, "the Bosnian Serb forces not only knew that the combination of the killings of the men with the forcible transfer of the women, children and elderly would inevitably result in the physical disappearance of the Bosnian Muslim population of Srebrenica, but clearly intended through those acts to physically destroy this group." That is what the Ottoman leaders clearly intended to do to the Armenians of Eastern Anatolia in 1915.

So what are we to make of the massively-funded Turkish government denialism of crimes committed by their predecessors in 1915? It goes beyond denialism. Under S.301 of the Turkish Criminal Code, citizens can be, and are, prosecuted for asserting that there was a genocide. Hrant Dink, a courageous newspaper editor, was assassinated and the government did nothing to bring his assassins to justice. Schoolchildren are taught to write essays refuting the genocide. The press restrictions are such that Turkey is rated 154th in league tables of press freedom, largely because of its ban on criticism of Ottoman behaviour.

Of course, it was a long time ago, but 100 years is still within living memory. Several elderly women who were small children when carried by their mothers across the burning sands, were invited to tea with President Obama in 2015, along with the world's most famous Armenian, Kim Kardashian. And, of course, the mental scars, the psychological trauma on their children and grandchildren, continues throughout the diaspora, and will continue until Turkey makes some acknowledgement of the crime, and some reparation.

International law may provide some assistance, as it has with art looted by the Nazis: there are assets expropriated in 1915 that can still be traced. Over 1,000 seized churches could be given back. One church, at Lake Van, was restored and returned a few years ago, which gives some hope of resolution. Armenians want their historic lands restored, but that is probably asking too much. I have suggested that the majestic and mysterious Mount Ararat that overlooks the capital, Yerevan, could be restored to Armenians as an act of reconciliation. What Armenians most want is an acknowledgement of the dreadful crime that was committed, and if Turkey chokes on an admission of genocide, it should at least admit that its Ottoman predecessor committed a crime against humanity—there can be no conceivable legal argument that the massacres and deportations did not amount to that.

Turkey, outrageously, claims that if the 1915 events did not amount to genocide, they amounted to nothing at all: "*c'est la guerre*," as if "military necessity" in war can justify the marching of hundreds of thousands of civilians to their death. That this is a war crime of utmost gravity was confirmed by the American and Australian military courts that convicted Japanese generals for the death marches in the Philippines and at Sandakan. Their victims were soldiers who were prisoners of war: to subject civilians to the same treatment is a crime that "military necessity" can never justify, any more than it could justify General Mladić's destruction of Muslims in Srebrenica on the ground of strategic advantage for his army and his cause.

Genocide, because it is the worst crime against humanity, calls for a special study of its causes and for special precautions against its recurrence. There are lessons to be learned from the way in which a new and seemingly progressive "Young Turk" government decided to solidify its support behind the banner of racial superiority, and how this in turn led its intellectual theorists to demonise and dehumanise the Armenian minority. Genocide scholarship serves a valuable purpose of identifying patterns that recur in the build-up to behaviour in which formerly happy neighbours are incited to hack each other to death, renouncing the very notion of "neighbourhood" as a living space that human beings of different creeds or colours can amicably occupy. Within living memory, murderous hatred has been inflicted on Hindus and Bengalis of Bangladesh, on Tutsis in Rwanda, Muslims of Bosnia-Herzegovina, Tamils of Sri Lanka, Chechens in Russia, Mayans in Guatemala, Chinese in Indonesia, Darfurians in Sudan, and on other victim groups; currently on Christians and Yazidis by ISIS. The list is long and it will lengthen unless the world remembers the Armenians and rejects the claim that their killing was no more than cruel necessity or, as polite genocide deniers always say, like the Australian Government, "It was a tragedy." It was not a tragedy. It was a crime.

THE EARLY DAYS: ILLUMINATING ARMENIAN WOMEN'S EXPERIENCES

Nikki Marczak

Introduction[1]

Just over 100 years ago, Armenian women and girls across Anatolia and beyond were witnessing their teachers and community leaders being executed, mourning their murdered husbands and sons, hiding weapons from gendarmes, taking food to arrested male relatives, negotiating with authorities, and comforting distressed children.[2] Amid the chaos of the First World War, the Ottoman authorities launched a coordinated and systematic genocide against the Armenian population. The narrative of the Armenian Genocide commonly begins with attacks on the Armenian elite followed by massacres of "battle-aged" men. Stories of women during the early days of the genocide have largely been omitted or positioned as peripheral to the "main event." Yet their experiences are revealing in a number of ways, not least in their exposure of perpetrator intent and brutality. Marion Kaplan wrote in 1982 that including women's voices in historical study can "sharpen our understanding of a past that has been interpreted without any reference to women at all,"[3] an assertion that underlies this essay. In viewing the early phases of the Armenian Genocide from the perspectives of women, a richer and fuller history of victim experiences and perpetrator tactics emerges.

Here I integrate women's stories into the following stages of the Armenian Genocide narrative: early persecution; disarming of the community; targeting

---

1   In April 2015, I was honoured to give the keynote address in Melbourne for the 100 Year Commemoration of the Armenian Genocide. The community connected deeply to the stories of Armenian women highlighted during my talk, to their losses and suffering and their survival and resilience. It was the profound response from Melbourne's Armenian community to the stories of women—the sense that they somehow captured an essence of Armenian identity—that compelled me to undertake further research.

2   Although women's experiences were not homogeneous (there were distinctions based on age and socio-economic position, as well as regional variation), patterns do emerge in practices employed by authorities and in women's responses.

3   Marion A. Kaplan, "Tradition and Transition: The Acculturation, Assimilation and Integration of Jews in Imperial Germany: A Gender Analysis," *Leo Baeck Institute Year Book* 27, no. 1 (1982), 7.

of community leaders and intellectuals (eliticide);[4] and the arrest, torture and killing of large numbers of men, although it should be noted that these did not necessarily happen in the same order in every region, and many aspects of the genocide overlapped, occurred concurrently or in close succession.

In genocide historiography, the concept of the male norm,[5] or the assumption that men's experience is the universal human experience, has created a dichotomy by which women's stories are seen as divergent or particular.[6] As Paula Hyman suggests, history has been written in a way that spoke "explicitly of men but implied that women were included in the category of man"[7] or, alternatively, presented women's experiences as so distinct and separate from men's that they are not included in the core narrative of the genocide. Further, as Pascale Bos argues, "when one introduces gender as an analytic tool, culturally dominant and male ways of categorizing what is historically important and what is not are challenged."[8]

In fact, nuances contained in the experiences of Armenian women illustrate a number of important dimensions of the genocidal process, including deliberate attacks on the family unit as the symbol of the group's continuity.[9] Further, examining events from women's points of view helps to crystallise perpetrators' intent to destroy the social and cultural fabric of the group, a crucial dimension of Raphael Lemkin's concept of genocide. The destruction of family, community and cultural life has unique effects on women. Perpetrators attacked women in ways that aimed to break down Armenian society and although women were not generally targeted with mass murder until later in the genocidal process, their treatment while male relatives were arrested and killed was a clear harbinger of increasing brutality.

A notable exception to the majority of male-centric historiography is the pioneering study "Women and Children of the Armenian Genocide" by Donald E. Miller and Lorna Touryan Miller. They develop the concept of "tragic moral choices" to describe how "women were placed in untenable situations where

---

4 "Eliticide refers to the killing of the leadership, the educated, and the clergy of a group." See Samuel Totten and Paul R. Bartrop, *Dictionary of Genocide* (Westport: Greenwood Press, 2008), 1:129.

5 "Since men lay claim to representing 'humanity' in all its universality, both in theory and in everyday life, it is women who have to be singled out for closer specification." Maria Wendt Höjer and Cecilia Åse, *The Paradoxes of Politics: An Introduction to Feminist Political Theory* (Stockholm: Academia Adacta, 1999), 17.

6 For more detail, see Pascale Rachel Bos, "Women and the Holocaust: Analyzing Gender Difference," in *Experience and Expression: Women, the Nazis, and the Holocaust*, eds. Elizabeth R. Baer and Myrna Goldenberg (Detroit: Wayne State University Press, 2003).

7 Cited in Ibid., 24.

8 Ibid., 24.

9 For more on targeting of the family unit, see Elisa von Joeden-Forgey, "The Devil in the Details: 'Life Force Atrocities' and the Assault on the Family in Times of Conflict," *Genocide Studies and Prevention: An International Journal* 5 no. 1 (2010), 1–19.

no uncompromised moral decision could be made; only tragic moral choices existed as options."[10] Unthinkable decisions women faced, often alone, included whether to leave children with Turkish families in the hope they might be saved, or to kill themselves and their children to avoid deportation, abduction or sexual violence. This concept contains echoes of Lawrence Langer's "choiceless choices,"[11] those decisions made by victims of the Holocaust that may be considered problematic in other circumstances, such as stealing, smuggling or suicide. In the moral grey zone of genocide, such dilemmas were additional tortures that cannot be judged retrospectively, nor perhaps even fully comprehended.[12]

The pain and victimhood embedded in these situations is clear. What is less overt, but equally important, is the concept of agency. In order to build on Miller and Miller's "tragic moral choices," I attempt to introduce an additional dimension of analysis to Armenian women's experiences by recognising and highlighting agency and resilience. Not only does the process of uncovering women's roles and responses serve to counterbalance the pervasive, one-dimensional image of the "female victim," it also tells much about how targeted communities respond to genocide, how individuals assert their dignity and humanity even within a prison of oppression. Such responses also entail gendered aspects. Survivor accounts often depict how women maintained their domestic roles such as comforting children in times of great stress, while also noting women's "resourcefulness" in attempting to rescue their male relatives or negotiate with authorities. Although I am conscious of the risk of glorifying women's actions,[13] testimonial literature does frequently include reference to women's adaptability to changing and ever more perilous situations. Their daily struggle to survive and their adaptation to changing circumstances and extraordinary challenges should not be relegated to the sphere of "unimportant" women's domestic issues but rather, understood as central to the genocide experience.

---

10   Donald E. Miller and Lorna Touryan Miller, "Women and Children of the Armenian Genocide," in *The Armenian Genocide: History, Politics, Ethics*, ed. Richard G. Hovannisian (New York: St Martin's, 1992), 168. See also Miller and Miller's comprehensive testimonial collection and analysis, *Survivors: An Oral History of the Armenian Genocide* (Los Angeles: University of California Press, 1999).

11   Lawrence Langer, *Versions of Survival: The Holocaust and the Human Spirit* (Albany, NY: Suny Press, 1982).

12   "Grey zone" describes moral ambiguity in the concentration camps during the Holocaust. See Primo Levi, *The Drowned and the Saved* (London: Sphere Books, 1989).

13   Early gender analysis of the Holocaust tended to identify "special vulnerabilities" and to idealise women's "special abilities" (coping skills, resourcefulness and sisterhood). See Bos, "Women and the Holocaust."

Theoretical approach

In 2005 Katharine Derderian wrote that "further scholarly examination of gender-specific experience in the [Armenian] Genocide would aid in the understanding of the Genocide as a whole and provide a crucial basis for comparative work with other genocides."[14] While my aim is not a comprehensive comparative analysis, the theoretical approach in this essay has been influenced by analyses of Jewish women's lives during the early stages of the Holocaust, especially Kaplan's contribution to Dalia Ofer and Lenore Weitzman's *Women in the Holocaust*.[15]

In *The Magnitude of Genocide*, Colin Tatz and Winton Higgins note the "comprehensive analytical toolbox" provided by Holocaust Studies, asserting that it provides useful frameworks and lenses for examination of other cases.[16] In line with their view, I argue that gender analysis within Holocaust Studies, as an area of research that has developed over several decades, provides us with a reliable framework for application to the Armenian case.

This essay explores how women were often at the forefront as victims of violence and intimidation, and forced to deal directly with Turkish authorities. It investigates the ramifications of the disappearance of community leaders and intellectuals on women and girls, including long-term effects of disruption to their education. I also show how Armenian women managed the multiple responsibilities of their daily lives and, in addition, took on traditionally male responsibilities like representing the family in political or social affairs.

Over recent years an increasing body of scholarship has emerged on the use of sexual violence as a genocidal strategy against Armenian women and girls. During the genocide, sexual violence, abduction, and forced marriage and conversion were ubiquitous and enshrined in government policy.[17] It would be a mistake, however, to restrict the study of women's experiences to these crimes. Women were affected during every stage of the genocide and their distinct

---

14 Katharine Derderian, "Common Fate, Different Experience: Gender-Specific Aspects of the Armenian Genocide, 1915–1917," *Holocaust and Genocide Studies* 19, no. 1 (2005), 5.

15 Marion Kaplan, "Keeping Calm and Weathering the Storm: Jewish Women's Responses to Daily Life in Nazi Germany, 1933–1939," in *Women in the Holocaust*, eds. Dalia Ofer and Lenore J. Weitzman (New Haven: Yale University Press, 1998).

16 Colin Tatz and Winton Higgins, *The Magnitude of Genocide* (Santa Barbara: Praeger, 2016), xii.

17 In addition to Derderian, see Matthias Bjørnlund, "A Fate Worse Than Dying: Sexual Violence during the Armenian Genocide," in *Brutality and Desire: War and Sexuality in Europe's Twentieth Century*, ed. Dagmar Herzog (London: Palgrave Macmillan, 2008); Ara Sarafian, "The Absorption of Armenian Women and Children into Muslim Households as a Structural Component of the Armenian Genocide," in *In God's Name: Genocide and Religion in the Twentieth Century*, eds. Omer Bartov and Phyllis Mack (New York: Berghahn Books, 2001); Anthonie Holslag, "Exposed Bodies: A Conceptual Approach to Sexual Violence during the Armenian Genocide," in *Gender and Genocide in the Twentieth Century: A Comparative Survey*, ed. Amy E. Randall (London: Bloomsbury Academic, 2015); and various texts by Lerna Ekmekcioglu.

experiences spanned every facet of life—sexual, social, familial, economic, physical, intellectual and more. In fact, there is a danger in defining women's experiences exclusively by sexual violence and trafficking, in that it can obscure or further sideline women's experiences of genocide. As Ofer and Weitzman argue, "While it is important to stress the distinctiveness of gendered experiences during the Holocaust, it is essential that women's experiences not be discussed exclusively in terms of motherhood or sexuality. To do so marginalizes women and, ironically, reinforces the male experience as the 'master narrative.' "[18]

The very beginning

The arrest and execution of Armenian community leaders and intellectuals marks the official start of the Armenian Genocide in the academic narrative and collective memory, partly because the roundups represented a sudden and significant escalation in violence against the Armenian population. Arguably, this has also been the result of an overwhelming attention in the genocide studies field on overt, physical tactics of genocide, most obviously mass murder. Survivors often began their testimonies with the arrests of community leaders or male relatives, not necessarily because this was the first episode of violence experienced, but possibly because they (and interviewers) assumed this was where the genocide story should commence. This starting point has the experiences of men as its foundation.[19]

Yet, prior or simultaneous to the roundups, both men and women were intensely affected by escalating persecution, rumours of violence in other regions, and the anxiety of anticipating what was to come. I have therefore chosen to begin not with the eliticide but with "early persecution," a category intended to capture the tense atmosphere before the arrests and murders. For instance, child survivor Ermance Rejebian said that before her father was arrested, she knew "something was afoot, because we would speak in whispers in our home."[20] Another survivor explicitly distinguished between the early reactions of men and women: "I could see and sense the men of our town gathering in groups, talking and looking very sad. The women used to sigh."[21]

---

18 Ofer and Weitzman, *Women in the Holocaust*, 16.

19 Only one woman was included on the list of Armenians to be deported or killed on April 24, 1915, writer Zabel Yesayan. See "Zabel Yessayan, Leading Female Writer of Armenian Awakening Period," *100 Lives* (blog), https://auroraprize.com/en/armenia/detail/10160/zabel-yessayan-leading-female-writer-armenian-awakening-period.

20 Testimony of Ermance Rejebian, USC Shoah Foundation Visual History Archive, http://vhaonline.usc.edu/viewingPage?testimonyID=56718&returnIndex=0.

21 Testimony of Takouhi Levonian, cited in Miller and Miller, "Women and Children," 158.

In the months, even years leading up to April 1915, there was an inherent danger for Armenian girls walking alone. Mothers would warn their daughters: "Horrific dangers are lurking around every corner. . . . So many young girls just disappear, even when they're just popping out to visit their neighbors."[22] The fear of sexual violence, which had been widespread during the 1909 Adana massacres, was palpable. Women and girls faced public taunts and a general sense of fear for their safety. As Derderian identified, "sexual intimidation created an environment of rumor and alarm."[23] The necessity of going out of the home on errands increased as men began to disappear or, fearing arrest, stayed hidden. Disguising one's "Armenianness" in public became imperative for girls and women. One survivor explained that a teenage girl "could not go out with her face uncovered fearing the Turks,"[24] and the risk intensified as public insults and humiliation came to be condoned among the Turkish population. Peter Balakian described one such attack on a cousin in his memoir, *Black Dog of Fate*. In an increasingly ominous atmosphere in Diarbekir, rumours of arrest, murder and deportation in other towns spread through the local community. Gendarmes began searching for weapons in houses and individuals started to disappear, including young women returning home from the bathhouse. The episode below conveys the gendered use of genocidal language and the growing acceptability of violence against civilians, both of which were used to instil fear in the Armenian community:

> I dressed fast and put on my *charshaff*, because if you look Muslim they might ignore you . . . in the distance I could hear women's voices screaming . . . and I was walking faster now when a group of Turkish men came out of a side street and began to throw stones at me. "Armenian. Whore. *Giaur* [infidel]." They chanted it, and they ripped my *charshaff* off and began spitting at me . . . throwing stones at me.[25]

Despite women's heightened sense of fear for their own safety and for their children, they continued to perform their accepted roles and daily tasks as caregivers for immediate and extended family members. Further, they drew on traditional knowledge and skills to respond to unusual and violent situations. Kaplan has described how Jewish women kept their households running

---

22 Astrid Katcharyan, *Affinity with Night Skies: Astra Sabondjian's Story* (London: Taderon Press, 2003), 20.
23 Derderian, "Common Fate," 5.
24 Testimony of Anna Boghossian, Armenian Assembly Oral History Project, Center for Armenian Research, University of Michigan-Dearborn, 1981, http://umdearborn.edu/casl/686475.
25 Peter Balakian, *Black Dog of Fate* (1999; New York: Basic Books, 2009), 220–21.

and comforted their children as persecution intensified before the Holocaust: "At the center of Jewish family life, holding it together and attempting to keep the effects of Nazism at bay, women's stories provide a history not of mere victims but of active people attempting to sustain their families and community, to fend off increasingly nightmarish dilemmas."[26] There are significant parallels in the Armenian case. Balakian describes his cousin's mother crying, wishing she were blind so she would not see her daughter hurt. Yet he emphasises her pragmatism and use of traditional cultural knowledge, soothing her daughter's wounds with beeswax and gauze soaked in milk, and a cloth dipped in egg yolk.[27]

Indeed, the role of women as caregivers and mothers permeates survivor testimony. Many child survivors retain vivid memories of how their suffering was tempered, mediated, by their mothers' efforts to reassure them, offer wise words or simple gestures like holding their hands. This is what Kaplan refers to as "the psychological work necessary to raise their family's spirits and tide the family over until better times."[28]

It is clear that even prior to the disarming of the Armenian population and elimination of the Armenian leadership, intimidation of women was imbued with genocidal intent, aiming to weaken the fortitude of the community. Women tried to keep their families' spirits up; ever more so once fathers, husbands and brothers began to disappear. The shattering of the family unit meant that women were suddenly launched into unfamiliar roles, such as negotiating with authorities, while also grieving for loved ones and apprehensive of the fate awaiting them.

Disarming the population

The disarming of the Armenian community had distinct impacts on women. First, women were often at the frontline of the violence, since they were likely to be in the home when searches were conducted. Second, with the home traditionally a female domain, women were deeply affected by the trauma of having their domestic spaces invaded and treasured items destroyed. Finally, they were often responsible for either hiding weapons or retrieving those hidden earlier. In order to terrorise the community, gendarmes would conduct

---

26 Marion A. Kaplan, *Between Dignity and Despair: Jewish Life in Nazi Germany* (Oxford: Oxford University Press, 1999), 3.
27 Balakian, *Black Dog*, 221.
28 Kaplan, "Keeping Calm," 43.

searches at all hours of the day and night and did so with excessive force.²⁹ In her unpublished autobiography written in 1922, Vartuhi Boyajian wrote:

> They dug the floors and the walls of the houses in search of guns and when they found any they would torture the people of that household to extort information about other houses or sources where guns were hidden. The torturing was so bad that Armenians would go secretly and buy guns to give it to them to escape torture. . . . The women who had guns for self defence would wrap them up into towels then carry them secretly to the elders of the Armenian Church who would turn them in to the Turkish government, to be in good standing citizens. But all was to no avail.³⁰

Armenian homes were often decorated with items handmade by the women and girls of the household and after the violent attacks, women were left not only with physical damage to their belongings, but also with a sense that any semblance of sanctuary had been obliterated. Theft or breakage of items created by the women using skills passed down over centuries was particularly distressing; a symbolic representation of the destruction of Armenian culture and identity. In addition, often the searches were simply an excuse to steal valuables from Armenian houses.³¹

Women's descriptions of chaos and terror during Turkish searches bring to mind Kaplan's portrayal of Jewish women's experiences of *Kristallnacht*, so named because of the "shards of shattered glass that lined German streets in the wake of the pogrom . . . from the windows of synagogues, homes, and Jewish-owned businesses plundered and destroyed during the violence."³² Yet "the night of broken glass" was experienced by many women as the destruction of their domestic spaces and intimate belongings, particularly bedding and pillows: "This image of feathers flying, of a domestic scene gravely disturbed, represents women's primary experience of the pogrom."³³ As Bos has

---

29 US Consul to Harput, Leslie Davis, U.S. State Department Record Group 59, 867.00/803, http://www.armenocide.de/armenocide/armgende.nsf/.

30 Vartuhi Boyajian, *My Autobiography–Written in Constantinople 1922: This is the Story of the Black Days of My Life*, unpublished testimony, Armenian Genocide Museum-Institute Archives, Yerevan.

31 "The Turkish soldiers, and also civilians, were going through Armenian homes, ostensibly searching for firearms and weapons and evidences of rebellion against the government, but really they were robbing of us whatever they wished to take." See Serpouhi Tavoukdjian, *Exiled: Story of an Armenian Girl* (Washington DC: Review and Herald Publishing Association, 1933), 25.

32 *Holocaust Encyclopedia*, United States Holocaust Memorial Museum, https://www.ushmm.org/wlc/en/article.php?ModuleId=10005201

33 Kaplan, "Keeping Calm," 46.

asserted, men and women not only experience but also remember and recount the same events in different and gendered ways.

Women's actions in times of intense stress can illuminate forgotten aspects of victim responses. In order to protect their families, and often at great risk to themselves, women attempted to hide or dispose of any items that might have led to arrest.[34] Echoing stories of Jewish families who burned book collections and documents in an attempt to avoid arrest by the Nazis, survivor Alice Muggerditchian Shipley recalled how she and her mother buried weapons along with her father's books and valuables under the basement floor. She was also responsible for burning her father's letters containing war and political information in the stove, while her mother cooked stuffed cabbages—an enlightening juxtaposition of traditional tasks and exceptional challenges. Alice had been so engaged with putting papers in the stove that she did not notice the cabbage burning; they ate it regardless.[35]

Hiding or handing over weapons did not necessarily prevent violence. One survivor remembered digging up a hidden weapon and placing it in the box for the gendarmes, only to have a senior official beat her mother with a cane: "I spread myself on mother so the blow would fall on me."[36] Gendarmes saw the searches as an opportunity to sexually assault Armenian women, the trauma of which was compounded if family members were present.[37] Such episodes elucidate genocidal intent, as the symbolism of attacking women in front of male relatives is an assault on the woman herself as well as a way to desecrate the sanctity of the family.[38] In addition to searches for weapons, Turkish soldiers would demand to know the whereabouts of men of the household. Vartuhi Boyajian recalled her neighbour's experience:

> It was Winter and the family was doing their laundry. The soldiers threw their laundry out in the mud outside and beat them up violently in order to make them confess where was the husband hiding. Then they threw them out of their home into the cold and took over their house leaving the poor

---

34 For instance, by throwing weapons into the river in the middle of the night. See the testimony of Massis Nikoghos Kodjoyan, in Verjine Svazlian, *The Armenian Genocide: Testimonies of the Eyewitness Survivors* (Yerevan: Gitoutyoun Publishing, House of the National Academy of Sciences of the Republic of Armenia, 2011), 203.

35 Alice Muggerditchian Shipley, *We Walked Then Ran*, privately published, 1983, 55.

36 Testimony of Paydsar Yerkat, in Svazlian, *The Armenian Genocide*, 366.

37 For example, survivor George Vetzigian said the Turks would invade Armenian houses, steal items and abuse young women in front of their relatives. See Carol Bedrosian and Laura Boghosian, "Survivors For All time: Stories of the Armenian Genocide," *Spirit of Change*, December 1, 2009, http://www.spiritofchange.org/Winter-2009/Survivors-For-All-Time-Stories-of-the-Armenian-Genocide.

38 von Joeden-Forgey, "The Devil in the Details."

woman with her kids outside on the frozen ice for days. They would beat her up three times each day, throwing out and destroying all her belongings and furniture, torturing her and her children until the day her husband would return and surrender. They assumed that the wife knew of his whereabouts. Several times they even put the house on fire but the helpless family did not have a clue where he was.[39]

When searches were carried out simultaneously with the arrests of men of the household, many women immediately took action to rescue their husbands. Here lies another parallel with the circumstances of Jewish women in Germany, who "summoned the courage to overcome gender stereotypes of passivity in order to find any means to have husbands and fathers released from camps."[40] Armenian women were suddenly responsible for liaising with authorities. When Astra Sabondjian's husband was arrested:

> she jumped into hostile territory to secure releases not only for her husband, but also for his closest friends, all high-ranking members of the Dashnag party. She argued with reason, pleaded with passion, threatened with caution, bargained with cunning, and they listened. She strode fearlessly into the Ministry of Interior demanding to be heard as though it was her right, she settled ransom payments at the Ministry of Finance, throwing money at them like confetti and persuaded every known newspaper contact of the international press propaganda machine to tell his story to the outside world.[41]

Not all women had such success, and their lack of political experience proved, in many cases, a ready target for officials. Shipley remembered how the women were tricked into handing over weapons with the promise that their imprisoned husbands would be released, only to have the authorities murder their husbands, and then the women too.[42] Gender analyses of the Holocaust often stress the common experience of women creating social networks in order to survive. Armenian survivor testimonies frequently describe women acting collectively in appealing for their husbands to be released or delivering food to their imprisoned relatives, as in the case of a group of women who gathered at

---

39 Boyajian, *My Autobiography*.
40 Kaplan, "Keeping Calm," 46.
41 Katcharyan, *Night Skies*, 72.
42 Testimony of Alice Muggerditchian Shipley, USC Shoah Foundation Visual History Archive, http://vhaonline.usc.edu/viewingPage.aspx?testimonyID=56527&returnIndex=0.

the prison where their male relatives were crowded into small cells, and were suffocating: "Some of the prisoners' wives protested to the Ittihad executioners; Atan bey had said with an ironic smile: 'Don't worry, we'll soon transfer your prisoners,' meaning, transfer them to the slaughterhouse."[43]

Women also took on the task of communicating horrific news to one another. Survivor Sarah Attarian accompanied her neighbour to the prison, only to discover inadvertently that the men had already been killed. Her neighbour collected some of the blood that had soaked into the dirt outside the prison to show the other women in the village. Their screams and cries upon being told of the murder of their relatives remained engraved in Sarah's memory.[44]

Eliticide

Men constituted the religious and intellectual leadership of the Armenian community. Their torture and murder was a structural component of the genocide, leaving the community with little capacity for social or political organisation and thus more vulnerable to further attacks. As scholars Samuel Totten and Paul R. Bartrop have written, "Eliticide is often committed at the outset of a genocide, and is perpetrated in order to deny a group those individuals who may be most capable of leading a resistance effort against the perpetrators. Concomitantly, it is used to instill fear in the citizenry of the targeted group and to engender an immense sense of loss."[45] This strategy too is one experienced in gendered ways, and the impact on women is, rather than a side effect of the genocidal process, central to it. Women often endured intimidation and brutality that accompanied the murder of their leaders. Girls' opportunities were diminished because of the destruction of educational infrastructure, and as the traditional transmitters of culture across generations, many women experienced the targeting of religious leaders and teachers as well as the desecration of sacred buildings as an attack on their identity.

Many Armenian women recalled with sadness the closure of their schools and arrest of beloved teachers. Survivor Perouze Ipekjian from Constantinople was in her graduation year when all her teachers disappeared.[46] Another survivor described her school uniform displaying one stripe to represent first

---

43 Hakob Manouk Holobikian, in Svazlian, *The Armenian Genocide*, 262.
44 Testimony of Sarah Attarian, USC Shoah Foundation Visual History Archive, http://vhaonline.usc.edu/viewingPage.aspx?testimonyID=56633&returnIndex=0.
45 Totten and Bartrop, *Dictionary of Genocide*, 129.
46 Testimony of Perouze Ipekjian, USC Shoah Foundation Visual History Archive, http://vhaonline.usc.edu/viewingPage?testimonyID=56592&returnIndex=0.

grade, and then sadly, "I would've had two stripes the following year."[47] Mari Vardanyan from Malatya recalled her education with pride—her school books, the opportunity to read aloud—and then the brutal end:

> I was always a good student, because my mother would teach me at home before sending me off to school. I liked school a lot. But then a paper was issued which said that whoever taught in an Armenian church institution would have to leave the country. And if they didn't leave the country in three days, their blood would be drunk out of a bowl. . . . I went to school, but the door was closed. I looked through the keyhole in the door and saw the priest praying inside. Our school never reopened.[48]

While both boys and girls had their schooling disrupted, there was a lifelong impact on girls. By the time the deportations ended, surviving girls were usually unable to resume their education as it was considered of little importance in the wake of genocide. Some were living in poverty, with returning to school an impossible option. Most had matured to "marriageable age" and with their primary role seen as repopulating the shattered community, engagements were arranged quickly. Education for girls and young women was limited to domestic skills and older family members refused the opportunities some yearned for: "I desperately wanted to finish my education. But my grandmother and my uncle both said it wasn't necessary; I had all the schooling I would ever need."[49]

Women related to community leaders were targeted with severe violence or forced to witness their family members tortured in a symbolic intersection of violence against women and men.[50] Authorities tormented women in the wake of their relatives' murders, as in the case of a woman sent the eyeballs of her professor husband.[51] These atrocities are indicative of a broader genocidal intent—one that used the initial murders of the community elite to terrorise remaining community members into submission. In this frightening atmosphere, women were faced with the challenge of caring for those men who had been tortured and then released. One professor was sent home in severe psycho-

---

47 Dirouhi Avedian, *Defying Fate: The Memoirs of Aram and Dirouhi Avedian* (California: H and K Manjikian Publications, 2014), 11.
48 Testimony of Mari Vardanyan, in Nazik Armenakian, *Survivors* (Yerevan: 4 Plus Documentary Photography Center, 2015), 133.
49 Dirouhi Kouymjian Highgas, *Refugee Girl* (Massachusetts: Baikar Publishing, 1985), 111.
50 For example, survivor Anaguel reported that her uncle had been a member of the Dashnag political party and that his wife was tortured so she would hand over his documents. See Miller and Miller, *Survivors*, 105.
51 Testimony of Alice Muggerditchian Shipley.

logical distress, frequently running outside naked and screaming of what the authorities had done to him. The women would run after him covering his body with bedsheets and returning him to the house.[52]

Finally, women were witness to their revered priests degraded, humiliated and brutally slain,[53] not only desecrating the sanctity of the church and removing any hope of a safe haven, but destroying a central element of women's spiritual and social life. The desecration of sacred spaces that were used by women for gathering and prayer, and the subversion of comforting rituals into signals of terror, such as the ringing of church bells to round up Armenian men, were often emphasised in survivor testimony. As Paydsar Yerkat recalled:

> I was woken up from a deep sleep by the ringing of the twin bells. I was surprised to hear them. From the window of my room could be seen the alley to the local church, St Karapet. I saw the men hurrying to the church silently and thoughtfully. The church was filled up, the doors closed. The private meeting lasted until midnight. No one was allowed to come out. The women took food to the prisoners in the church, moaning and crying. ... The Armenian men came out from there covered in blood, with beaten mouths and noses.[54]

As the community leaders disappeared, some women maintained their religious and cultural traditions as a way to manage the intense grief and to distract their children. Shipley recalled hearing women crying from their homes as the prominent men were handcuffed and taken away, and that her mother "pulled us away from the windows and read many encouraging verses from the Bible and gave us more verses to memorize."[55]

Forced army recruitment, imprisonment, murder and massacre

Over time, Armenian women lost husbands, fathers, sons and brothers to arrest, imprisonment, conscription and murder. Saying goodbye to fathers was a trauma that survivors never forgot, and those who were children frequently

---

52   Ibid.

53   For instance, Veronika Gaspar Berberian described how her grandfather, a priest, was decapitated as he knelt, praying, and his head used as a football by the Turkish soldiers. See Svazlian, *The Armenian Genocide*, 360.

54   Testimony of Paydsar Yerkat in Ibid., 366.

55   Shipley, *We Walked*, 53.

highlight the immediate impact on their mothers. Serpouhi Tavoukdjian remembered the heartbreak of her father's last night at home; as he gathered them for one last prayer, her mother was "ill from grief."[56] Nvart Assaturian described the night when the men in Bitlis, including her father, were arrested: "We waited and waited, and he was not coming . . . the Turks began knocking on the door, and my mother was sitting in the bed, and crying and praying . . . since then I cannot forget that night, and my mother's crying and praying."[57]

Occasionally, arrested men were returned to their families, but in a horrific state, and women immediately resumed their role as the men's carers. This included nursing their wounds, as in the case of a woman who bathed her husband's skin that had turned black from daily beatings.[58] Publicising the torture was even used as a strategy of intimidation to show the remaining population what the authorities were capable of. Some women were sent the bloodied clothes of their beaten relatives, while Balakian writes of his cousin's father being tortured and crucified, his mutilated body left on the doorstep (and his decapitated head at the edge of the street) for his wife to find.[59]

Women's roles were profoundly affected by the loss of male relatives. The structure of the Armenian household had been determined by gender and age, with young married couples moving into the husband's parents' house, often with uncles and aunts living under the same roof.[60] Relationships between family members were ordered according to generational protocols, with older women holding authority over young women and some new brides forbidden from speaking to their elders until the birth of their first child, or until grandparents had passed away.[61] Young mothers, usually teenagers, had traditionally relied on older women to help them with new babies. As Dirouhi Kouymjian Highgas writes, "My major upbringing was gladly undertaken by my grandmother. Older women in the household often took over the care of babies born to such young girls."[62]

Men's absence had serious repercussions on gender roles and intergenerational relationships, an aspect of the genocide that has so far been neglected

---

56 Tavoukdjian, *Exiled*, 24.
57 Testimony of Nvart Assaturian, USC Shoah Foundation Visual History Archive, http://vhaonline.usc.edu/viewingPage.aspx?testimonyID=56720&returnIndex=0.
58 Testimony of Mikayel Mkrtich Chilingarian, in Svazlian, *The Armenian Genocide*, 268.
59 Balakian, *Black Dog*, 222–23.
60 For example, see the testimony of Zarouhi Ayanian, Center for Armenian Research, University of Michigan-Dearborn, http://umdearborn.edu/casl/686475.
61 Miller and Miller, *Survivors*, 55.
62 Highgas, *Refugee Girl*, 14.

in academic research. Existing rules of relationships and communication were broken, as young women had to become "the head of the family"[63] or the sole protectors of sons and younger brothers,[64] positions historically occupied by fathers. Further, while the eldest man had been responsible for dealing with "social and political interactions,"[65] women both young and old now took on the unfamiliar tasks of liaising with authorities, as well as daily activities that had previously been the province of men, including shopping for food.[66] There were also financial consequences. Just as some Jewish women sought employment when their husbands were arrested, Armenian women took on paid jobs to support their children in the absence of an income, overturning traditional gender roles and, for those who had occupied a high socio-economic position, class status as well. Some even had to manage the moral dilemma of taking jobs washing or sewing uniforms for Turkish soldiers.[67]

Women began to straddle multiple roles. Without abandoning their traditional responsibilities, they quickly learnt how to advocate to authorities or use illegal means to rescue male relatives or protect their families, including bribery. Kaplan notes that actions by Jewish women "not only broke gender barriers but also bypassed normal standards of legality,"[68] and likewise, Armenian women took huge risks in stepping out of gender constraints and engaging in common but illegal methods of survival. Vergine Rouben Nadjarian recalled how her mother hid, negotiated and bribed to save their lives at every opportunity, including trading jewellery for shelter in Turkish homes. Yet she continued to conform to traditional gender expectations of self-sacrifice, telling her mother, "If you die, I'll die with you."[69] Another woman took a handful of gold pieces to a senior official in exchange for the release of her husband, and when he returned home, she dressed him in cotton for a month to protect his wounds.[70] The dual persona that women came to embody is exemplified by Astra Sabondjian, who, in addition to negotiating on behalf of her husband and collecting information for his illicit newspaper, visited her hus-

---

63 Testimony of Garegin Touroudjikian, in Svazlian, *The Armenian Genocide*, 522.
64 Eliz Sanasarian, "Gender Distinction in the Genocidal Process: A Preliminary Study of the Armenian Case," *Holocaust and Genocide Studies* 4, no. 4 (1989), 452.
65 Miller and Miller, *Survivors*, 55.
66 Several testimonies refer to shopping having been a male duty. For instance, Zarouhi Ayanian, Center for Armenian Research, University of Michigan-Dearborn.
67 Testimony of Haiganoush Bedrosian, USC Shoah Foundation Visual History Archive, http://vhaonline.usc.edu/viewingPage.aspx?testimonyID=56699&returnIndex=0.
68 Kaplan, "Keeping Calm," 44.
69 Testimony of Vergine Rouben Nadjarian, in Svazlian, *The Armenian Genocide*, 284–85.
70 Miller and Miller, *Survivors*, 66.

band in prison every week and brought him fresh bandages and ointment for his wounds.

Significantly, women were forced to make life-changing and tragic decisions without the support of husbands, brothers or fathers. Rubina Peroomian writes:

> In almost every household, with the men of the family murdered or imprisoned, it was now up to the women to assume responsibility and make the difficult decisions, first, to accept the loss of the murdered or imprisoned husband or son . . . [and deciding] whether or not to entrust a young child to the care of a volunteering neighbor—with the hope of returning and reclaiming the child.[71]

As in the case of Jewish women sending their children out of Germany in the hope they might survive, some Armenian women had to decide whether to accept offers from non-Armenian families to take in their children. Knowing they would never see their children again, and that they would be converted and assimilated into Muslim Turkish society, these decisions encompassed the sorrow of losing loved ones and further, the pain that accompanies loss of culture and tradition. Many implored their children not to forget their heritage. The grief of mothers is recorded in their own testimonies and remembered by the children, with a survivor describing being sent to a Turkish official's house and the absence of a goodbye kiss from his mother, which he attributed to her inability to bear the sadness of bidding him farewell.[72]

Survivor Bertha Nakshian Ketchian recalled daily searches by officials and pressure from a Turkish captain to give her away. Her story is pertinent in multiple ways, illustrating the predicaments women faced and their changed roles, and demonstrating that authorities knew in advance the atrocities awaiting deportees: "Grandmother Mariam, now the head of the household, would slowly open the door . . . the brutal presence of angry soldiers was terrifying . . . the captain concentrated on staring only at me." When Mariam continually refused to give Bertha away, he responded: "You'll be sorry. . . . You are all going on a long, troublesome journey. She is very little and will not survive it, or she will be taken by the Arabs."[73]

---

[71] Rubina Peroomian, "Women and the Armenian Genocide: The Victim, the Living Martyr" in *Plight and Fate of Women During and Following Genocide*, ed. Samuel Totten (New Brunswick: Transaction Publishers, 2009), 9.

[72] Testimony of Sarkis Agojian, quoted in Rouben P. Adalian, "The Armenian Genocide," in *Century of Genocide: Eyewitness Accounts and Critical Views*, eds. Samuel Totten, William S. Parsons and Israel W. Charny (New York: Garland Publishing, 1997), 70.

The concepts of tragic moral decisions and choiceless choices are perhaps most explicitly revealed in acts of suicide or family murder.[74] Suicide and acts such as drowning or abandoning children were common on the deportation marches (usually to avoid violence, abduction or sexual abuse) but even at this early stage, some saw suicide and the killing of their children as their only option. After the murder of her father, Nektar Hovnan Gasparian's mother decided to end the remaining relatives' lives. Nektar herself survived, but remembered: "She had arsenic with her; she gave it to a few girls of the village; she drank it and made me and my sister Anoush drink it."[75]

Such actions demonstrate both the lack of genuine options for Armenian women as well as the spectrum of responses. Decisions to choose death over deportation or abduction, or excruciating acts of sacrifice in giving away children in order to potentially save their lives, contained elements of victimhood but paradoxically also agency and resilience. Decision-making by women involved complex gendered dimensions in that the role of mothers and "appropriate female behaviour" was highly prescribed. Sometimes women's responses aligned with gender expectations; in other situations, they chose to act outside of their traditional roles. Cases also occurred where moral dilemmas had adverse consequences for women's intergenerational relationships, such as when grandmothers had a different view from mothers as to whether or not children should be given away.

Concluding thoughts

Forgotten elements of the complex crime of genocide, or those historically viewed as marginal, surface in women's stories. Scholars of the Holocaust who pioneered gender analysis uncovered significant and meaningful details, and by applying aspects of their theories and frameworks to the Armenian case, gendered experiences of the early days of the genocide are brought out of the shadows. The rounding up of community leaders, long known as the official start of the genocide, tells the story with men as the central characters. But the genocidal process relied on tactics that targeted both men and women in distinct, yet intersecting ways. The challenges faced by women are as vital to the history of the genocide as the executions and massacres of men. Beginning the analysis with early persecution, for instance by including escalating

---

73   Bertha Nakshian Ketchian, *In the Shadow of the Fortress: The Genocide Remembered* (Massachusetts: Zoryan Institute for Contemporary Armenian Research and Documentation, 1988), 13.

74   Suicide among Jews in the early Nazi period was also common, see Konrad Kwiet, "The Ultimate Refuge: Suicide in the Jewish Community under the Nazis," *Leo Baeck Institute Yearbook* 29, no. 1 (1984), 135–67.

75   Testimony of Nektar Hovnan Gasparian, in Svazlian, *The Armenian Genocide*, 198.

public attacks and insults against both women and men, sexual intimidation of women, and pressure to cover their faces, may help formulate a more gender-inclusive narrative.

What emerges clearly by viewing the events from women's points of view is the intent to annihilate the family unit and prevent the continuity of the community. Women's experiences highlight the unique essence, the real tragedy of genocide—the social, cultural, physical *and* biological destruction of the group. This is seen in the shattering of community structures, traditional ways of life, established familial roles, and the capacity for cultural transmission to new generations. Yet within the constraints imposed, many Armenian women responded in ways that asserted their resilience. Their actions and decisions straddled traditional gender expectations and attempts to take on new and challenging tasks. While this essay focuses on the beginning of the genocide, their fortitude continued to manifest during the next phases of torment—deportation marches under horrific conditions, systematic sexual violence, massacres, starvation, and eventually unimaginable suffering in desert concentration camps.

Testimonies describing the treatment of women expose their persecution, but also their strength. These were women who watched as their homes were invaded and torn apart, who tried to soothe crying children and tend to the wounds of tortured husbands. Women who read Bible stories as their relatives were shot in or outside the church, supported each other in groups to appeal to authorities, and bribed officials to release husbands and protect their children. Women who used every skill and every ounce of tenacity they had to survive.

FINDING A WAY: WOMEN'S STORIES OF DAILY SURVIVAL AFTER THE 1965 KILLINGS IN INDONESIA

Annie Pohlman

Introduction: the 1965–1966 massacres in Indonesia

In this essay I explore the experiences of women who lived through the mass killings of 1965–1966 and the strategies they developed to survive in the aftermath of that violence. Mass violence swept across Indonesia in the months and years following a military coup in Jakarta on 1 October 1965, and it had a profound impact on the lives of millions. In its wake, the Indonesian Army carried out a propaganda campaign to incite violence against its main political rival, the Indonesian Communist Party (*Partai Komunis Indonesia* or the PKI) and its supporters. With the willing participation of numerous civilian militia groups, the Army orchestrated the eradication of the Left in Indonesia. Approximately half a million people were killed and a further 1 million were rounded up during anti-Communist purges and held in political detention. Many died during torture or from hunger, disease, forced labour or a lack of medical care.[1] Although political groups are excluded from the 1948 United Nations Convention on the Prevention and Punishment of the Crime of Genocide, the 1965–1966 mass killings were genocidal in intent.[2] As several scholars argue, these killings were intended to wipe out the political Left from the Indonesian polity.[3] The leading scholar on the Indonesian case notes that the violence of 1965–1966 was "a successful exercise in national obliteration."[4]

---

1   Robert Cribb, "Genocide in Indonesia, 1965–1966," *Journal of Genocide Research* 3, no. 2 (2001), 219–39; Douglas Kammen and Katharine McGregor, eds., *The Contours of Mass Violence in Indonesia, 1965–68* (Singapore: NUS Press and NIAS Press, 2012).

2   See Beth van Schaack, "The Crime of Political Genocide: Repairing the Genocide Convention's Blind Spot," *Yale Law Journal* 106, no. 7 (1997), 2259–91; Anton Weiss-Wendt, "Hostage to Politics: Raphael Lemkin on 'Soviet Genocide,' " *Journal of Genocide Research* 7, no. 4 (2005), 551–59.

3   See Cribb, "Genocide in Indonesia," 219–25; Helen Fein, "Revolutionary and Antirevolutionary Genocides: A Comparison of State Murders in Democratic Kampuchea, 1965 to 1979, and in Indonesia, 1965 to 1966," *Comparative Studies in Society and History* 35, no. 4 (1993), 796–823; Jess Melvin, "Mechanics of Mass Murder: How the Indonesian Military Initiated and Implemented the Indonesian Genocide" (PhD thesis, University of Melbourne, 2014); Annie Pohlman, "Incitement to Genocide against a Political Group: The Anti-Communist Killings in Indonesia," *Portal: Journal of Multidisciplinary Studies* 11, no. 1 (2014), 1–22.

4   Cribb, "Genocide in Indonesia," 237.

During this period of mass killings and arrests—that continued apace until March 1966—the Indonesian Army under Major General Suharto took government. What followed was three decades of authoritarian, military-backed rule, under a regime that named itself the "New Order" (1966–1998). Throughout this military regime, those with any connection to the former PKI experienced a range of repressive measures, and these were carried out not only against former members of the PKI but also former members of any of the organisations associated with the party, such as the women's organisation Gerwani (*Gerakan Wanita Indonesia*, the Indonesian Women's Movement), the trade union federation, SOBSI (*Sentral Organisasi Buruh Seluruh Indonesia*), and the farmers' and peasants' association, the BTI (*Barisan Tani Indonesia*). Measures were also taken against anyone imprisoned during the arrests that followed the coup, regardless of whether they had connections to the PKI.[5] Prior to 1965, Communist supporters made up nearly one-quarter of Indonesia's then estimated 100 million population.[6] Under the new military rule, Leftist associations were banned and therefore affiliation with such organisations was denied by many for fear of persecution. Anti-communism was a core pillar of the New Order, which maintained a vigilant and militant stance against Leftist politics over its 33-year rule.[7]

Repression against former prisoners and associates of the PKI took many forms. Particularly for those politically detained following the coup—some of whom remained incarcerated for a decade or more—the New Order government imposed a range of restrictions designed to impede their reintegration into society.[8] Those known as ex-*tapol* (an abbreviation of "*tahanan politik*" or "political prisoner") were targeted upon release from prison with restraints on employment, movement, speech, residence and political participation. Furthermore, the family members of ex-*tapol* and those killed during the massacres, faced similar restrictions, all of which the New Order implemented without legal process and in the name of social inoculation against the alleged danger of a communist revival.[9] By the 1980s, these restrictions had developed

---

5   Amnesty International, *Indonesia: An Amnesty International Report* (London: Amnesty International, 1977); Greg Fealy, *The Release of Indonesia's Political Prisoners: Domestic Versus Foreign Policy, 1975–1979* (Clayton, Victoria: Centre for Southeast Asian Studies, Monash University, 1995).

6   Rex Mortimer, *Indonesian Communism Under Sukarno: Ideology and Politics, 1959–1965* (Ithaca: Cornell University Press, 1974), 366.

7   Robert Goodfellow, *Api dalam Sekam: The New Order and the Ideology of Anti-Communism* (Clayton, Victoria: Monash Asia Institute, 1995); Ariel Heryanto, *State Terrorism and Political Identity in Indonesia: Fatally Belonging* (London: Routledge, 2006); Katharine E. McGregor, *History in Uniform: Military Ideology and the Construction of Indonesia's Past* (Honolulu: University of Hawai'i Press, 2007).

8   Asia Watch, *Human Rights in Indonesia and East Timor* (New York: Human Rights Watch, 1988), 5–6.

9   Asia Watch, *Human Rights*, 6; Julie Southwood and Patrick Flanagan, *Indonesia: Law, Propaganda, and Terror* (London: Zed Press, 1983), 75–80.

into the more formal "clean self" and "clean environment" restrictions—to be "clean" meant that one had no familial or other ties with persons killed or arrested following the coup. Those found to be "unclean" were barred from various forms of employment, citizenship, expression and movement.[10]

Aside from these formal restrictions, those seen to have former Leftist connections also experienced a range of social stigmas and economic difficulties. People identified as ex-*tapol*, and their families by association, were targeted by military and government officials through various forms of heightened surveillance.[11] Former political prisoners had their identity cards stamped with the initials "E/T" (ex-*tapol*), becoming easily identifiable to officials.[12] Forms of monitoring and restriction of movement were further reinforced by social surveillance by distrustful neighbours and community members; many former prisoners have spoken of how neighbours conducted monitoring on "unclean" former Communists in their midst.[13] Barred from a wide range of educational and employment opportunities, many former prisoners, their children, grandchildren and other family members suffered significant financial difficulties.

While the worst of these repressive measures were lifted following the end of the New Order regime in 1998, the stigma of association with former Communists and political prisoners remains to this day.[14] To date, the Indonesian government has delayed or blocked attempts to investigate or redress the violence of 1965; there has been no official apology or reparations made to survivors or victims' families.[15] Given the impunity for historical cases of gross human rights violations in Indonesia, survivors and their advocates speak out about their experiences at some risk; those who choose to take part in truth-telling about past abuses do so under threat of reprisal from security services and hard-line groups within their communities.[16]

---

10   See Justus van der Kroef, "Indonesia's Political Prisoners," *Pacific Affairs* 49, no. 1 (1976), 34–60; Annie Pohlman, "A Fragment of a Story: Gerwani and *Tapol* Experiences," *Intersections: Gender, History and Culture in the Asian Context* 10 (2004), http://intersections.anu.edu.au/issue10/pohlman.html.

11   See Asia Watch, *Human Rights*, 65–73; Fealy, *The Release*.

12   Tapol, "All Forms of Discrimination Must End," *Tapol Bulletin* 130 (1995), 5–7.

13   Carmel Budiardjo, *Surviving Indonesia's Gulag: A Western Woman Tells Her Story* (London: Cassell, 1996), 103–10; Tapol, "All Forms of Discrimination," 5–7.

14   Steven Miller, "Zombie Anti-Communism? Democratisation and the Demons of Suharto Era Politics in Contemporary Indonesia," in *After 1965: Causes, Responses and Memories of the Indonesian Genocide*, eds. Katharine McGregor, Annie Pohlman and Jess Melvin (New York: Palgrave MacMillan, forthcoming).

15   International Centre for Transitional Justice (ICTJ) and the Commission for Disappeared Persons and Victims of Violence (KontraS), *Derailed: Transitional Justice in Indonesia Since the Fall of Soeharto* (Jakarta: ICTJ & KontraS, 2011); Kimura Ehito, "The Struggle for Justice and Reconciliation in Post-Suharto Indonesia," *Southeast Asian Studies* 4, no. 1 (2015), 73–93.

16   Sri Lestari Wahyuningroem, "Seducing for Truth and Justice: Civil Society Initiatives for the 1965 Mass Violence in Indonesia," *Journal of Current Southeast Asian Affairs* 32, no. 3 (2013), 115–42; Annie Pohlman,

Since the end of the New Order, however, many survivors have indeed chosen to speak about their experiences. Survivors' testimonies have revealed how those killed and imprisoned during the mass violence of 1965–1966 experienced egregious violence, many suffering inhumane and dehumanising treatment.[17] Those left behind when loved ones were rounded up also experienced violence and severe forms of hardship. Yet such stories are rarely examined in detail and are often treated as peripheral to narratives about those who experienced violence first-hand.[18]

In this essay, I examine the stories of two women who lost husbands, Ibu Arum and Ibu Moeliek,[19] and the impact this had upon them and their families. I explore the suffering and resilience of these women and pay particular attention to their experiences in terms of financial hardship and the strategies they developed and deployed to survive. I also highlight the experiences of women in finding ways to persevere in the wake of genocidal violence, ensuring the survival of their children and other family members in the face of extreme violence, marginalisation and poverty.

Women speaking of survival after the violence

The topic of survival underpins many of the testimonies of women survivors, the term having multiple meanings for individual women. In some women's testimonies, survival meant immediate safety from direct threats of attack and imminent danger. When describing the weeks and months after the 1965 coup, women talked about having to hide or flee when soldiers and mobs of youth militias came to their homes in the night, sometimes taking members of their family or attacking entire households, looting and killing, even setting fire to the house. These stories convey the nightmare and panic of having to grab

---

"A Year of Truth and the Possibilities for Reconciliation in Indonesia," *Genocide Studies and Prevention: An International Journal* 10, no. 1 (2016), 60–78.

17 Southwood and Flanagan, *Indonesia*, 112–18; Kammen and McGregor, *The Contours*.

18 For exceptions, see Anton Lucas, trans., "Survival: Bu Yeti's Story," in *The Indonesian Killings 1965–1966: Studies from Java and Bali*, ed. Robert Cribb (Clayton, Victoria: Centre of Southeast Asian Studies, Monash University, 1990), 227–39; Yayan Wiludiharto, "Penantian Panjang di Jalan Penuh Batas: Kisah Keluarga Korban," in *Tahun yang tak Pernah Berakhir: Memahami Pengalaman Korban 65, Esai-esai Sejarah Lisan*, eds. John Roosa, Ayu Ratih and Hilmar Farid (Jakarta: ELSAM, TRuK and ISSI, 2004), 61–85; Komnas Perempuan, *Gender-Based Crimes Against Humanity: Listening to the Voices of Women Survivors of 1965* (Jakarta: Komnas Perempuan, 2007); Budiawan, "Living with the Spectre of the Past: Traumatic Experiences among Wives of Former Political Prisoners of the '1965 Event' in Indonesia," in *Contestations of Memory in Southeast Asia*, eds. Roxana Waterson and Kwok Kian-Woon (Singapore: NUS Press, 2012), 270–91.

19 "*Ibu*" is a term that means both "wife" and "mother." All names given in this essay are pseudonyms, except when initials are employed in the source document. For example, see Komnas Perempuan, *Gender-Based Crimes*, 128.

children and meagre possessions and flee, uncertain whether they would find safety.[20]

For other women, "survival" referred to the daily effort, over years and decades, to secure necessities for themselves and their families. The way this topic circulated through women's testimonies differed. First, it related to finding shelter and sufficient food. In many cases, necessities included discussions about their children's access to schooling and other opportunities. Stories of survival were also relayed in descriptions individual women gave of their work or the belongings they sold or sometimes stole. Furthermore, the topic of survival was evident in stories centred on making difficult decisions and sacrifices. Many spoke of extreme poverty and marginal living that involved daily struggles to provide food, shelter and other immediate needs for themselves, their children and other family members.

Many women had been income earners prior to the upheaval but, with the loss of a husband, the family's income dramatically reduced in most cases. In the first few months after a husband was arrested or killed, women often resorted to selling household goods and furniture and later perhaps even the family home. As one woman, "AR"—part of whose testimony is recorded in a report by the Indonesian National Commission on Violence against Women—recounted:

> We had all been selling things for a long time, that was how I took care of my three children who had such bloated stomachs [from starvation] that kept on getting bigger. We sold the cupboard, the bed, [I] kept selling until . . . we ended up sleeping on the floor. Luckily I had foster parents there [and] they often gave me rice. I didn't have anything there, not even any jewellery. I didn't think of myself at that time, I never thought I would be stuck in such a hole. Once I tried to sell things behind the school, but it was hard to sell anything because I was the wife of a PKI member. Only one or two people bought from me, I was broke again, [but I] kept going so I could feed the children. Everywhere I went I was ridiculed by people, that was how it was for me.[21]

---

20 This chapter draws on selected interviews with women survivors conducted by the author between 2002 and 2012, and on transcripts of interviews held by two Indonesian non-government organisations, the Lontar Foundation and the Indonesian Institute for Social History (*Institut Sejarah Sosial Indonesia*). Partial interview transcripts are also taken from the Komnas Perempuan (Indonesian National Commission on Violence Against Women) report (*Gender-Based Crimes*). The author conducted approximately 150 interviews with women survivors of the 1965–1966 mass killings as part of a large oral historiographical study into women's experiences during this period in various parts of Sumatra and Java, Indonesia. For a description of these interviews, see Annie Pohlman, *Women, Sexual Violence and the Indonesian Killings of 1965–1966* (London: Routledge, 2015), 21n1.

21 Cited in Komnas Perempuan, *Gender-Based Crimes*, 128.

This section of AR's testimony contains experiences that were common to many women after the death or detention of husbands. The loss of income, compounded by the social marginalisation and stigma faced by those associated with "Communist sympathisers," almost always meant direct and often severe economic hardship for family members.[22] Whether the process happened over mere weeks or over years, families lost incomes, possessions, homes and land. In the testimonies of many women, this process is described as a relentless and distressing erosion of not only the family's sources of income and wealth but of their position within communities.

Research into the experiences of women who live through periods of conflict tends to focus on the gendered and gendering effects of that violence. Quite rightly, such research has revealed the broad range of gendered violence, particularly sexualised forms of violence, perpetrated frequently as part of conflict, crimes against humanity, war crimes and genocide.[23] Where more research is needed is into women's lives in the aftermath of conflict; that is, into the years and decades of survival and rebuilding. As Tristan Borer argues, "[a]lthough it is clear that war is gendered, less recognised are the ways in which the post-war period is equally gendered."[24] As recent research into the lives of women in post- genocide situations has shown, more work is required to understand the social, economic and varying institutional constraints and opportunities faced by women in the immediate and long-term periods following mass violence.[25]

Ibu Arum

By her own account, Ibu Arum had a hard life, one in which she "worked every day to survive."[26] Born in the late 1930s in a poor area of southern

---

22 See Budiawan, "Living with the Spectre," 270–72; Wenhsien Huang, "Women and Political Detention in Indonesia," *Amnesty International*, April 7, 1975, ASA 21/WH/CF.

23 For example, see Nira Yuval-Davis, *Gender and Nation* (London: Sage, 1997); Binaifer Nowrojee, *Shattered Lives: Sexual Violence During the Rwandan Genocide and its Aftermath* (New York: Human Rights Watch, 1996); Beverly Allen, *Rape Warfare: The Hidden Genocide of Women in Bosnia-Herzegovina and Croatia* (Minneapolis: University of Minnesota Press, 1996).

24 Tristan Anne Borer, "Gendered War and Gendered Peace: Truth Commissions and Postconflict Gender Violence: Lessons from South Africa," *Violence Against Women* 15, no. 10 (2009), 1170.

25 Catherine Ruth Finnoff, "Gendered Vulnerabilities after Genocide: Three Essays on Post-Conflict Rwanda" (PhD thesis, University of Massachusetts, 2010); Jennie E. Burnet, *Genocide Lives in Us: Women, Memory, and Silence in Rwanda* (Madison: University of Wisconsin Press, 2012); Judy Ledgerwood, "Death, Shattered Families, and Living as Widows in Cambodia," in *Plight and Fate of Women During and Following Genocide*, ed. Samuel Totten (New Brunswick and London: Transaction, 2009), 67–82.

26 The transcript for the oral testimony by Ibu Arum (a pseudonym) is taken from the testimonial archives of the Indonesian Institute for Social History (ISSI), used with permission.

Sumatra, she was orphaned during the Japanese occupation (1942–1945) by the time she was five. Raised by an uncle who worked in a rubber factory, she never attended school and married when she was 15. She and her husband worked as day labourers on local plantations and cut and sold firewood from the nearby forest. Together they worked to accumulate a marginal income that paid for a small house and fed their three children.

As with many poor men in the area, in the mid-1950s her husband became involved in the Indonesian Communist Party's organisation for farmers and peasants, the BTI (*Barisan Tani Indonesia*), as well as another local labourers' union.[27] During the 1950s and early 1960s, the BTI's membership grew substantially throughout many regions of Indonesia, particularly among landless peasants whose labour was critical to farming and forestry in Java and Sumatra.[28] Attracted by the PKI's strong stance on land reform, as well as numerous programmes aimed at supporting the mostly landless agrarian labourers, the BTI, like other PKI-affiliated bodies, grew into an organisation with millions of members.[29]

In her testimony, Ibu Arum noted that in her area following the coup, a wave of killings and arrests occurred that lasted until early 1966. As in other parts of Sumatra, plantation workers in their region, many of whom had been members of the BTI and other unions, became targets during the massacres because of their affiliations with the PKI.[30] Ibu Arum recalled that at night she could hear people being shot in the plantation near their home: "But people didn't talk about, they'd [refer to these events] only in code. Codes like, 'there's an operation going on in there,' things like that." As she explained, she and all the other villagers who lived near the plantation knew what was happening and were frightened:

> We were all terrified, when everything exploded and they were looking for people, they were rounding them up, and it went on for some time, the rounding up of people.... They were all the people accused of being in the PKI, or that they must have been in Gerwani (the PKI-affiliated women's

---

27 See Karl J. Pelzer, "The Agrarian Conflict in East Sumatra," *Pacific Affairs* 30, no. 2 (1957), 151–59.

28 See Rex Mortimer, "Class, Social Cleavage and Indonesian Communism," *Indonesia* 8 (1969), 1–20; Ernst Utrecht, "Land Reform in Indonesia," *Bulletin of Indonesian Economic Studies* 5, no. 3 (1969), 71–88.

29 See Ernst Utrecht, "Land Reform and Bimas in Indonesia," *Journal of Contemporary Asia*, 3, no. 2 (1973), 149–64.

30 Joshua Oppenheimer and Michael Uwemedimo, "Show of Force: A Cinema-Séance of Power and Violence in Sumatra's Plantation Belt," *Critical Quarterly* 51, no. 1 (2009), 84–110; Hilmar Farid, "Indonesia's Original Sin: Mass Killings and Capitalist Expansion, 1965–66," *Inter-Asia Cultural Studies* 6, no. 1 (2005), 3–16; Ann Laura Stoler, *Capitalism and Confrontation in Sumatra's Plantation Belt, 1870–1979* (New Haven: Yale University Press, 1985).

organisation), that's what they said. Then they'd be taken, then taken away. And then they disappeared ... in the forest.

In this initial wave of killings and arrests, Ibu Arum and her family were left alone. It was a few months later, when the military were carrying out a "clean-up" operation that her husband was arrested. These clean-up operations went on in some parts of Indonesia until approximately 1970. The Indonesian Army worked with local governments and other civilians to identify and detain remaining PKI supporters (often called "*PKI malam*" or "night PKI"), particularly in rural areas.[31] Aimed at rounding up PKI supporters who had escaped initial purges, these clean-up operations also targeted those seen to be closely aligned with the "Old Order"—the retrospective name given to President Sukarno's government by the Suharto regime to distinguish it from the "New Order" post-1966.[32] Throughout the late 1960s, government departments, various branches of the military and a wide range of formal labour sectors were also cleansed of suspected "PKI elements"; those removed were then sent to one of the many detention camps established for the purpose of holding hundreds of thousands of political prisoners.[33]

Ibu Arum recalled how soldiers led the clean-up operation amongst the plantation workers and how local members of their community also participated: "One of our neighbours, he was the one who got involved in this, that's what he did." As Ibu Arum explained, "The [soldiers] would come out at night and take people. And he was the one who wrote down each of their names. . . . Our neighbour, he wrote down names on a list of people from around here, all of them. . . . I'm not sure why he did it, but they [the soldiers] told him to do it, and they paid him to do it too, that's what happened." Ibu Arum's husband was one of those whose name was added to the list of unionists and other alleged PKI supporters given by their neighbour to the soldiers.

> One evening, they came for him. His name was on the list. He was out in the plantation still, getting firewood to sell along with my uncle, and they took him from there, in the forest. . . . It was only about one kilometre from our home. They [a group of soldiers] followed him into the middle of the

---

31 See Justus van der Kroef, "Indonesian Communism Since the 1965 Coup," *Pacific Affairs* 43, no. 1 (1970), 34–60.

32 See HD. Haryo Sasongko and Melanie Budianta, eds., *Menembus Tirai Asap: Kesaksian Tahanan Politik 1965* (Jakarta: Lontar Foundation, 2003).

33 See van der Kroef, "Indonesia's Political Prisoners," 34–38; van der Kroef, "Indonesian Communism," 34–40.

plantation and arrested him there. Then they took him to the local military command post [*Kodim*].

Ibu Arum's uncle was not arrested, and came back to tell her that armed soldiers had taken her husband. Ibu Arum was terrified about what might happen to her husband at the command post. "We knew what was happening there. People said that at the command post, people were being beaten and tortured. They said they were tying people up, beating them. . . . I was scared to go to the command post, but I was also scared for [my husband]." The command post was located in the nearby town and she and a few other women whose husbands had been kidnapped made the three-hour journey on foot.

When they arrived, the soldiers harassed them and ate the food they had brought for their husbands. Ibu Arum recalled how she and another woman were slapped across the face for asking to see their husbands, and both told to wait in a side-room of the command post. "So we went into the room, and there were people getting electric shocks [in the next room], crying, we could hear them doing it. . . . I could hear them being beaten, thrashed." After waiting for a few hours, the women were told to go home without seeing their husbands.

Thus began a new and more "terrible way of living," as Ibu Arum described it, for herself and for the other women from the plantation whose husbands had been arrested. "Once a week, we would walk there [to the command post], we would leave at 5a.m. and get there by 8a.m., we would take food in for the men, because they had none. . . . There would be four, maybe five of us at a time, whoever could go, but someone would stay at home with the children." As in many of the detention camps across Indonesia during the late 1960s, the political detainees held at the command post were starving.[34] Ibu Arum's husband, along with others, received almost no food rations from their jailors and relied on what little food family members were able to bring. However, the food that she and the other women brought was almost always taken by the soldiers and only some of it passed on to detainees.

As Ibu Arum explained, sustenance for the women themselves and their children was also a constant struggle. Over the three years Ibu Arum's husband and the other men from the planation were detained, Ibu Arum and her small circle of friends cooperated to keep themselves, their husbands and their children fed as best they could. Without this cooperation, Ibu Arum insisted, none of them would have survived:

---

34   See Carmel Budiardjo, "Political Imprisonment in Indonesia," *Bulletin of Concerned Asian Scholars* 6, no. 2 (1974), 20–23.

We all had children, most of them small children, all of us wives. The children were little, some of them just babies. I myself had three little ones . . . one was eight, the second one was five, and the third one was just two. . . . All of our men had been put inside, and we all really struggled. So we went to work and we worked together. I went to work back in the plantation. The rubber plantation was nearby, just behind where our houses were. I got out and worked hard. I also went to the forest to collect firewood, to sell. My friends did this too. . . . One of us would stay with the children, the [others] would go work, so that we would have food.

This small group of women took turns working at the plantation or scavenging for firewood to sell at the market. One woman would always stay with the children and, as some of the older children grew up, they too went to work hunting for firewood or looked after the younger ones. The children would also make the weekly journey to the command post to deliver what little food they could spare for the imprisoned men. Cooperation between the women "kept us all alive, thanks be to God. Without [it], we would be dead. Starved."

After three years, Ibu Arum's husband and the other men were gradually released. Each of the men was forced to "report back" to the command post once a week (*wajib lapor*); each time they had to pay the soldiers 1000 Rupiah (roughly the cost of feeding an extended family for at least a few weeks) to stay out of detention and they were often forced to perform free labour. The mandatory bribes and additional forced labour meant that Ibu Arum's family, as with other families from the plantation, struggled for subsistence. Yet, as Ibu Arum explained, "we were blessed . . . we were together." As she also made clear, they had been "blessed" because none of their husbands had been murdered or starved to death while in detention: "they all came home, and not many did."

Ibu Moeliek

Ibu Moeliek was born in the early 1930s in West Sumatra.[35] Though interrupted by the Second World War and the Japanese occupation (1942–1945), followed by the struggle for independence from the Dutch (1945–1949), Ibu Moeliek received a primary education and was married in her mid-twenties to a high-ranking local member of government. Her husband, Pak "A," was a supporter of the PKI and became a leader within the BTI, and Ibu Moeliek

---

35 Interview, recorded with permission, with Ibu Moeliek and Ibu Jusufa, together with Narny Yenny, September 2005, West Sumatra.

herself became quite heavily involved in running one of the *Taman Melati* (Melati Gardens) kindergartens in their city. These crèches were set up by Gerwani—the popular women's organisation closely aligned with the PKI—to help women in communities across Indonesia.[36] Aside from her work with the *Taman Melati*, Ibu Moeliek became increasingly involved with organising other activities through the city's Gerwani branch.

Shortly after the coup, anti-PKI violence broke out in the city and surrounding villages. Ibu Moeliek's husband, Pak A, as a public official with close links to the PKI, knew that he would become a target. After an angry mob came looking for him at his office in town, Pak A told his wife that he had to flee, saying that she and their four young children would be alright. "But we weren't. And [he] left, ran into the forest." In that part of Sumatra, the city lies on the coast and the hills behind are covered with dense rainforest. During the anti-Communist purges that started in the region mid-October 1965 and continued for some months, many members of the PKI and affiliated organisations went on the run, attempting to hide in the forest. Another woman from this area explained that soldiers and groups of civilian militias would go "pig hunting." She described how, when the mob caught someone, "they'd slaughter them near the mountain top. They'd be pulled along by their feet . . . suspended by their feet, by their hands . . . like they were carrying a pig. After they cut [the victim's throat], blood would spill out everywhere. They'd all come down together, [calling], 'We've got one! We've got a pig!' "[37]

After Pak A had fled to the forest, Ibu Moeliek explained how people came looking for him. "I was still at home with the children. [Shortly after] Pak A left, for three nights the police came looking for him. They came at one in the morning, 2 a.m., sometimes 3 a.m.. Yelling, harassing us." This went on for some time while Pak A was on the run and she recalled how the harassment by policemen, soldiers and mob members frightened her and her young children. "We were all terrified [every] time they came. Our youngest wasn't even four years old yet, the next one was in kindergarten, the third one was in Year Two at school and the oldest one well, he was suffering. I had to find food for all five of us."

After five months of hiding in the forest, Ibu Moeliek's husband was captured by a mob of civilian militias and soldiers. Dragged out of the forest along with other PKI members who had been hiding, Pak A was taken to the city's main police station. Ibu Moeliek found out from friends that he had been captured and went to the police station to see him when she could:

---

36 See Saskia E. Wieringa, *Sexual Politics in Indonesia* (New York: Palgrave, 2002), 240–41.
37 Interview, recorded with permission, with Ibu Eny and Narny Yenny, September 2005, West Sumatra.

I had the chance to go see him there. I went to see him with the children. . . . He was detained there for five months, but after one time [after I had gone to see him], two days later I found out that he'd been shot. They said it happened when they [the detainees] were taken out and taken across the road near the [town] market. He was shot there near the police station, in front of that market. Another man was shot too, with [my husband]. They were shot from behind by a policeman, in the back of the head . . .

For the five months Pak A was detained at the police station, Ibu Moeliek took their children to see him whenever able, bringing food with her. As similarly described by Ibu Arum, detainees held at the city's police station were starving. Ibu Moeliek was never able to find out the exact details of her husband's death but believed her husband and the other victim had been taken from the police station and executed. She believed the public nature of his execution was due to his "position within the PKI" and that he was made an example of because of the public office he had held within the government.

In Ibu Moeliek's testimony, she emphasised that from the time her husband fled into the forest, she and her children suffered a great deal. She explained that without her husband's income they were starving. "There was nothing I could do. At first, I just kept crying with my children because how would I be able to feed them? We had nothing anymore . . . and then, after what happened at the police station, when my husband was no more, then we really suffered." During those first few months, Ibu Moeliek gradually sold household items to pay for food and then she sold "whatever else I could find." Eventually, she had sold everything in their house:

> By then, we had nothing to eat. My children had no father to get food for them. So I worked. So then I went out and cleaned, I cleaned peoples' clothes . . . I would work for whoever would let me, I would clean their clothes and get a little bit of money. Then my oldest girl, she was still little, but then she started helping me to clean clothes too.

Ibu Moeliek explained that, for a time, they managed to survive on the money brought in by herself and her oldest daughter (the second child). She received no help from family or friends who had all "turned away" from her, but she added that, "Not everyone was bad to us. Some people felt sorry for us. They saw a mother with four hungry children and felt sorry for us . . . but many people, they cursed us, rejected us. . . . [They] cursed the children and called them 'PKI children' and things like that." The term "*anak* PKI" or "PKI child" became a common epithet used against the children of those who were murdered or detained following the 1965 coup.[38]

Her own parents were very old and were only able to help on occasion. The only time Ibu Moeliek was able to get help from her husband's family was just before her oldest child died. As she explained during our interview:

> I went many times [in the beginning]. I went back and asked them again for rice for my child when he was dying. I came home that day with half a small bag of rice and they told me never to come again. They would not give us anymore, not again. That's what my parents-in-law said to me. . . . [T]hey were rich. But they wouldn't help us.

Ibu Moeliek explained that her parents-in-law were angry with their son for his involvement in the PKI and blamed him for being killed. They cut all ties with their son's children.

Ibu Moeliek described a sequence of events she called "the most devastating" of her life. Shortly after going to see her parents-in-law to beg for food, her oldest child, a son, died. He had been sick for a while and Ibu Moeliek blamed the lack of food that would have "kept him strong." Shortly after, she was arrested and taken to the police station:

> I was kept inside for a month. The three [remaining] children were left all by themselves, to find food for themselves, even the little one. The oldest one [her second child, a daughter] sold off the rest of our possessions, everything. That's how they were able to get food. They came to see me when I was in detention, and they were starving. . . . It broke my heart. My children were starving, I wasn't there to get them food. I was devastated, and terrified about what would happen to them.

Ibu Moeliek did not speak much about her treatment during detention at the police station; as she explained, her focus was on getting out as fast as she could to take care of her children. At the end of the month she was released along with some other women; only a small number of women had been detained at the police station, whereas "hundreds of men were being kept there," all of them "packed tightly into rooms, like animals, starving." As with most former political prisoners, Ibu Moeliek was required to make "reports" to local authorities for many years.

---

38 See Andrew Conroe, "Generating History: Violence and the Risks of Remembering for Families of Former Political Prisoners in Post-New Order Indonesia" (PhD thesis, University of Michigan, 2012).

After her release from detention, Ibu Moeliek needed to find a "better-paid job"; cleaning clothes did not bring in enough money. She found work as a housemaid for a family in another part of the city and the income was sufficient to feed her children. A year or so later she found another job as a housemaid for a different family who let her and her children live in the back section of their house. She stayed for nearly 10 years and had enough money to feed her children and, eventually, to send them to school. Once she and her children had moved in with this second family, Ibu Moeliek reflected, their "lives got better, not everything was hard all the time. I was happy. We had food, the children were able to go to school, and they [the family she worked for] were good to us." After 10 years, and with her children mostly grown up, she married a man who had also been a political prisoner. After his death in the early 2000s, Ibu Moeliek went to live with one of her daughters and her grandchildren.

Finding a way

Ibu Arum's and Ibu Moeliek's experiences during and after the mass killings and arrests of 1965–1966 share many similarities. Like so many women, they faced a range of increasingly demanding and dangerous circumstances and choices, including attacks by soldiers, police or civilian militias. The numerous deprivations imposed by the loss of income and connections had to be negotiated and new social relations managed. As their testimonies highlight, the immediate priorities of finding food and safety became the main focus.

In her testimony, Ibu Arum focused on the difficulties that she and her young children endured during the three years of her husband's detention. For her, the only way she was able to survive this period was due to the mutual help and cooperation between herself and a small group of like-situated wives. As she outlined, by working together to secure income for food, as well as sharing the childcare, they survived. Ibu Moeliek, by comparison, was cut off by relatives and from other support mechanisms. She and her family were on the verge of starvation and her oldest child, already ill, perished from lack of food. Ibu Arum's husband survived detention, whereas Ibu Moeliek's husband was taken from detention and publicly executed. Both endured and both survived, but like so many other women affected by the mass violence of 1965, they lost loved ones as well.

Both testimonies give witness to women's daily acts of survival in the face of violence, severe economic stress and social marginalisation. Their stories reveal some of the ways in which women negotiated these circumstances and the choices they made in order to survive. Moreover, the testimonies of Ibu Arum and Ibu Moeliek reveal the social, economic and other constraints faced by women in the immediate and long-term periods after mass violence, which are so often neglected in the histories of this period.

NORTH KOREA: GENOCIDE OR NOT?[1]

The Honourable Michael Kirby AC CMG

On March 21, 2013, the UN Human Rights Council established the Commission of Inquiry on Human Rights in the Democratic People's Republic of Korea ("North Korea"). I was asked to chair the Commission, which was required "to investigate the systematic, widespread and grave violations of human rights in North Korea, with a view to ensuring full accountability, in particular for violations that may amount to crimes against humanity."[2] One of the thornier issues those of us on the Commission had to wrestle with was whether the human rights violations in question, which indeed claimed many lives, constituted genocide. We found ourselves in highly contested territory: how was genocide to be defined? Did the available evidence of the North Korean authorities' human rights abuses fall within the accepted definition?

My colleagues and I thus had to confront the complexities of the concept of genocide and its legal status before we could make a finding, one way or another, about its attribution to the transgressions we were examining. In what follows I sketch the historical background to this conundrum, and the actions of the North Korean government as revealed in the evidence before us. On that basis I go on to explain why we came to the conclusion we did.

The (very) late arrival of the genocide concept

The world had not heard of "genocide" before 1944. Yet the world has known the phenomenon of genocide all too well since time immemorial—as Steven Pinker graphically reminds us in his historical overview of human violence.[3] We can read many accounts of what we now call genocides in the Old Testament, Thucydides' history of the Peloponnesian War, Polybius' account of the sacking of Carthage in the Third Punic War, and in countless other an-

---

1   This paper's origins are a presentation to the Department of Statistics and Mathematics at Queen's University of Ontario, Canada, June 8, 2015.
2   "Commission of Inquiry on Human Rights in the Democratic People's Republic of Korea," UN Human Rights: Office of the High Commission, accessed October 28, 2016, http://www.ohchr.org/EN/HRBodies/HRC/CoIDPRK/Pages/AboutCoI.aspx.
3   Steven Pinker, *The Better Angels of Our Nature: Why Violence Has Declined* (London: Allen Lane, 2011).

cient sources, as well as in the work of today's forensic anthropologists and archaeologists. That is before we come to the more premeditated medieval genocides such as the Crusades, and the modern ones associated with slave trade, colonialism, ethnic nation building and regime maintenance, right up to the Holocaust itself and beyond.

At its most basic, genocide refers to the deliberate destruction of a recognisable group of people, eliminated because of who they are rather than what they have done or might do. "Killing-by-category," Pinker calls it.[4] Why did it take humanity until 1944 to find a word for such a horrific and ubiquitous phenomenon? Perhaps because it was such a banal accompaniment of the almost ceaseless warfare in human affairs. A war occurs between tribes A and B; A wins a decisive victory, massacres all the B men to preclude a counterattack, opportunistically enslaves the B women and children, and seizes B's territory. Tribe B is then effectively obliterated. Until the twentieth century, the A leaders had no need to account for their actions because there were no authoritative witnesses, and certainly none with cameras, or telegraphic or wireless links to a foreign press. Above all, there was no rule of law as such to bring leaders to account.

This situation changed with the genocide orchestrated from April 1915 by Turkish authorities against Armenians and other Christian minorities in Asia Minor. Now the witnesses included foreign diplomats and consular staff, and correspondents equipped with cameras, telegraph and shortwave radio. Reports of the atrocities found their way into Western newspapers and sparked mass mobilisation of groups supporting Armenian survivors, including in far-off Australia.[5] The governments of Britain, France and Russia issued a declaration condemning the outrage. Yet the outrage itself still lacked a name, let alone any legal sanction against it.

Raphael Lemkin, a Polish-Jewish jurist, became obsessed about this problem in the interwar period, all the while focusing on the Armenian killings. What was this crime, and what should we call it? In 1944 he came up with an answer in a very long, forbidding book published in the USA,[6] by which time his own people (including family members) had fallen victim to the self-same crime at the hands of the German occupiers of his country.[7] The missing

---

4   Ibid., 386.

5   Peter Stanley and Vicken Babkenian, *Armenia, Australia and the Great War* (Sydney: NewSouth, 2016).

6   Raphael Lemkin, *Axis Rule in Occupied Europe: Laws of Occupation, Analysis of Government, Proposals for Redress* (Washington, DC: Carnegie Endowment for International Peace, 1944).

7   The fascinating story of Lemkin's mission, in apparent opposition to his compatriot and colleague Hersch Lauterpacht's project to found post-war human rights development on a more individualistic basis, has re-

name was "genocide" and he laboured for many years to see it stand for a justiciable crime.

Thanks largely to Lemkin, the still newly created United Nations Organisation adopted in 1948 the Convention on the Prevention and Punishment of the Crime of Genocide ("the Genocide Convention"). Until then, genocide had rated just one official mention—in the indictment of October 1945 served on the defendants in the first Nuremberg trial of major Nazi officials. In consequence of the new convention, "genocide" found its way into indictments before ad hoc international tribunals dealing with atrocities in Cambodia, Rwanda and the former Yugoslavia. Today it constitutes part of the jurisdiction that the 1998 Rome Statute confers on the International Criminal Court (ICC).

Unfortunately, Lemkin's achievement was incomplete. Countries whose authorities had committed historic wrongs connived to attenuate the definition of genocide in the convention, lest they be accused of the crime themselves. I will return to the problems of definition below.[8] Suffice to say that the definition in the Genocide Convention, with all its shortcomings, became the one and only authoritative definition for both analytical and legal purposes, and is reproduced in the crimes schedule of the Rome Statute that constitutes the ICC.[9] Above all, the definition insists on the "intent to destroy [a group] in whole or in part," and political or class groups are not mentioned as recognisable victims of genocide, which has proved problematic in a number of cases, including Cambodia and, indeed, North Korea.

Of course, most thoughtful people today probably consider that they know, with a fair degree of accuracy, what genocide means. The same could be said for lexicographers. The *Macquarie Dictionary* defines it as "extermination of a national or racial group as a planned move." The *Shorter Oxford English Dictionary* gives an even briefer definition: "annihilation of a race." The *Chambers English Dictionary* uses the same definition but adds the adjective "deliberate": "the deliberate extermination of a race or other group." This may be an unnecessary elaboration as it is difficult to imagine that a whole race (or part thereof) could be exterminated except by deliberate conduct, even if it remains true to the Genocide Convention's insistence on intent. Of itself, the

---

cently been told by international lawyer Philippe Sands, *East West Street: On the Origins of Genocide and Crimes Against Humanity* (London: Weidenfeld & Nicolson, 2016).

8 For a more detailed critique of the definition, see Colin Tatz and Winton Higgins, *The Magnitude of Genocide* (Santa Barbara: Praeger, 2016), 17–32.

9 See UN General Assembly Resolution 260, "United Nations Genocide Convention," Article II, December 9, 1948, https://treaties.un.org/doc/publication/unts/volume%2078/volume-78-i-1021-english.pdf; and the crimes schedule of the "Rome Statute of the International Criminal Court," Article 6 and 25(e), July 1, 2002, https://www.icc-cpi.int/nr/rdonlyres/ea9aeff7-5752-4f84-be94-0a655eb30e16/0/rome_statute_english.pdf.

connotation of "race" is too large to permit chance, accidental or unthinking extermination of so many human beings.

On the basis of their general knowledge or reading, most people would probably sense that the Khmer Rouge regime's systematic destruction of between 1.5 and 1.7 million people in Cambodia constituted genocide.[10] When it comes to international law, though, such matters are not decided by intuition, feelings or common assumptions. Nor can they fall into the widespread (often rhetorical) tendency to equate any large-scale heinous crime with genocide. The specificity of this crime needs to be respected.

To decide whether conduct of indisputably oppressive regimes that disregard fundamental human rights amounts to genocide requires the decision-maker to be more precise. He or she must look exactly at what constitutes genocide in international law. This obligation takes the decision-maker to an examination of the origins of the notion of genocide in international law.

Considering genocide in North Korea

My role in the UN Commission of Inquiry into Human Rights Abuses in North Korea obliged me to embark upon that journey. The purpose of this essay is to explain where the journey took me, where it ended up, and the controversies surrounding the destination I reached together with my colleagues.[11] The Inquiry found convincing evidence of many human rights violations and crimes against humanity. Was there proof of genocide though? On the evidence before us, we answered that question in the negative. Some readers of the report and some scholars have found that conclusion surprising.

Our inquiry followed many years of disturbing reports about North Korea. Although a member of the United Nations since 1993, its authorities had not cooperated with the UN human rights machinery. They had not permitted successive special rapporteurs—appointed by the Human Rights Commission (and then Council, abbreviated to HRC)—to visit their territory, nor had they invited the High Commissioner for Human Rights. North Korea had essentially closed its borders, allowing only a trickle of tourists who were kept under close watch and restricted in their movements and contacts. For these reasons, North Korea came to be known as a "hermit kingdom."

Accessing up-to-date, accurate and representative evidence to respond to

---

10   Tatz and Higgins, *The Magnitude*, 106.

11   UN Human Rights Council, "Report of the Commission of Inquiry on Human Rights Violations in the Democratic People's Republic of Korea," February 7, 2014, https://documents-dds-ny.un.org/doc/UNDOC/GEN/G14/108/66/PDF/G141866.pdf?Open Element.

the nine-point mandate for our inquiry was bound to be extremely difficult.[12] As expected, the North Korean government, through its mission in Geneva, effectively ignored our requests to permit Commission members and staff to visit the country. It maintained this stance throughout the inquiry. In the end, a copy of our draft report was emailed through North Korea's Geneva embassy to the country's Supreme Leader (Kim Jong-un), with a warning that he might himself be personally accountable for the crimes against humanity found in the report under the "command principle."[13] This too was ignored. The North Korean authorities, however, were aware of the inquiry. They regularly denounced it and its members. When they criticised the inquiry and its procedures, the Commission's members and other UN representatives offered to come to Pyongyang to explain their mandate, to report and answer questions. This offer was also ignored.[14]

Faced with such intransigence, the Commission was reminded of the importance of the compulsory procedure of *subpoena* (literally "under the power"), developed in national legal systems to ensure that parties, witnesses and records relevant to a proceeding are bought before judicial officers charged with making findings about transgressive conduct. While the HRC strongly and repeatedly urged the North Korean government to cooperate with the inquiry, its pleas were also ignored. Yet obviously, this want of cooperation could not be allowed to obstruct the Inquiry in the discharge of its mandate, any more than a national court or inquiry would simply surrender in the face of non-cooperation.

The three members of our Commission of Inquiry came from differing cultural and legal traditions. Two (Marzuki Darusman from Indonesia, and Sonja Biserko from Serbia) came from countries that follow civil law traditions, ultimately traced back to France and Germany. My own experience had been in the common law tradition derived from England as applied in Australia. Most UN inquiries are carried out by professors and public officials from civilian countries. Ours gave a great deal of attention at the outset to the methodology we should adopt to overcome, as far as possible, the hostility and non-cooperation of the subject country.[15]

The Commission was not itself a court or tribunal. It was not authorised to prosecute, still less to arraign and to determine North Korea's guilt, or that

---

12 "Report of the Commission," 6–7.
13 Ibid., 25.
14 Ibid., 23–25.
15 Ibid., 10–15; Philip Alston and Sarah Knuckey, *The Transformation of Human Rights Fact-Finding* (Oxford: Oxford University Press 2016), 25, 69, 89.

of any named officials. The object of UN commissions in the area of human rights is to be "effective tools to draw out facts necessary for wider accountability efforts."[16] Self-evidently, all such inquiries must themselves conform with UN human rights law. This means that they must accord natural justice (due process) to those who are the subject of inquiry, and protection to those who give or produce testimony, and may for that reason be at risk. Our Commission took these obligations seriously. The methodology adopted included:

1. Advertisement to invite witnesses to identify complaints and offer testimony;
2. Conduct of public hearings to receive such testimony as could be safely procured in public (with other evidence being received in private);
3. Film recording of such public testimony and placing it online, accompanied by written transcripts in relevant languages;
4. Inviting national and international media to attend and cover the testimony and draw it to global attention;
5. Production of a report written in simple, accessible language;
6. Indicating clearly in the report of the findings made by the Commission and the evidence upon which such findings are based;
7. Provision of a draft of the report to the nations and individuals most closely concerned, with an invitation to offer suggested corrections or comment on factual or legal conclusions;
8. Publication with the report of any such comments (that were received and published from China);[17] and
9. Engaging with media in all forms to promote knowledge of—and to secure support for—the conclusions and recommendations.[18]

The Commission was aware that false testimony from witnesses could potentially damage the credibility of its findings. It therefore took care to limit the witnesses to those who, on preliminary interview by the Commission's Secretariat, appeared to be honest and trustworthy. It also secured an unusual

---

16 UNSC, "The Rule of Law and Transitional Justice in Conflict and Post Conflict Societies," August 23, 2004, https://www.un.org/ruleoflaw/files/2004%20report.pdf; UNHRC, "Impunity: Report of the Secretary-General," February 15, 2006, http://repository.un.org/handle/11176/258488. See also Geoffrey Palmer, "Reform of UN Inquiries," *For the Sake of Future Generations: Essays on International Law, Crime Justice in Honour of Roger S. Clark*, eds. Suzannah Linton, Gerry Simpson and William A. Schabas (Leiden: Brill-Nijhoff, 2015), 597–616.

17 "Report of the Commission," 27–36.

18 Michael Kirby, "The UN Report on North Korea: How the United Nations Met the Common Law," *Judicial Officers Bulletin* 27, no. 8 (2015), 72–73.

agreement with the government of South Korea, to allow North Korea to send representatives or advocates, or to engage lawyers, who could make submissions and (with the Commission's leave) ask questions of witnesses. This offer was communicated to the North Korean government, which ignored it. In giving testimony, witnesses before the Commission were examined in a manner appropriate to "examination in chief," that is, with non-leading questions. This course permitted them to give their testimony in a generally chronological order, in their own language, and in a way they felt comfortable. The Commission did not cross-examine witnesses unless it found it essential to clarify apparent inconsistencies, or to address particular doubts that the evidence had raised in the minds of Commission members. The non-leading mode of most of the examination allowed witnesses to speak for themselves.

The Commission substantially organised the mass of testimony it procured under the headings of the nine-point mandate it had received from the HRC. In each case, analysis of the issues and the overall effect of the testimony were supplemented by short extracts from the transcripts. These passages add light and colour to the report, which third person chronicles commonly lack. Part of the power of the Commission's report derives from the care devoted by the members and the Secretariat to providing a readable text. The purpose was to ensure that the findings, conclusions and recommendations grew naturally out of the preceding passages of testimony, evidentiary extracts, recommendations and analysis.

The North Korean government criticised the report on the basis of the alleged "self-selecting" character of the witnesses, among other points. The Commission repeatedly responded with appeals to permit its members to visit the country and to conduct a transparent investigation among a wider pool of witnesses. This offer was also ignored. Moreover, the testimony of more than 80 witnesses (taken and recorded in Seoul, Tokyo, London and Washington DC) was placed online and is still available there. This means that people everywhere throughout the world (except in North Korea) can view the witnesses and their testimony for themselves and reach their own conclusions as to their truthfulness, balance and representativeness.

North Korea's objections, and alternating "charm offensive" and bullying tactics following publication of the report, are recorded online. Sharp (but respectful) exchanges between the country's ambassadors at the UN in Geneva and New York and myself as the Commission's Chair, are also available on the internet. These allow both the political actors and the general international public to evaluate the Commission's report. Certainly, in the first instance, the political actors in the organs of the UN indicated their strong support for the inquiry through overwhelming votes endorsing the report in the HRC, the UN

General Assembly and the Security Council. In the latter, the human rights situation in North Korea was added to the agenda of the Security Council following a procedural vote, not subject to the veto, by a two-thirds majority (11 for, two abstentions, two against).

Two permanent members of the Security Council (China and the Russian Federation) voted against the procedural resolution that added the report to the Council's agenda. One substantive matter on which the concurring decision of the permanent members would be essential concerns the Commission's recommendation that the case of North Korea be referred to the ICC. If that occurred, prosecutorial decisions might be considered and, if so decided, trials would be conducted to render those arguably guilty of grave crimes accountable both before the people of North Korea and the international community.[19] So far, that substantive resolution has not been proposed, still less voted on.

In December 2015, the Commission's report returned to the Security Council. By a further procedural motion, the Council affirmed that the topic was within its agenda. Again, China and the Russian Federation disagreed, but their negative votes again did not count as a veto, since the resolution was procedural. No so-called "double veto" was invoked to challenge the assertion that the resolution was procedural. The Chinese ambassador asserted that North Korea presented no danger to the peace and security of its neighbours. Notwithstanding this argument, the Security Council adopted the resolution. By its own actions, North Korea itself quickly demonstrated the serious error of the Chinese characterisation of its dangers: in January 2016 it conducted a fourth nuclear weapons test and, a month later, tested an intercontinental missile. Ostensibly, it carried out the latter test to place a satellite in space. Yet no observer was misled into thinking that its objectives were purely peaceful. In September 2016 it undertook a fifth and larger nuclear test.

As noted above, the Commission recommended that North Korea's human rights violations should be referred to the ICC.[20] Under the Rome Statute that established the court, in exceptional cases the Security Council can confer jurisdiction notwithstanding the fact that the country concerned is not itself a party to the statute. Although the Council has not so far invoked this exceptional jurisdiction in North Korea's case, following the country's fourth nuclear test on January 6, 2016 and a new missile launch, the Council adopted a strong resolution imposing new and severe sanctions on the country.[21]

---

19 "Report of the Commission," 361, 370.

20 "Rome Statute," Article 13(b).

21 Richard Roth, Holly Yan and Ralph Ellis, "UN Security Council Approves Tough Sanctions on North Korea," *CNN*, March 3, 2016, http://www.cnn.com/2016/03/02/world/un-north-korea-sanction-vote-index/html.

The Commission's findings of crimes against humanity referred to the definition of such crimes under international law. It found ample evidence in the testimony of such crimes in the conduct of political prison camps; in the ordinary prison system; in the way the regime targeted religious believers and others considered subversive influences; in the victimisation of people who attempt to flee the country; and in the targeting of other countries' citizens as victims, in particular through a deliberate campaign of abduction of foreigners.[22]

As well, the failure to address the state's obligations to feed its population on top of natural disasters (floods and droughts) was found to have resulted in a major famine in the mid-1990s.[23] It caused death by starvation of up to 2 million people,[24] and severe stunting of infants, deprived of essential nourishment. Famine crimes (including the North Korean case) have been examined in depth by international lawyer, David Marcus,[25] who proposes four grades of negligence or recklessness, the top two to be considered criminal: the least deliberate (incompetent government that cannot manage a food crisis); the next level (an indifferent government that does not act even though it has the capacity to); second worst (when governments develop policies that create famine and although they are aware of the consequences, persist in implementing them); and, finally, the first-degree famine crime where governments intentionally use starvation as a tool of annihilation.[26] Marcus argues that the first and second-degree cases are distinguished by the intent (or *dolus specialis*). He also argues that famine crimes of this extent, used to eliminate a particular group, may align with the Genocide Convention.

Genocide scholar Adam Jones explains that as a tyrannical regime following in the footsteps of Mao Zedong and Josef Stalin, the North Korean government has added to political persecution a strong element of racism with its philosophy that Koreans constitute the world's purest or cleanest race. After the fall of the Soviet Union and China's withdrawal of foreign aid, 1994 saw a major famine, while international humanitarian aid was diverted from local populations to the leadership who sold it on the black market for profit.

---

22 "Report on the Commission," 319, 323, 330, 333, 335, 345.
23 Ibid., 144.
24 Adam Jones, *Genocide: A Comprehensive Introduction*, 2nd ed. (Oxon: Routledge, 2011), 68. The Commission found "the death of at the very least hundreds of thousands of human beings." Report, 208. Although it is true that some observers have estimated millions of deaths in the 1995 famine in DPRK, more recent estimates have suggested that the number of deaths was substantially lower, no more than 800,000 and probably less.
25 David Marcus, "Famine Crimes in International Law," *American Journal of International Law* 97 (2003), 245–81.
26 Tatz and Higgins, *The Magnitude*, 30.

Forced requisitions of crops and food for the army exacerbated the situation, and any protesting civilians were labelled political enemies and punished with exile to Gulags for slave labour or execution.[27]

All of this is true. Yet in the context of the Commission of Inquiry's terms of reference, and with the Genocide Convention providing the international legal definition, was there evidence of genocide? This was the question that the Commission addressed in a special section of its report.

The definition of genocide

Although the Commission's mandate from the HRC did not expressly raise the issue of genocide (as distinct from human rights violations and crimes against humanity), some of the submissions it received urged that a case of genocide had been established. This was particularly so in relation to the starvation of the general population (but especially the prison and detention camp population),[28] and the drastic reduction in the population of Christian and other religious believers in North Korea.[29] Here too there is a parallel with the Cambodian case, which can be said to align with the international legal definition of genocide in its targeting of Buddhist monks, Muslim Cham communities, and ethnic Chinese and Vietnamese, but not in relation to its killing of Cambodian citizens who were viewed as political or class enemies.

In the North Korean case, Christian Solidarity Worldwide, a civil society organisation representing Christians, appeared before the Commission in London and offered a well-prepared and persuasive submission that the evidence of genocide against religious groups (especially Christians) was sufficiently established. This related particularly to the 1950s and 1960s when, even according to North Korea's national census and other official materials, the Christian population in the country declined rapidly and substantially.

Unsurprisingly, at the partition of the Korean Peninsula in 1945, the proportion of the Christian population of North Korea approximated that of South Korea. Before the end of the Second World War in August 1945, during the years that Korea was a unified kingdom and empire—even as a colony of Japan (1911–1945)—it had been a unified country, with a common language and culture, including religious culture.[30] According to the statistics issued by the North Korean census authorities, the percentage of the population identi-

---

27 Jones, *Genocide*, 216.
28 "Report on the Commission," 350.
29 Ibid., 351.
30 Ibid., 9–21.

fying as Christian in 1945 was 24 per cent. This was roughly the same as in the south. It is roughly the same proportion as exists in South Korea today.

In North Korea, however, the percentage identifying in the census as Christians plunged rapidly, so that today it stands at less than one per cent. Christians, Chondoists and Buddhists dropped from 24 per cent in 1950 to 0.016 per cent in 2002.[31] The Commission was invited to accept the inference that this reduction was the result of the regime's hostile attitudes and actions towards faith communities, and Christians in particular. Such hostility would have been consistent with a large amount of evidence before the Commission proving the regime's suppression of any challenge to the ideology propounded by its successive Supreme Leaders. So was there sufficient evidence to justify a conclusion of genocide in that case? Was the evidence supported by the testimony relating to the suffering of the people (especially children) of North Korea during the famine in the mid-1990s? That period was labelled by the regime (with its attraction to traditional Marxist slogans) as "the arduous march."

Before the Commission reached a conclusion on this subject, it consulted a number of experts on the international law of genocide. These experts included Professor William Schabas and Sir Geoffrey Nice QC. The former had written extensively on the legal aspects of genocide.[32] The latter had extensive trial experience before the International Tribunal for the former Yugoslavia, dealing with allegations (and the proof) of the international crime of genocide. Each of these experts cautioned the Commission that it should not feel under any obligation to find the "gold standard" international crime of genocide. As noted earlier in this essay, in law, genocide has unique features. It has specificities that have to be applied in formal decision-making. It is not a general offence arising from any mass death toll due to serious human rights offences.

The components of genocide in international law

In dealing with this issue, the Commission collated the testimony that might arguably fall within the crime of genocide:

> According to the Commission's findings, hundreds of thousands of inmates have been exterminated in political prison camps and other places over a span of more than five decades. In conformity with the intent to eliminate class enemies and factionalists over the course of three generations, entire

---

31 Ibid., 351.
32 William Schabas, *Unspeakable Atrocities: Justice, Politics, and Rights at the War Crimes Tribunals* (Oxford: Oxford University Press, 2012), 106.

groups of people, including families with their children, have perished in the prison camps because of who they were and not for what they had personally done. This raises the question of whether genocide or an international crime akin to it has been committed.[33]

Having reflected on those findings, the Commission addressed the definition of genocide in international law, which specifies the groups covered as national, ethnic, racial or religious in character.

The Commission concluded that the North Korean government's clearly deliberate conduct, that had destroyed human life en masse, had been "based principally on imputed political opinion and state assigned social class," and that "such grounds are not included in the contemporary definition of genocide under international law."[34]

Because the number and horror of the crimes revealed in the Commission's report demanded still closer analysis, it went on to consider how the acts of murder and extermination might be classified:

> Such crimes might be described as a "politicide." However, in a non-technical sense, some observers would question why the conduct detailed above was not also, by analogy, genocide. The Commission is sympathetic to the possible expansion of the current understanding of genocide. However, in light of finding many instances of crimes against humanity, the Commission does not find it necessary to explore these theoretical possibilities here. The Commission emphasises that crimes against humanity, in their own right, are crimes of such gravity that they not only trigger the responsibility of the state concerned, but demand a firm response by the international community as a whole to ensure that no further crimes are committed and the perpetrators are held accountable.[35]

The Commission acknowledged that the category of possible elimination that might come closest to the definition of genocide in the present international law would be that relating to religion:

> In its testimony before the Commission, Christian Solidarity Worldwide submitted that there were indications of genocide against religious groups, specifically Christians, in particular in the 1950s and the 1960s. The Com-

---

33 "Report on the Commission," 350.
34 Ibid., 351.
35 Ibid.

mission established, based on the [North Korean government's] own figures that the proportion of religious adherence [had greatly declined]. The Commission also received information about purges targeting religious believers in the 1950s and the 1960s. However, the Commission was not in a position to gather enough information to make a determination as to whether the authorities at that time sought to repress organised religion by extremely violent means or whether they were driven by the intent to physically annihilate the followers of particular religions as a group. This is a subject that would require thorough historical research that is difficult or impossible to undertake without access to the relevant [North Korean] archives.[36]

In this way the Commission came to its conclusion that genocide, as it is currently defined in international law, was not made out on thetestimony. The reasons for extermination were fundamentally political and ideological. That is not currently a ground for the establishment of genocide in international law. Nonetheless, the evidence of many acts amounting to crimes against humanity was overwhelming. Such acts were enough to invoke the duty of the international community to respond. It would have pushed the boundaries of the Commission's report needlessly to have reached a finding of genocide.

Conclusion

Genocide is a special crime of the greatest horror. That is why UN inquiries, scholars, historians and even politicians have to be careful in the use of the word. Throwing around the term "genocide" and drawing analogies to horrible events that do not fit the treaty definition of genocide, is dangerous. It tends to downgrade the unique and particular elements of the crime as presently defined.

One could certainly argue that genocide in international law should extend to crimes of extermination based upon actual or perceived political conviction or belief. So much was proposed during the elaboration of the Genocide Convention by the representative of Cuba. The USA's representative opposed the suggestion. In the end, the "political ground" was not adopted. This was another reason, based on the *travaux préparatoires*, for the Commission to hold back.

Time may establish that, in this respect, the Commission was excessively cautious. Evidence might appear that the extermination of religious believers

---

36 "Report on the Commission, 351.

that occurred in North Korea was motivated by their religious beliefs. If that were so, it would be enough to constitute genocide, accountable in international law as it stands today. Time might eventually also see the enlargement of the definition of genocide to include extermination on political grounds. Any such elaboration would operate in law prospectively only, even if—analytically speaking—it might apply to North Korea's actions in the 1950s, 1960s, or even up to the present day, based on the continuation of the relevant acts of deadly violence based on racial or religious grounds.

If we are to build international law and tribunals that are respected as a true regime of law, we must do so on a foundation of authentic components. Those components will include establishing the preexistence of the norm invoked. In the immediate instance, that is the norm of the definition of genocide contained in present international law.

On each occasion when alleged victims and civil society organisations urged the Commission to push the envelope of international law and practice into problematic areas, it held back. It observed the principle of due process and natural justice. It took care to warn the North Korean government and its Supreme Leader of their own potential personal liability for international crimes. When it came to considering the international crime of genocide, it accepted the orthodox, current definition. On the basis of that definition it declined to record a finding of genocide.

Whilst this conclusion may strike some as surprising, even needlessly cautious and disrespectful to the victims in North Korea, it was the conclusion that the rule of law appeared to demand on the evidence adduced. One of the essential ingredients for preventing, combatting and responding to genocide is the existence of international law. In that sense, the Commission's approach contributes to a world in which genocide is no longer just a morally repugnant affliction of humanity, but constitutes an international crime for which perpetrators can face prosecution.

Part 4
Culture and Memory

REALITIES, SURREALITIES AND THE MEMBRANE OF INNOCENCE

Tony Barta

A funny thing happened to me on the way to Genocide Studies: I was called a surrealist. I was not so sure it was a compliment when I first heard it 30 years ago. And I only heard it through Colin Tatz, who then told the world about it. I had delivered my very first paper on genocide, at a conference called "On Being a German- Jewish Refugee in Australia." The problem was that I wanted to discuss how the genocide in everyone's minds, the Holocaust, inhibited consciousness of the violent past that had enabled us to meet on ground named after the colonial secretary, Lord Sydney. The question was equally suppressed where I had settled with my family, the city named after Lord Melbourne.

The conference went well. The trouble came when I attempted to explain to a Jewish audience at the Hakoah Club that these cities might be named after civilised gentlemen, but they were founded on genocide. That did not fit with the consciousness of many in the audience. I caused unease, then outrage. Konrad Kwiet, behind me, urged, "Mention your mother, mention your mother." She was sitting in the front row. It did not come to that. I was thrown from the platform by a young Zionist who went on to become an important lawyer. When it came to publishing the papers, the editors, John Moses and Kwiet, decided to include mine, though according to Tatz, they asked him whether my "surrealistic" vision belonged there.[1]

Generally, when we talk about the surreal we mean something strange, outside everyday reality, disconcerting. For me, the word had a quite different resonance. I recalled a debate in the seventies about how knowledge is socially constructed and made culturally meaningful. Objective historical knowledge in the present is only achieved with a sense of how subjectivity constructs the past. Philosopher Robert Solomon's book *The Passions* argued for a more extensive and intensive embrace of subjectivity. His chapter devoted to the individual nature of all perspectives was titled "Surrealism."[2]

---

1 Tony Barta, "After the Holocaust: Consciousness of Genocide in Australia," *Australian Journal of Politics and History* 31, no. 1 (1985), 154–61; Colin Tatz, "Confronting Australian Genocide," *Aboriginal History* 25 (2001), 16–36; the recollection is reprinted in Colin Tatz, *With Intent to Destroy: Reflecting on Genocide* (London: Verso, 2003), 102–03.

2 Robert C. Solomon, *The Passions* (New York: Anchor Doubleday, 1976), chap. 3; see also, Clifford Geertz,

Solomon wished to distinguish his position from one that says individual perspectives *create* reality. He believed, as do I, that in a comprehensive sense, there is only one reality but any person can only comprehend that reality in part, and from an individual perspective:

> Surreality is Reality from a point of view, limited by our personal experience and edited for brevity and manageability as well as for dramatic considerations. Objective reality is all here now, all at once. Subjective surreality, on the other hand, can handle only a small piece of Reality at any one time.

That definition takes us straight to the problem I encountered at the Hakoah Club. Anyone interested in the multiplicity of perspectives, paradigms and interpretations that jostle within genocide studies, needs to ponder surreality. My own perspective on genocide, and genocide studies, would be to highlight this interplay between historically constructed expectations, blind spots, prejudices and decisions, the context that produced them—and subsequent outcomes. Solomon gives a special place to "values"; the source of values, he says, is the passions. I would never exclude emotion or indeed physiological drives and pathologies. Yet, because I am especially interested in *intentions, interests* and *unintended consequences*, I look to the limitations of knowledge or feeling in a potentially disastrous situation. In Solomon's example:

> The psychologist Kurt Lewin compares the "lifeworlds" of two men crossing dangerously thin ice in a carriage; one knows the danger, the other does not. The "facts" (the Reality) are the same for both of them; their surrealities could not be more different.

The thin ice in genocide studies is a complex of historical realities very few actors are likely to know. Many of us assume people in Nazi Germany knew where things were headed. Mostly they did not. Such psychological realism is crucial in the key question of *intent*. Intent looks readily demonstrable if searching the documents yields a smoking gun. But reading documents often means reading actions. By their actions we must know them.

My argument has always been that the intentions of a settler "taking up" land outside Melbourne can seem to him (and to us) genuinely innocent of

---

The Interpretation of Cultures (New York: Basic Books 1973); Peter L. Berger and Thomas Luckmann, *The Social Construction of Reality* (Harmondsworth: Penguin, 1967); Alfred Schutz, *On Phenomenology and Social Relations* (Chicago: University of Chicago Press, 1970).

genocidal intent. A genocidal *outcome* nevertheless results. Only by construing the actions within a broader complex of culture and societal and individual interests, can we begin to understand the *larger factors* in play. Some reasons will have been personal (to impress a parent or a fiancée), some as impersonal as a worldwide colonial project. It seems obvious that a history will benefit more from a sense of different surrealities when it has information specific to an individual. Culture and interests are not, however, only personal, any more than a consciousness of history is. The ways these matters are construed, at the time and later, depends on our conceptual framework, most importantly on the way we conceive of *relations*. How are the thoughts and actions of an individual to be understood *in relation to* the larger contexts of economy, coercive power, society, culture, ideology?

Layers of surreality

It does not take much theorising to agree that people acting in the past (that is, their present) acted within a history we are now able to conceptualise into different factors and contexts. The question is how to represent their realities and surrealities to enhance our understanding. Too often we simply resort to our old friend "common sense." This is both vital and hazardous in genocide studies. Vital because it reminds us to check our reference base, and hazardous because it leads to false assumptions about empathy and equivalence.

Our common sense assumption is that the most direct access to a surreality in the past is through the memory of a person who experienced the situation. Common sense also tells us there are complications in the ways people remember and represent their own experience. *Remembering Genocide*, edited by Nigel Eltringham and Pam Maclean, reminds us that memory is not a passive storage system, not an image bank of the past, but an active, dynamic, shaping force. The editors quote Raphael Samuel's warning that it is "historically conditioned to the emergencies of the moment. . . . Like history, memory is inherently revisionist and never more chameleon when it appears to remain the same."[3] That said, memory is unparalleled and indispensable in the access it gives us to the past.

Each of us can think of memorable instances even as we remember the caveats about memory and retelling. Often we listen with a special consideration of a general kind, assuming a further surreality of trauma, which involves

---

3   Pam Maclean, "To be Hunted like Animals: Samuel and Joseph Chanesman Remember Their Survival in the Polish Countryside during the Holocaust" in *Remembering Genocide*, eds. Nigel Eltringham and Pam Maclean (New York: Routledge, 2014). The quote from Raphael Samuel is from *Theatres of Memory* (London and New York: Verso, 1994), 1.x. See also works by Zoe Waxman and Pascale Bos on gender and memory.

the protection of self and others, the effects of repeated recounting, and confidence or doubt about creating conviction in the listener. Nevertheless, the stories told do carry weight. This is especially so in the case of the Holocaust where we rely on the accounts of survivors—and a small number who did not survive—to convey the surreality of victimisation. Because the imagery of the slaughter is so hellish, with its herding, gassing and burning of bodies, it is also the most surreal in a more conventional sense, but that is not what I mean here. What I am trying to chase down is our access to the experience and the larger realities recognised or unrecognised in that particular experience.

Our sense of victim experience is by far the most powerful and pervading due to the extensive testimonies of survivors. Testimony and memoir are also by far the most common source for reconstructing the surreality of perpetrators. We have the accounts of Franz Stangl, Rudolf Höss and a few other officers, and we have the trial records. If the most damning testimony in trials was that of victims it was because the self-exculpating testimony of the accused was not considered to give the court access to the all-important *mens rea*, the incriminating state of mind at the time of the offence. No amount of badgering could elicit from Adolf Eichmann a confession of murderous intent. It had to be proven by inferences from deliberately euphemistic documents, the testimony of his victims—and from his actions.[4]

Because action (or *inaction*) is so challenging to construe, "bystanders" are always problematical in their links to a genocide. Sometimes they are literally bystanders at an episode of discrimination or violence, yet more often they are far from the scene and very often genuinely innocent—in which case, they may be better described in Tatz's conceptualisation, as "beneficiaries." In the case of the Nazi genocide of Europe's Jews, we have been almost as much fascinated by the surrealities of "ordinary Germans" as we are with the "ordinary men" who became killers. Those far from the scene aroused more interest in earlier decades, when collective guilt became a legacy of post-war preoccupations. Books like Milton Mayer's *They Thought They Were Free* and William Sheridan Allen's *The Nazi Seizure of Power* were staples of teaching in the 1970s. In biographies of ordinary Nazis or "The Experience of a Single German Town," we found access to the lives of Germans before the worst atrocities were perpetrated.

---

4 Essential documents remain in several versions including Heinrich Himmler's speeches to his officers, especially the address at Poznan: http://www.nizkor.org/hweb/people/h/himmler-heinrich/posen/oct-04-43/ausrottung-transl-nizkor.html. See also Rudolf Höss, *Death Dealer: The Memoirs of the SS Kommandant at Auschwitz*, ed. Steven Paskuly, trans. Andrew Pollinger (Boston: Da Capo Press, 1996); Gitta Sereny, *Into That Darkness: An Examination of Conscience* (New York: Vintage, 1974); Gitta Sereny, *Albert Speer: His Battle with Truth* (New York: Vintage, 1996); Bettina Stangneth, *Eichmann Before Jerusalem: The Unexamined Life of a Mass Murderer* (New York: Knopf, 2014).

Such access has been one basic ambition of modern history over the past two centuries. Where traditional accounts were more concerned with making a meaningful narrative, we have more recently wanted to know "how it actually was." For some historians that still means the formation of policy, for others an account of large events that swept up individuals. The experiences of individuals have now achieved a dominating popularity, with biography a staple of historical bestsellers. What is known as "ethnographic history" attempts to read the actualities of individual perspectives—surrealities—by interpreting historical episodes within an understanding of cultures. History must situate both culture and individual experience within economic, societal and political contexts, and these contexts are also needed to understand any episode of genocide.

Genocide Studies in the academy are scarcely 30 years old; ethnographic history is about a decade older. How many genuinely ethnographic accounts of genocide have we produced in that time? The studies of specific Nazi atrocities by Christopher Browning, Jan Gross and Claude Lanzmann take us very close to the action—of ordinary men committing massacres or filling a lorry with Jews for gassing. Gross follows neighbours in a Polish village doing their part. Konrad Kwiet's "From the Diary of a Killing Unit" shows how the mentality of bicycle policemen transforms once they are far from the familiar streets of Vienna.[5]

The notion that individual actions need to be read very carefully, alongside maximum historical information and theoretical assistance, has become standard in ethnography. Here, as Inga Clendinnen reminds us, neither common sense nor its bedfellow, intuition, are much help. Engaging in open discussion of interpretive options "reduces the role of untestable 'intuition' by making the business of interpreting actions a public affair: it inhibits the casual offloading of our own expectations onto unlike others."[6] The interpretation of cultures, as Clifford Geertz argued, can only proceed by a hermeneutic process that goes beyond attentive observation. *Understanding* and *creating understanding* is something elaborate, educated and subtle. To *illuminate* an action, we need to consider what will be most effective from the plethora of theories and methods our libraries hold.

In studies of Australian genocide, the groundwork of ethnographic history

---

5 Konrad Kwiet, "From the Diary of a Killing Unit" in *Why Germany?: National Socialist Anti-Semitism and the European Context*, ed. John Milfull (Oxford: Berg, 1993), 75–90; Christopher Browning, *Ordinary Men: Reserve Police Battalion 101 and the Final Solution in Poland* (New York: HarperCollins, 1993); Jan T. Gross *Neighbors: The Destruction of the Jewish Community in Jedwabne, Poland* (Princeton: Princeton University Press, 2001).

6 Inga Clendinnen, *Reading the Holocaust* (Melbourne: Text, 1998), 138.

began quite early, before the term was invented. More recently, records, memories and local studies have not produced many analyses in terms of colonial settler culture.[7] Explicating genocidal realities in the USA has been similarly fitful.[8] Perhaps because we have a stronger ethnographic tradition in studying peoples further from home, the accounts of genocide in Cambodia, Rwanda and Central America are more culturally engaged. They have given us some of the best examples of where an anthropologically curious and ethnographically persistent kind of genocide study can take us.

Alexander Hinton has reflected on some of the challenges. He has spoken of his early interest in Buddhism, in folk psychology, emotion, stories. How could Cambodians do this? The cover of his book *Why Did They Kill?* has an apt summary: "Hinton considers this violence in light of a number of dynamics, including the ways in which difference is manufactured, how identity and meaning are constructed, and how emotionally resonant forms of cultural knowledge are incorporated into genocidal ideologies." The foreword to another of his books, *Annihilating Difference*, asks:

> What combination of hatred and fear leads people to see their neighbours not as fellow human beings entitled to lead their own lives but as an intolerable presence that must be isolated and eliminated? Human rights activists seek to monitor, curb, and punish such atrocities. They identify proximate causes or individuals who bear special responsibility. But in a fundamental sense they do not really explain these abuses. For a deeper explanation, they must turn to other disciplines. In this quest, anthropology has much to offer.[9]

---

7   Some sources are indicated in Tony Barta, " 'They appear actually to vanish from the face of the earth.' Aborigines and the European Project in Australia Felix," *Journal of Genocide Research* 10, no. 4 (2008), 519–39. Judith Wright, *The Cry for the Dead* (Melbourne: Oxford University Press, 1981) stands out among memoirs that also try to indicate the genocidal realties and surrealities of settler culture. On Wright, and Clendinnen, see Tom Griffiths, *The Art of Time Travel: Historians and Their Craft* (Melbourne: Text, 2016).

8   Some of the most illuminating histories do not have genocide in their vocabulary. Ned Blackhawk, *Violence over the Land: Indians and Empires in the Early American West* (Cambridge, Mass: Harvard University Press, 2006) refers to "genocidal" events, also plainly addressed in Jeffrey Ostler, *The Plains Sioux and U.S. Colonialism from Lewis and Clark to Wounded Knee* (New York: Cambridge University Press, 2004); Stephen Howe, "Native America and the Study of Colonialism, Part 1: Contested Histories," *Settler Colonial Studies* 3, no. 1 (2013), 102–26, and "Native America and the Study of Colonialism, Part 2: Colonial Presents," *Settler Colonial Studies* 4, no. 1 (2014), 105–19. Not to be missed: Ken Burns and Stephen Ives, *The West* (New York: Insignia Films, 1996), DVD.

9   Alexander Laban Hinton, ed., *Annihilating Difference: The Anthropology of Genocide* (Berkeley: University of California Press, 2002), 1–6. Nancy Scheper-Hughes adds, "Public anthropology [is about] making things public that are private. Making invisible things into public issues, making visible secrets that empower some and disempower others who are not privy to the information." Located in Aleksandra Bartoszko, "Being Radical without Being a Leftist: Interview with Nancy Scheper-Hughes," *antropologi.info* (blog), http://www.antropologi.info/blog/anthropology/2011/nancy-scheper-hughes.

Not all historians value the help of other disciplines, and we certainly do not want to erase the differences. Individual proclivities—and surrealities—will shape the ways we seek to create understanding.

Surrealities of writers and readers

Writing history is not easier than other forms of writing. Our own personal dispositions are crucial to the perspectives we adopt. We will all conventionally acknowledge a rather formulaic subjectivity, derived from our own historical context and life experience. We are inclined to be reticent, perhaps mercifully, about our own surrealities, the interplay of intimate, emotional and societal factors that are probably crucial to the kind of history we write and read. Even such an obvious personal constriction as the languages we know and do not know, something that is just as obviously linked to the largest dynamics of world history, rarely rates a mention. In Australian history our language limitations are manifest—and almost always passed over in silence. To recognise how many hundreds of languages have disappeared would be to implicate our everyday selves in genocide. The Great Australian Silence was upheld by the writers and the readers of the history they complacently shared.

If every historian writes from a unique personal experience and a shared historical encounter, there is also a more institutional factor in the shaping of historical consciousness. Greg Dening once memorably compared the mindsets of academic disciplines to an old horse ploughing its furrow and we all know examples (ourselves included) that fit. The strictness of our blinkers, the matters we choose for attention, the assumptions we bring to the interpretive venture, the paradigms we apply—all these are brewed in the surreality we inhabit. To the extent the surreality inhabits us, it commands our focus and our scope. How much is nature and how much nurture is interesting to pursue; all of us have our own mix.[10]

Where does this matter in genocide studies? Almost everywhere. What we give attention to, when and how persistently we examine a question of genocide, indeed whether we even see a question of genocide: every impulse of our enquiry is provoked, vetted, or encouraged by our individual surreality. As we shall see again, when we turn to our audience, each surreality is of course a construct of history, society, culture and ideology. These are the very large contexts that control something as fundamental as the definition of genocide we adhere to, or which elements of the standard definitions (Lemkin's

---

10 The draught horse Eustace makes a repeat appearance in Greg Dening, *Performances* (Melbourne: Melbourne University Publishing, 1996). See also Griffiths, *The Art*, chap. 6.

1944 chapter, or the clauses of the UN Convention) we deploy. When we add the more intimate contexts—family, friends, academic environment, those we wish to win approval from—we can see that the whole field of genocide studies is likely to be skewed by dominating, but not usually acknowledged, surrealities.

The influence of such factors is over and above (*sur*) or underneath (*sous*) our choice of which reality we focus on and how we go about it. To concentrate on legal questions, as William Schabas does, or on massacres, as Lyndall Ryan and Benjamin Madley do, means breadth and depth in our understanding of genocide. There is no reason to promote one expertise over another. Nor can inclinations towards empirical or theoretical pursuits claim any superiority. I will end up arguing that all treatments of genocide are not created equal because I believe all writers should attend to the surrealities of their subjects and attempt to follow them through to their historical contexts—social, cultural, political, economic. I have an open bias towards intellectual constructs, utilising what Geertz called "made in the academy concepts" to interpret events. But I also have a bias towards less explicit representations, the kind that leaves much implicit, that relies more on artistic flair to give us access to the worlds of others. Writers (and filmmakers) with such talents have usually had them nurtured outside of the academy. We all have examples of true stories or made up ones that have the power to transport us into the experiences of others. Fiction relies on this power but memoirs can have it, too. (I once had the nerve to suggest to Raimond Gaita that he write no more books because he had achieved close to perfection in *Romulus, My Father*.) If we want the feeling of taking part in an atrocity, or surviving one, we will turn to a writer who knows the art of recreating a surreality.

Imagination is the heart of the matter. Each interpretive enterprise relies on the talent of the writer that will enable the reader to inhabit something of another's reality. Fiction has the most immersive potential and its poetics can sometimes cultivate, rather than smother, our critical faculties. A more prosaic kind of explication might foreground the analytical capacity of writer and reader, but the surrealities in play will only come through if the more imaginative arts allow them to. For access to individual cases we still rely mainly on memoir, fiction and encounters through film. The art of novelists (Lion Feuchtwanger to Jonathan Franzen) and filmmakers (Leni Riefenstahl to Edgar Reitz) have given us more insight into Nazi allegiance on the one hand and the ideology of innocence on the other. The closer we get to the realities of Nazi Germany, and the surrealities of German people, the less we will see these characterisations as alternatives.[11]

Strategies of meaning-creation implicitly have a target audience. For academic work it is other academics. Within that audience we will have in mind a more circumscribed set we may or may not be part of, and certain individuals whose opinion we value. We may hope to strengthen ties within professional networks or at least not alienate colleagues. For whom, with what intellectual interests and prejudices, am I writing? What qualities am I searching for in a wider circle of possible readers? With which elements of their surrealities am I seeking to make a connection?

The perspectives of our audience are not really the end-point of our work. They are the primary ones. Their surrealities govern the reception of the accounts we give. I learned about their power the hard way in that first encounter at the conference in Sydney. Recently, at the other end of my career, I stopped to check with a large lecture hall that my reference to Clifford Geertz had some resonance. It did not. The great ethnographer had not been dead 10 years and for this audience of genocide scholars he was scarcely a whisper. We can assume very little, even in a specialist audience, about a shared set of references, understandings, responses. As with all representations—visual, written, musical—we cannot assume that our surreality evokes a similar reverberation in someone else's.

All historians strive to make past understandings real to their readers. Where we rely on translation, as in so much writing on the Holocaust, we need to be aware that almost any word or set of words can skew the meaning of the original. We can build up crippling scruples about tone and nuance. Beyond the hideous distortions in the language of the Nazis (memorialised by Viktor Klemperer) are the historical, cultural and intimately personal specifics faced by all translators. Anyone bilingual knows the pull of one language or the other for just the right, often untranslatable word. For the difference a word makes in conveying a meaning—and with it a surreality—see the attention J.M. Coetzee pays to Franz Kafka and his translators. He needs a page to show how one sentence of interior experience can be wrong, word after word.[12] The experience examined is making love. Should we have less care with the experience of separating children from mothers for killing?

Film has a special place in the representation of surrealities because it deploys, and employs, powers that are the most deeply learned and practised in human communication. To read the face and voice and demeanour of another,

---

11 Tony Barta, "Recognizing the Third Reich: Heimat and the Ideology of Innocence," in *History on/and/in Film*, eds. Tom O'Regan and Brian Shoesmith (Perth, 1985), 131–39. For earlier examples, see Tony Barta, *Screening the Past: Film and the Representation of History* (Westport: Praeger, 1998), chap. 8, and chap. 9, a discussion of television and history with Pierre Sorlin. Also Tony Barta, "Consuming the Holocaust: Memory Production and Popular Film," *Contention* 5, no. 2 (1996), 161–75, and the 2014 film *Labyrinth of Lies*.

12 J.M. Coetzee, "Translating Kafka," *Stranger Shores, Essays 1986–1999* (London: Vintage, 2002), 88–103.

a skill that predates literacy by millennia, is acquired in the first months of life. Even as we watch for signs of deception we build our confidence in our ability to access another's experience by watching and listening. This encounter is the basis of "documentary" interviews with survivors, and sometimes perpetrators, of genocide. There is almost always a degree of acting in such accounts and the acting in fictional films also depends on our suspension of disbelief. Once we become critically aware of how film manipulates our senses to supposedly give access to the inner reality of another person, suspicions can multiply. Some of the most successful art makes us aware of artifice even as it inducts us into an extreme rendering of a past horror. Think of Lanzmann's stolid persistence in *Shoah*, the little girl with the red coat in Steven Spielberg's monochrome *Schindler's List*, and the old-format framing throughout *Son of Saul*. All attempt to heighten the simultaneous awareness of surrealities as historical reality.

Surreality as reality: interests and ideology, intent and innocence

We have thousands of attempts to link the prejudices and political choices of Germans to the Holocaust. In Germany, the question resides less in media representations than in quite personal connections to the broad-brush verdicts of collective guilt (you *must* have known) or collective innocence—how *could* we have known? Historical judgement between these opposed surrealities has tended to come to questions of historically formed culture and ideology. Unsurprisingly, most Germans have responded negatively to accusations and analyses they see as lacking realism and subtlety.[13]

Raphael Lemkin opened himself to this criticism even as he brought an important aspect of collective responsibility to light. He was a lawyer before he was an historian and his interest in subjectivity did not, so I thought, go much beyond the crucial *mens rea*. But there turns out to be another Latin tag on which he also placed weight in his judgement of intent. In the preface to *Axis Rule* he quotes three words followed by a translation: *facit cui prodest*—he in whose interest it was, did it.[14] Lemkin insisted that the crimes carried out

---

[13] Dirk Moses has made many contributions to the understanding of post-war surrealities in Germany. Of special relevance here is his discussion of Jürgen Habermas and Martin Walser in "The Non-German German and the German German: Dilemmas of Identity after the Holocaust," *New German Critique* 101 (2007), 45–49.

[14] Raphael Lemkin, *Axis Rule in Occupied Europe: Laws of Occupation, Analysis of Government, Proposals for Redress* (Washington: Carnegie Endowment for International Peace, 1944), xiv. Subsequent quotations are also from the Preface; Tony Barta, " 'He in Whose Interest It Was, Did It': Lemkin's Lost Law of Genocide," *Global Dialogue* 15, no. 1 (2013), 12–23 .

far from hearth and home could not be separated from "important political and moral considerations based upon the responsibility of the German people treated as an entirety":

> All important classes and groups of the population have voluntarily assisted Hitler in the scheme of world domination: the military, by training the reserves and working out plans for conquest; the businessmen, by penetrating and disrupting foreign economies through cartels, patent devices, and clearing agreements; the propagandists, by organizing Germans abroad and preparing fifth columns in countries to be occupied; the scientists, by elaborating doctrines for German hegemony; the educators, by arming spiritually the German youth.

Germany's Nazi elite was crammed into the dock but in his "Proposals for Redress" he makes plain that the larger societal involvement implies something very close to collective guilt regardless of the subjective sense of individuals. The surrealities massaged by ideology are trumped by the objective realities of *interest*:

> Indeed, all groups of the German nation had their share in the spoils of occupied Europe. The German Hausfrau used for her family the food of all occupied countries, Polish geese, Yugoslav pigs, French wine, Danish butter, Greek olives, Norwegian fish; the German industrialist used French and Polish coal, Russian lumber; the German employer in agriculture and industry used for his greater profit imported conscript labor; the German business man bought up foreign interests and properties, taking advantage of the debasement of non-German currencies; the importer benefited through low prices and compulsory credits; and by Hitler's decree of July 28, 1942, the access to women in occupied countries was facilitated for German manhood by fiat of law.

In their first essay on genocide, Ann Curthoys and John Docker highlighted the benefits Lemkin listed, and his insistence that all groups who shared the spoils of occupied Europe shared responsibility for the atrocities. Their concern was less Germany than the consciousness of genocide in Australia.[15] Unlike Lemkin, they were not arguing for guilt, but for a recognition of the suppressed reality of colonisation: genocide.

---

15   Ann Curthoys and John Docker, "Introduction: Genocide: Definitions, Questions, Settler-colonies," *Aboriginal History* 25 (2001), 1–15.

Robert Manne insisted many years ago that the black armband/white blindfold controversy was not about guilt. It was shame we should feel.[16] Suppression and *re*pression of the shameful remains the reality/surreality interface in Australian history. There are notable signs of consciousness changing. The weasel word " Reconciliation" is giving way to "Recognition" and "truth-telling." Even "Treaty" has reappeared. "Genocide" is still too confronting for older Australians and is not pushed to the fore by Aboriginal spokespeople.[17] There are incremental gains to be achieved. There may be generational change under way that may even allow the idea of a treaty onto the agenda. The changes in historical consciousness are due more to Indigenous initiative and public presence than to the labours of historians. Musicians, actors in film and television have made more difference than politicians, with footballers in the front line.

Only a few historians even by the 1990s would attach something as universal as sport and as searingly individual as suicide to a whole history of colonisation. For Colin Tatz, the crisis in Aboriginal communities was not only a matter of alcohol and family violence. "It is a legacy of past violations by a hostile and even genocidal society." Men who did not kill themselves still had a low chance of surviving past 50. Their surreality was closer to football than colonisation but Tatz makes the connection. The Ceduna Rovers won the Far West premiership in South Australia in 1958. "By 1987, less than 30 years later, all but one of the 18 young men were dead."[18]

Colin Tatz gave his collection of powerful essays a powerful title: *With Intent to Destroy*. The provenance of the phrase could not be more impressive. Since my first failed attempt to indicate elements of shared responsibility different from explicit genocidal intent, my aim has been to broaden the readings of ultimately genocidal interests and actions. How individual surrealities, focussed on the innocent pursuit of interests, help create a reality in which a genocide is produced, is part of the problem. The other part, determinedly repressing what might surface as intent, is the membrane of innocence.

There was a prologue to my disaster at the Hakoah Club, and an epilogue. In the days before the conference an old friend of my parents asked what had

---

16 Robert Manne, "Sorry Business: The Road to the Apology," *Monthly*, March, 2008, 22–31; Tony Barta, "Sorry, and Not Sorry, in Australia: How the Apology to the Stolen Generations Buried a History of Genocide," *Journal of Genocide Research* 10, no. 2 (2008), 201–14.

17 Some Indigenous leaders, most eminently Marcia Langton and Noel Pearson, have on occasion used the word genocide, and it has recently been revived in public discourse by Stan Grant, *Talking to My Country* (Sydney: HarperCollins, 2016).

18 Colin Tatz, *Aboriginal Suicide is Different: A Portrait of Life and Self-destruction* (Canberra: Aboriginal Studies Press, 2001), 5. On March 31, 2017, ABC news reported that Indigenous youth are 17 times more likely to be in judicial detention.

brought me to Sydney. Quick as a flash came the perfect response to my mention of Aboriginal genocide. "That wasn't us," he said. "That was the poms."[19]

The day after the debacle I returned to the Club to pick up the jumper I had shed before my talk. The woman in the office had not been present but she had heard. It was a pity, she said, that I was not there the previous week. Charlie Perkins had come to address the same audience. He had said how much he could feel their suffering. "You could have heard a pin drop," she said. "He held them in the palm of his hand."

Perkins knew about surrealities. He had lived them and studied them and negotiated them all his life. He knew the strength of the membrane. I came to see he was right. Most Australians still respond to any association with genocide in ways that preclude negotiation. The Perkins' principle is to allow recognition of a reality in the only way possible, within someone's surreality. To recognise that there were many Indigenous peoples and that the many means employed to destroy their unique identities must be classed as genocide may still be a bridge too far.[20] Yet the 30 years of bridge building must, we hope, make eventual recognition more certain.

Tatz coined a memorable and pertinent phrase when he wrote of breaking through "the membrane that locked or blocked out the unthinkable notion of genocide having occurred in this moral country." It was a membrane of innocence, impervious to a word evoking a distant horror. Tatz lists the many writers who had tried to get Australians to face the facts, some detailing atrocities against Aboriginal peoples, but none connecting massacres and other brutalities of European Australia with the foreign concept, "Genocide":

> No one was reading the Polish international jurist, Raphael Lemkin, who coined the word for the destruction of the genus of a people in 1944. No scholar was looking at the fine print, or at the fact that the United Nations had created an international law which equated physical killing with such acts as imposing birth control measures and forcibly transferring children. We were all steeped in Auschwitz, Treblinka, Sobibor and Belzec, in mon-

---

19 A British historian has also returned the weight of responsibility to the colonial power. Tom Lawson, *The Last Man: A British Genocide in Tasmania* (London: I.B. Taurus, 2014). See also John Docker, "A Plethora of Intentions: Genocide, Settler Colonialism and Historical Consciousness in Australia and Britain," *International Journal of Human Rights* 19, no. 1 (2015), 74–89. For a contrary view of the effect in historical consciousness, see Rebe Taylor, "Genocide, Extinction and Aboriginal Self-determination in Tasmanian Historiography," *History Compass* 11, no. 6 (2013), 405–41.

20 Another Aboriginal language has been buried with Tommy George, the last fluent speaker of Awu Laya on Cape York. He fought a billionaire miner and won but could not save a basic element of his culture. Perhaps because it was a double funeral with his son, there was a report with headline and pictures in the *Weekend Australian*, August 13–14, 2016.

strous SS men, in Himmlers, Heydrichs and Hoesses. Who needed to look further than these men and their doings for an understanding of genocide? Who could look any further?[21]

Tatz was one who did look further. His attack on the membrane of ignorance and innocence was sustained and effective. Work on Australian genocide by other scholars combined with Indigenous activism began to bring international attention to bear on our history. I believe the most cited and defining intervention was Tatz's 1999 paper "Genocide in Australia," supported by his path-breaking work on racism. He succeeded in installing genocide studies as an academic discipline with institutional support and founding *Genocide Perspectives* to stimulate Australian scholarship in an environment of ignorance, ideology and interests resistant to any association with genocide.

Directly confronting the resistance remains something very few Australian historians do. Despite the landmark interventions of two Prime Ministers—Paul Keating's Redfern speech should be the credo taught to every generation of schoolchildren—the key recognition of Australia as a nation founded on genocide scarcely surfaces in our histories. They keep reinforcing the membrane anchored in the ideology of the society at large. But a smaller group of our academic colleagues have recognised something we should be proud of: that genocide, from its invention, is an activist concept as well as a hermeneutic one. Like Raphael Lemkin, we want it to have an effect in changing the world.[22]

---

21 Tatz, "Confronting Australian Genocide," 18–19.
22 Donna-Lee Frieze, ed. *Totally Unofficial: The Autobiography of Raphael Lemkin* (New Haven: Yale University Press, 2013); Tony Barta, "Liberating Genocide: An Activist Concept and Historical Understanding," *Genocide Studies and Prevention* 9, no. 2 (2015), 103–19.

THROUGH GERMAN EYES: AMATEUR PHOTOS AND TRANS-GENERATIONAL RENEGOTIATIONS OF THE HOLOCAUST

Kirril Shields

Introduction

In a trunk in my garage I have a sizable collection of photos gathered over a span of years. They are black and white images taken during Hitler's reign and each contains some reference to the Third Reich. Often they show uniformed men lounging with friends. Others reveal youth in Hitler Youth uniform, or a group of soldiers on military parade, and some contain little to no evidence of the Nazi party, with possibly just a flag in the background or a framed picture of Adolf Hitler on a wall. Others portray European Jews in their homes, in a *shtetl*, or in the camps, and a few have been taken by Allied soldiers as they moved across Europe from late-1944 to mid-1945. Similar in their production, each has been taken with a personal, hand-held camera. There are no press photos in the collection, no propaganda cigarette cards then common in Nazi Germany: the images are amateurish and often blurred, off-kilter, sometimes over-exposed, and the majority are mundane. They show (mostly) men and some women carrying out banal institutional and vocational activities: butchers, mechanics, cooks, soldiers, couriers, doctors, nurses and ditch diggers, to name just some. Their setting is slightly more adventurous, revealing a host of European regions—French beaches, the outskirts of Moscow, the very northern tip of Finland. I began collecting these images many years back when, on a five-month cycling trip through Europe, I kept coming across markets where stallholders sold individual photos, sometimes albums. I have since continued buying from online sources, as well as from the odd antique shop.

As mentioned, the majority of photos glimpse the day-to-day workings of the Reich from various working class perspectives. Contrastingly, though fewer in number, some images are at a remove from everyday settings. Not pictures of Hitler and his high-ranking entourage, but images whose innocuous look belies their more disturbing truth (although this might be true of any photos of the Third Reich). In this essay I look at two particular photos to interrogate photography as a memorialising link to the Holocaust, and by doing so discuss literal and representational modes of interacting with this past. The photos I explore represent particular types of German images. The first has been taken by a German and reveals individuals who are clearly victims of the regime. The second photo is an image taken by a member of the SS, showing his comrades enacting a similar role to that of the photographer. The gaze is similar, since both are from the viewpoint of perpetrators, yet the subject matter varies. Given their agenda and content, each is fraught with ethical and historiographical complexity. Individually and collectively, amateur German images are a problematic means of remembering the Holocaust, and the act of reinstating such images as insight into this history adds to the complexity. In questioning these photos' legitimacy, I explore Marianne Hirsch's idea of postmemory—inherited memories passed down the generations through, for example, the medium of the photo (to name one narrative form)—alongside Roland Barthes' discussion of the photo's *punctum*, those moments that arrest a viewer's gaze and reconfigure initial readings. I then discuss trans-generational shifts, assessing the photos' potency as legitimate representations of the Nazi regime.

The photos

Krakow Jews, 1939

The first image depicts three Jewish males who appear reluctant to have their photo taken. Behind them are parked German military vehicles. Their faces show a mixture of irritation and confusion, and not one of the men looks pleased. Handwritten on the back in German is "Krakow, 1939." This photograph reminds me—not only in its subject matter and mode of production and gaze, but in the feeling it generates—of images found in the SS Auschwitz album, in which imprisoned women and men are forced to look into the lens of a camera held by an SS officer. Similarly, there is a resemblance to that iconic image of the boy with raised arms whose family is being evicted from the Warsaw Ghetto, a photo discussed at length by, among others, Hirsch and Susan Sontag. The photo is also reminiscent of Walter Genewien's collection of images that he took as a "tourist" of the Warsaw Ghetto while a member of Germany's Wehrmacht. In these types of photos a sense of resigned reluctance pervades, sometimes mixed with a streak of anger and often disbelief (or annoyance), notable in facial expressions or body language. In all cases, the subjects are required—it would seem—to look into the camera and not into the distance, or elsewhere. Alternatively, they are viewed from a distance as one might look at zoo animals, people captured both literally and figuratively for the pleasure of the photographer. They are, as Hirsch signals, photos of people shot on camera not long before being shot with bullets.[1]

The second photograph shows eight members of the SS *Totenkopf*—the SS branch that worked in the camps—at Mauthausen concentration camp. The men who committed crimes such as the gassings are having their picture taken by another perpetrator, or with a timer, or by an inmate. Such images are rare; there are limited records showing the men who were not high up in the SS hierarchy, but who carried out the crimes. A plethora of photos exists of Heinrich Himmler and Rudolf Hess for example, a small number of Josef Mengele, but very few of SS minions directly operating the killing machine. Here we witness men who are physical and masculine in some ways, yet verge on the bland, even the ugly. They are middle-aged and of middling weight. Their uniforms are loose, hair unkempt, their postures relaxed. In this depiction of uniformed mundanity, it is possible to infer the presence of families, the routine of work, and an aura of camaraderie. Somewhat ironically, while their physicality (or lack thereof) provides an antithetical redressing of SS mythology, these men are literally the overseers of life and death. These are the men responsible for keeping order in Germany's concentration camps in both a bureaucratic and physical sense, overseeing underling Trawniki guards, administering punishment, helping with selections, and carrying out gassings, shootings and hangings.

---

1 Marianne Hirsch, *The Generation of Postmemory: Writing and Visual Culture After the Holocaust* (New York: Columbia University Press, 2012), 13.

SS *Totenkopf* Guards, 1940s

Both photos either explicitly show, or allude to, the Holocaust, displaying literal and/or connotative connections to aspects of that past. "Literal" in that each photo, as John Frohmayer suggests, presents the viewer with evidence of the Holocaust, the irrefutable acknowledgement that such events took place.² Photos such as these remove "doubt . . . they affirm 'having-been-there' of the victim and the victimizer, of the horror."³ Each photo, therefore, becomes a small piece of a larger historical narrative. Similarly, there is a semiotic connection to this past, each photo symbolic of a wider narrative, and each contains multiple signifiers to substantiate this broader history, though such readings are somewhat dependent upon prior knowledge. For example, in photo two, the men stand around a table and a bench carved from stone taken from the quarry at Mauthausen; the photo confirms the presence of the quarry and its infamous "stairs of death," a long stairway prisoners climbed while carrying heavy stone blocks. The table and chair come to represent the oppression of the Nazi slave labour camp system.

The photographers were most likely members of the SS who have taken

---

2   Cited in Marianne Hirsch, *Family Frames: Photography, Narrative, and Postmemory* (Massachusetts: Harvard University Press, 1997), 24.

3   Hirsch, *Family Frames*, 24.

these as mementos, capturing moments of comradeship and the subjugation of others. The gaze (the photographer's viewpoint) is purposefully informative. Each has a certain wish, an ideology embedded within it; the *Totenkopf* men evidently wish to "put their hearts on their sleeve" for an ideology is marked literally on their uniforms, in the patches on their collars, their belt buckles, the caps, and the iconic death's head emblem. This and the way they hold themselves, and their lack of a smile, show a group of men intent on fulfilling political and gendered roles that, given the signs inscribed in the photo, require a balance of seriousness and mateship. In the photo of the Jewish men, it is the ideologue's viewpoint that positions their victims. German politics becomes evident for there is a clear divide, an "us" versus "them" distinction. This photo, taken by a Nazi, captures the captured (and makes evident the societal position of slave as compared to victor). Claude Lanzmann believes images like these deprive the viewer of anything outside of the Nazi gaze and are therefore problematic, as the perpetrator's intentions guide the onlooker.[4] Similarly, Ulrich Baer suggests that Nazi images rob their Jewish subject matter "of any interior life and self-directed means of expression, while the Nazi photographer is endowed by historians with motives, feelings, and a rationale for his actions."[5] These photos record "nothing but the 'ruination' and death of the Jews ... while they reveal a complex 'mental' stance and even the overall 'existential attitude' of the German behind the camera."[6] Agency becomes the privilege of the German, not the victim, and a viewer's reaction might be empathic to the victimised yet more understanding of the subjugator; action might be more easily conceptualised and understood than subordination. In the photo of the *Totenkopf* group, the image may negate this appropriation of agency, for the men are too average, too normal to determine people's fate, an ordinariness suggesting these men are not the masters of their own fate; they are merely the ciphers of a hierarchical ideology.

In both cases, the images convey a distinct message, one that privileges the German over the victim. The Germans as conquerors wanted to record their success. Those persecuted had little desire to remember the humiliation, other than to document atrocities for future generations. As losers in this battle, those imprisoned in the German photos are often positioned to feel like oddities, and their expressions reveal as much. To add to this visual bias, the Germans had affordable technology and many owned a small camera, so the

---

4   Ulrich Baer, *Spectral Evidence: The Photography of Trauma* (Cambridge, MA: MIT University Press, 2002), 138.
5   Ibid., 136.
6   Ibid.

bulk of amateur photos of the period situate the victim politically and ideologically as the "Other." A contemporary viewer, therefore, imagines 1930s and 1940s Europe from the viewpoint of the Germans, or the Germans' accomplices, and it is only once the Russians begin incursions into former occupied Europe in 1943, followed by the Americans and British in late 1944, that the tone of the amateur photo differs. German photos are bestowed a sense of authority, and yet these images are unjust and unethical: mass-produced death, either literally or through association, is documented with some glee and admiration or, at best, with a level of curiosity.

Historical veracity

When discussing photos as individual snapshots of a time and place, the audience glimpses the past through a small and specific window that does speak to a larger narrative, but homes in on the specificities of the photo itself. The abundance of amateur photos, however, suggests a collective means of seeing this past, a cohort of images building a common remembrance. In both cases the contemporary viewer is, in the words of Gary Weissman, a "non-witness," as we have no first-hand knowledge of events.[7] We are at an historic, cultural and temporal remove, and our role in these photos is more voyeur than participant. We are the non-witness to another's victimisation and torment. Sontag notes that "torment, a canonical subject in art . . . is often represented . . . as a spectacle, something being watched (or ignored) by other people. The implication here is: no, it cannot be stopped—and the mingling of inattentive with attentive onlookers underscores this."[8] The nature of the amateur German photo suggests we remain voyeurs, watching from an advantaged dislocation, peering at images that are (consciously or not), boastful. Unlike photos that might catch a unique situation, a "one-off" occurrence, the prevalence of German amateur photos reiterates the fact that a victim's torment is not halted post-photo; rather, it continues, and we as spectators become witness to a photographer's ongoing political and ideological habits. We see his world the way he wishes us to see it. We see the world the way Germany, at that point in history, wished us to see it.

Amateur photography was a very much accepted and encouraged practice throughout the Reich. Rolf Sachsse notes in his study of Nazi photography that "[t]he power of the state rested not so much on the contribution of grand

---

7 Gary Weissman, *Fantasies of Witnessing: Postwar Efforts to Experience the Holocaust* (Ithaca: Cornell University Press, 2004), 18.
8 Susan Sontag, *Regarding the Pain of Others* (London: Penguin Books, 2003), 38.

visual images provided by professionals, artists and photo-journalists, as on the simple praxis of shooting photos by anybody who could hold a camera in his or her hand."[9] The everyday photographer, invited by the state, contributed to the nation's collective identity, and the every-persons' photo acted as propaganda. Aleida Assmann writes that, "the new decentralized medium of photography, which was put into the hands of the citizens to coproduce and maintain a shared collective memory, was central here."[10] She continues: "The project of the NS State . . . was to transform, as far as possible, external propaganda into personal practice, choice and habit. Together with the mass distribution of new private cameras, a visual regime was constructed and implanted into the minds of the citizens who then collectively practiced, shared and consolidated the iconic photos of the NS state themselves."[11] Nazi amateur photos have an agenda embedded in them, not solely contrived by the individual, but sponsored by the government. They build a certain type of Germany akin to propaganda posters or Nazi movies. Individual photos become political messages, and while such images contain the normal and banal of the everyday—alongside battle scenes and comrades in arms—the collective effect intends to support and uphold Nazi ideology.

This becomes problematic when generations removed peer proudly through family albums, or when amateur German photos gain status as historical records. The emphasis shifts from the Holocaust *per se*, to the Reich more generally, possibly dissipating the importance of the Holocaust. Similarly, amateur photos present alternatives to those known as iconic of, and synonymous with, the Holocaust—images brutal in their content, such as the Jewish man kneeling on the edge of a pit awaiting execution. Iconic images, while often horrific, have become, some contend, too commonplace. Their presence on book covers, for example, at museums, or on television shows, dissipates their authority and their shock value. Caroline Dean, in her examination on empathy after the Holocaust, notes that, "assertions that we are numb and indifferent to suffering, that exposure to narratives and images of suffering has generated new and dramatic forms of emotional distance . . . are by now commonplace in both the United States and western Europe."[12] Alternative records such as amateur photos, therefore, might replace the iconic and over-used. Regardless of an interred bias, they offer a

---

9 Rolf Sachsse, *Die Erziehung zum Wegsehen: Fotografie im NS-Staat* (Dresden: Philo Fine Arts, 2003), 133.
10 Aleida Assmann, "Look Away in Nazi Germany," in *Empathy and its Limits*, eds. Aleida Assmann and Ines Detmers (London: Palgrave Macmillan, 2016), 132–33.
11 Ibid., 133.
12 Caroline Dean, *The Fragility of Empathy After the Holocaust* (Ithaca: Cornell University Press, 2004), 2.

new perspective, no matter how mundane, for each photo is authentic and documents a specific moment in time, attesting to what Roland Barthes observed in *Camera Lucida*, that photos adhere to the embedded referent and "can never deny the thing has been there [documenting] . . . absolutely, irrefutable [the] present."[13] In their discussion of street scene photos of European Jewish populations, Hirsch and Leo Spitzer note that images of the period hold documentary value.[14] Such photos—including those featured in this essay—contain historical veracity, and are first-hand evidence of what occurred. The photos discussed by Hirsch and Spitzer, for example, construct "an authoritative historical archive while also hoping to reactivate and re-embody it as memory."[15] These are images of a Jewish population taken by street photographers. Therefore, their use to reactivate or invigorate a past needs certain considerations, but different considerations to those arising when dealing with the German gaze. Especially when, as noted, this gaze was purposeful propaganda attempting to build a National Socialist Europe.

The return of the German gaze

When Hirsch discusses the notion of postmemory, she is suggesting on the one hand that "memory can be transmitted to those who were not actually there to live an event," specifically children whose parents survived the Holocaust.[16] She is also discussing intergenerational transference of memory through "the aesthetics of remembrance in the aftermath of catastrophe."[17] Hirsch writes that "postmemory's connection to the past is not actually mediated by recall but by imaginative investment, projection, and creation,"[18] which is, when considering victim narratives and perspectives, an approach to this past that might have its concerns, yet remains morally tenacious if viewed from the vantage point of the victim. What if this production of memory, individually and more widely generated, derived from photos akin to those shown here? How might individuals or communities inherit these images if they become accessible historical documents? Similarly, how might a museum curate such images? Susan Crane contends that, "the normalcy of understanding, facili-

---

13 Roland Barthes, *Camera Lucida: Reflections on Photography*, trans. Richard Howard (New York: Hill and Wang/The Noonday Press, 1981), 76–77.
14 Marianne Hirsch and Leo Spitzer, "Incongruous Images: 'Before, During, and After' the Holocaust," *History and Theory: Studies in the History of Philosophy* 48 (2009), 9.
15 Ibid., 14.
16 Hirsch, *Generation of Postmemory*, 105–06.
17 Ibid., 104.
18 Ibid., 106–07.

tated through communication, as well as collective memory, is threatened by atrocity images. The 'universal language' theory would hold that any human eye will register the same content in any image, and thus replicate the intention of the photographer."[19] According to Crane, therefore, images taken by perpetrators hold a certain power, and by their very vantage point, viewers are imbued with the photographer's perspective.

One way of negating the potency of such photos lies in the importance placed on them as historical records. Similarly, the importance attached to them as cultural artefact—deny the photos moral legitimacy through education and negate the risk of them becoming normalised and accepted viewpoints. There is also the assumption of knowledge a viewer brings to these images, realising something of this past and positioning these images accordingly, thereby neutering their potency as Nazi propaganda. In their exploration of Jewish photos of the past, Hirsch and Spitzer write:

> Not only may these viewers be able to contextualize the images historically, inserting them within the broader tapestry of cultural/collective or personal/familial resemblance, but they also bring to them an awareness of future history—of events-yet-to-come that could not have been known to the subjects of the photographs of their photographers at the time when the photos were taken.[20]

While aspects of this statement might not relate to the photos examined here—in that events-yet-to-come were seemingly known or predicted by the Nazi photographer, for the Germans would win!, would be victorious!—the idea that contemporary audiences contextualise images with this history in mind remains applicable. Audience knowledge, the building of such knowledge, and curatorial positioning that adds to knowledge, are important tools in the negotiation of amateur German photos. In the case of the two photos here, however, pragmatic suggestions present their own concerns, presupposing as they do that the viewer has sufficient knowledge of the Holocaust, and that curatorial practices ensure Holocaust narratives are not pushed aside by alternate stories that question the historicity of the Holocaust. These presuppositions have proved less than dependable on occasions.

Alternatively, as Crane suggests in her paper "Choosing Not to Look: Representation, Repatriation, and Holocaust Atrocity Photography," these photos

---

19 Susan Crane, "Choosing Not to Look: Representation, Repatriation, and Holocaust Atrocity Photography," *History and Theory: Studies in the Philosophy of History* 47, no. 3 (2008), 311.

20 Hirsch and Spitzer, "Incongruous Images," 15.

are possibly best removed from the public and "should perhaps fall under the same category as Nazi medical experiments: they have been rendered inadmissible because they are ethically compromised materials, made without the participants' consent."[21] Whilst this idea is appealing at first blush, the vast number of German images circulating between private collectors on internet sites such as eBay and Gumtree undercut the proposal. Amateur German photos are accessible in bulk, taking up viewership on sites such as Instagram and Facebook. "Collection of wartime atrocity images and gruesome war trophies by combatants and civilians alike," noted Crane in 2008, "has become not typical, but also not unusual . . . [and] have dramatically increased with the advent of the Internet."[22] Eight years has lapsed since Crane's observation, and technology has only heightened the accessibility of such German images. Instagram account "die_soldaten," for example, posts glorified images of the Wehrmacht and the SS and has almost 18 thousand followers. "germanmilitarypower" boasts over 30 thousand followers, and "the_ wehrmacht_and_ss" over 10 thousand, and these sites, and many others, upload amateur and press photos taken from the German perspective on a daily basis. We return, therefore, to the overarching debate: how to deal with photos whose Nazi gaze proudly shows trauma inflicted on others, or makes banal and dull (or glorifies) the perpetrators and, by association, their crimes.

More theoretically, though not separate from educative and curatorial considerations, amateur German images invert what Barthes calls the *punctum* of the photo. In *Mythologies*, Barthes suggests the political photo "has the power to convert" and goes into some detail revealing how politicians assemble images to sell themselves, to convince an audience of aptness and show credentials.[23] Photos examined here might be less overt than politicians' propaganda, yet work in similar fashion. We see the world as the photographer wishes us to see it: we look at a world through a specific set of German eyes that reveal a time and a place. In the case of both photos—and of photos of the genre more generally—the viewer projects into them what the photographer expects (or hopes); in this way the photo has a function, "to inform, to surprise, to cause to signify, to provoke desire."[24] The onlooker is educated by the photo and gets to know something about the educator. A triadic symbiotic relationship arises: the viewer learns about the subject matter, and, in doing so, comes to understand, in some measure, the photographer. In this case, the German

---

21 Crane, "Choosing Not to Look," 309.
22 Ibid., 320.
23 Roland Barthes, *Mythologies*, trans. Annette Lavers (London: Vintage Classics, 2000), 91–93.
24 Ibid., 28.

gaze seeks to show the power relationship between Germans and the victim; in the process, without even seeing the person behind the camera, we gain insight into the photographer. We learn something about their gender, race, mindset, politics, hobbies and interests, profession, family life, their dress, what they eat and drink, and their dislikes.

Knowledge is literal and connotative: we can see these things and we can read into these images. Barthes goes on to highlight aspects of the photograph that he calls the *studium* by introducing the notion of the *punctum*, those moments in the photo that "shoot out of it like an arrow, and pierces me. . . . A photograph's punctum is that accident which pricks me (but also bruises me, is poignant to me)."[25] When Hirsch and Spritzer discuss photos taken of a Jewish population walking in pairs or in small groups down a street in an Eastern European city, the *punctum* is that moment that arrests your gaze and your imagination. In these photos of European Jewry, this moment might be the yellow star pinned to the clothing. The viewer is "pierced" by a small detail that "annihilates the rest of the image"[26]: the abnormal in an otherwise normal scene. The *punctum*, writes Barthes, "changes my reading, that I am looking at a new photograph, marked in my eyes with a higher value."[27] The street photo conveys, on an initial viewing, two or three people from a certain period enjoying a day out. At that moment of piercing, when we spy the yellow star, the photo invokes another narrative, one that undermines and revises initial readings.

If we look to the two photos in this study, there are moments in either that indicate this *punctum*, such as the SS uniform, and yet the *punctum* is not what is shown, but what is not shown. The photos' secondary narrative, their encoded meaning, destroys the innocence or normalcy of the images. The photo tells, without literally showing, that death awaits the Jewish men, or that these SS men are the killers. Such images invert Barthes' concept of the *punctum* for they reveal the photos' hidden intentions; agendas pushed just out of view of the audience. For an onlooker to decipher these encoded messages, the *punctum* needs to be there, somewhere. To the unfamiliar, the men in uniform are just men in uniform in an old photo, and while some may gawp over the fact that these individuals are part of the infamous SS, there is little to signal their actual roles. Similarly, while the photo of the Jewish men reveals the Holocaust, the true situation lies just beyond the frame of the photo itself. So there is a need to negate the image as seen at face value, otherwise misread-

---

25 Barthes, *Camera Lucida*, 27.
26 Ibid., 20.
27 Ibid., 26–27.

ing occurs. The *punctum* needs to deflate the nefarious gaze that privileges the German. Similarly, a certain embedded pathos is present in these photos, one not necessarily accentuated by the visible content. Sympathy should be extracted rather than nationalistic pride, but this is not so easy without that *punctum*. Crane argues that, "with atrocity images, we have tended toward preservation as if by moral imperative, but if that choice means retention of, and indeed conservation of, the Nazi gaze, we should consider the alternatives."[28] The inclusion of the *punctum* allows for a more nuanced and ethical positioning, less binary in its approach to Nazi images than noted in Crane's suggestion, and provides a more general audience, those without the scholarly background, the encoded knowledge that bruises, internally ruptures, and pierces. The alternative to this *punctum*, Crane argues, is to "choose not to look" or to choose on behalf of onlookers the photos they should or should not view,[29] an idea undermined by the multitudinous amateur Nazi photos already present in the public domain.

The insertion of a *punctum*, a moment of acknowledgement that annihilates what comes before, serves two purposes. First, it draws an audience to the image, since surface level readings only attract a certain degree of interest. Second, the photo is contextualised, made to fit within the wider context of the Holocaust, thus providing a modern audience with an "honest" reading. Deny the photos their place in the Holocaust and take them solely to show Jewish men or men in uniform, and the true atrocity of what they represent stays hidden. This attempt to quash a viewer's initial experience would therefore negate some of the Nazi gaze when this gaze does not show the atrocity first-hand. What, though, of those many hundreds of thousands of photos not directly tied to the horrors, to the atrocities of the Nazi regime, yet are part of this "everyday" propaganda machine? What about those vernacular photos that show Nazi life?

Cultural memory and sympathy

The risk in providing amateur German photos currency as historical documentation is that they legitimate the Nazi perspective. "Legitimate" in that the emphasis currently placed on the Holocaust becomes sidelined, not consciously (though conscious decisions still antagonise in the form of Holocaust denial, for example), but because of an ulterior narrative. In the more banal photos of Nazi life, day-to-day existence is pleasurable and seemingly whole-

---

28 Crane, "Choosing Not to Look," 322.
29 Ibid.

some. There is, as mentioned before, nothing innocuous about these narratives, aside from their place in time and history as seen retrospectively. Revisionist narratives about the Holocaust have already emerged in other artistic and aesthetic endeavours, such as the genre of fiction, in book form, including *The Hand that Signed the Paper*.[30] In Helen Demidenko/Darville's novel, Ukrainian history is rewritten to privilege a Ukrainian family who work in, or marry members of, the SS. Originally touted as semi-biographical and told from the perspective of the Australian/Ukrainian granddaughter of these former SS, the writer eventually revealed she was British in heritage with no connection to this past whatsoever. By then the book had won two prestigious Australian literary awards and had sold multitudes of copies. With amateur photos, we could be seeing a similar movement in the popularity of internet realms that privilege a German gaze. Given the numerous amateur German photos for sale on the internet or in antique shops—due, possibly, to the death of family members whose possessions are not wanted—the social and cultural repercussions are multifaceted and complex. For example, what were once private photos are now in the public domain, which sanitises the true story behind the photo, while those who bore witness to the atrocities, whether victim or perpetrator, are no longer alive to provide context. Generational memory is shifting, and with it cultural and societal attitudes.

Associated with this trans-generational transmission is an assumption, writes Sontag, that the photo, in contrast to the painting or the novel (for example), intends to show and not evoke, suggesting objectivity. Photos are believed to be real-life moments that bear witness and are therefore "true." The audience might react with interest, but with a limited ability to decipher bias and subjectivity.[31] We have inured within us the belief that photos are factual representations of life moments that tend to contain fewer, if any, insinuations, especially if images are at a remove from politics and the press. Vernacular photos such as family holiday snaps, individual portraits, school mementos, photos of picnics and weddings are seemingly no place for politics. This attitude is coupled with the problem of temporal distance. We therefore, supposedly, do not question a photograph's intentions. Similarly, the distance between now and the event itself further lessens a photo's impact on contemporary psyches. And there has been, interestingly, mixed reaction from scholars regarding the potency of amateur Nazi images on a contemporary audience.

Exploring the divide between present and past in her discussion of post-

---

30 Helen Darville, *The Hand that Signed the Paper* (Sydney: Allen and Unwin, 1994).
31 Sontag, *Regarding*, 42.

Holocaust empathy, Dean suggests that distance might lead "to insufficient or disingenuous sympathy" by later generations.[32] Both Dean and Dominik LaCapra, among others, explore the notion of empathy post- Auschwitz and find the notion tenuous, yet for differing reasons. LaCapra writes that "empathy itself, as an imaginative component not only of the historian's craft but of any responsive approach to the past or the other, raises knotty perplexities, for it is difficult to see how one may be empathetic without intrusively arrogating to oneself the victim's experience or undergoing (whether consciously or unconsciously) surrogate victimage."[33] Here LaCapra suggests Nazi photos do privilege the victim, and yet the audience may adopt a position of "surrogate" victimisation, a somewhat nihilistic approach to another's suffering. Assmann notes a divergent stance in some approaches to Nazi images, suggesting photos of victims—including the trains and the camps—initially tokens of Nazi superiority, now evoke an antithetical and appropriate emotional response. She contends that "the same photos that had been taken in a state of utter lack of empathy with the victims [pre-1945] were suddenly charged [post-1945] with enormous empathy with the victims."[34] New generations who look at iconic Nazi photos or artwork in which Nazi images are incorporated, and see victimisation over perpetration, often reinvigorate sympathy for the victim, Assmann notes.

Conversely, Caroline Dean questions the role of Nazi photos and our modern-day social conscience, and though she looks specifically at photos of atrocity, one of the questions raised is pertinent when discussing "banal" Nazi images: do Nazi photos excite or numb us?[35] In answering this question, Dean looks to a gap identified by a group of "heterogeneous scholars" that separates "representation from responsibility . . . between emotional allegiance to empathy and a sense that this term [empathy] can no longer capture modern historical experience."[36] Dean examines three terms she believes question the legitimacy of empathy in contemporary Western society, and all three are products of post-Holocaust generations. She suggests that "expectancy, excitement, voyeurism . . . violate the dignity of memory by taking the historical event out of context, by appropriating it for our own pleasure and rendering meaningful empathy impossible."[37] While Dean looks at contemporary

---

32 Dean, *Fragility*, 3.
33 Dominik LaCapra, *History and Memory after Auschwitz* (Ithaca: Cornell University Press, 1988), 182.
34 Assmann, "Look Away," 136.
35 Dean, *Fragility*, 6.
36 Ibid., 7.
37 Ibid., 24.

artwork as a case study, and refers to processes of historiography more generally, these three ingredients are potentially implicit in the photos featured here. To collect these images and to post them on social media is an example of appropriation, for in either case there is some degree of nihilism and self-pleasure. There is something politically wilful in the reappropriation of amateur Nazi photos, and this approach mimics, to a degree, the initial intentions of the photographer. Furthermore, collecting Nazi photos can become a hobby that seemingly ignores peoples' fates. If fate were a consideration, some reference to the Holocaust, rather than none, might accompany amateur German photos found on numerous Instagram accounts. It might also be the case that, as we play a voyeuristic role, and knowing something of the Holocaust more generally, there remains a certain expectation placed on these photos: a contemporary audience expects a certain type of narrative rather than *the* historical narrative. These images, for example, excite by emphasising uniform over civilian or machinery over humanity, the battle rather than the casualties. Similarly, they highlight the "Germanic type" who dominates "Others." Expectancy, excitement and a voyeuristic element are not the products of a less than sympathetic contemporary audience, but the products of modern society more generally. James Dawes, in his publication *Evil Men*, argues that "empathy and the altruism effect . . . can be contingent on social constructs, artefacts of a particular society's way of socializing its subjects into collaborative prosocial behaviour, and they can nonetheless still feel as implacable as biology in shaping the lives of those subjects."[38] Empathy, according to Dawes, does not come naturally, and social conditioning establishes the preconditions for sympathetic outcomes or reactions.

Originally taken as a somewhat less blatant form of propaganda, Nazi amateur photos become historical artefacts in a global society where empathy is forced or false, and sympathy for those victimised might already be under stress. This poses a danger to the collective memory of the Holocaust or, at the very least, a problematic combination. Sontag believes that "remembering is an ethical act, has ethical value in and of itself. Memory is, achingly, the only relation we can have with the dead."[39] Similarly, Assmann writes that blocked empathy leads to blocked memory.[40] Given the photo's original intention, sympathy remains stalled and empathy becomes something of a hollow reaction, as the photographer's prerogative was neither. If sympathy/empathy were unintended, then the memorialisation of the victims might be altogether

---

38   James Dawes, *Evil Men* (Massachusetts: Harvard University Press, 2014), 197.
39   Sontag, *Regarding*, 103.
40   Assmann, "Look Away," 144.

negated. It could be difficult to inspire sympathy, much less empathy, when a contemporary reading of such images defers to the original gaze. Amateur German photos are not going to evoke large-scale emotional reaction that privileges the victim, as this was never their intention. Their pathos accentuates the victor: jubilation rather than humiliation, and so forth. What such images might do in their quantity and gaze is to remove an emotional reaction for the victim, and instead fascinate over the perpetrator. As Hirsch and Spitzer note, the incongruity of retrospectively adopting old photographs, "tell[s] us more about what we want and need from the past, than the past itself."[41] Here we might be witness to the onset of a new generation of memorialisation, helped by the Nazi photo that adds to current knowledge, but from a perspective with a dubious moral and ethical content. Oddly, the very thing these photos meant to do some years ago, might now be acting out.

Conclusion

While the normalising of the Nazi gaze seems a bleak forecast, amateur photos of the Reich do offer some alternate readings of this past, allowing further insight and investigation. They do show the history in a broader context and in highlighting atrocity there is always a victim: there cannot be one without the other. Amateur German images, therefore, are not without their reference to those victimised even if they never intended these photos to signal victimisation. The two photos used as case studies are, I believe, apt but somewhat extreme examples of the types of photography the Germans took with their small cameras. They show the murdered and the murderers, whereas most photos are content with day-to-day generalities. Vernacular showings of life in the Reich, though, are most potent when normalising the German viewpoint. The Holocaust is no longer a central feature, neither is war nor the carnage of battle. These amateur photos lack the *punctum*, and even locating them within the historical narrative of the time does little to provide the moment that "annihilates" the image. The two photos cited literally and figuratively refer to the Holocaust, and alongside those found in the Auschwitz album for example, they have a kinship to iconic images used to evoke post-Holocaust empathy. Ironically, the more macabre and telling of disaster, or the more iconic an image becomes—the more powerful the *punctum*—the more sympathy might be extracted from post-generations. Countless other photos, used as Nazi propaganda, though relatively boring in their content, show life under National Socialism to be convivial, healthy, productive and, even in times of war, rela-

---

41 Hirsch and Spitzer, "Incongruous Images," 23.

tively pleasant. These images are the more acceptable, for in them death is not apparent, nor is killing. They build an overall oeuvre that privileges normalcy over the macabre or iconic, but they do not call on an individual's imagination. They are possibly too dull for the modern audience, too normal for them to be of interest. And possibly this normality becomes their undoing as historical reference; cultural reappropriation and trans-generational shifts are less likely the outcome of the mundane. Similarly, though somewhat contradictory to this lack of excitement, amateur German photos fit within what Inga Clendinnen calls a strange opposition in relation to the Holocaust, a continuum "which begins with the familiar and extends to the profoundly strange."[42] This disparity is particularly true of images revealing everyday machinations of the Reich. Because, by their very historicity, their setting and subject matter (their Third Reich vernacularity), these photos are beyond a contemporary viewer's comprehension. That may be, among other factors, the strongest antidote to their potency. And yet while they show day-to-day life of the Third Reich, this in itself reveals a lack of normalcy, for life under Hitler's reign must have been anything but normal.

---

42 Inga Clendinnen, *Reading the Holocaust* (Melbourne: Text Publishing, 1988), 31.

FAITH AFTER GENOCIDE

Deborah Mayersen

Introduction

"And then one day, God replaced the light with the darkness."[1] In this way, Miriam Katin begins her account of surviving the Holocaust, presented in graphic novel format. For graphic novelists depicting genocide, like Katin, theological questions can be a pressing issue. Characters—and their authors—grapple with the seeming chasm between the existence of a benevolent deity and the occurrence of this most terrible of crimes. Where was God as genocide unfolded? Is it possible to have faith in its aftermath? This essay will examine how three graphic novels explore these complex and challenging issues. In many respects the graphic novels are very different: *We Are On Our Own* is a Holocaust memoir; *Smile Through the Tears* a non-fiction account of the fate of a Tutsi family during the Rwandan genocide; and *Deogratias* a fictional account of a perpetrator of the Rwandan genocide. Yet each pose searing questions about the role of God, and the role of organised religion, during genocide.

This analysis begins by briefly examining broader theological responses to genocide in the post-Holocaust period. It then explores the graphic novel as a space in which to depict and grapple with genocide. After introducing the reader to each of the graphic novels under discussion, the essay examines how each uses text and images to pose challenging questions about the role of God, and of organised religion, during genocide. It examines the anger and feelings of abandonment experienced by the protagonists as their prayers go unanswered. I explore their sense of betrayal as religious leaders prove corrupt and complicit with the genocidaires. My analysis shows how each grapples with deep theological questions about God's existence, nature and role during genocide. Finally, I reflect on how the three graphic novels each come to vividly contrasting conclusions.

---

1 Miriam Katin, *We Are On Our Own: A Memoir* (Montreal: Drawn and Quarterly, 2006), 5.

Theology after genocide

Theological debate about the role of God in the world, and particularly Jewish theological debate, was profoundly challenged by the Holocaust. Traditional Judeo-Christian conceptions of God as omniscient, omnipotent and omnibenevolent have always conflicted with a world in which pain and suffering exists, but for many this conflict became intolerable in the wake of the Holocaust. Survivors expressed their anguish in memoirs, none more famously than Elie Wiesel in *Night*:

> Never shall I forget that night, the first night in camp [Auschwitz], which has turned my life into one long night, seven times cursed and seven times sealed.
>
> Never shall I forget that smoke.
>
> Never shall I forget the little faces of the children, whose bodies I saw turned into wreaths of smoke beneath a silent blue sky.
>
> Never shall I forget those flames which consumed my faith forever.
>
> Never shall I forget that nocturnal silence which deprived me, for all eternity, of the desire to live.
>
> Never shall I forget those moments which murdered my God and my soul and turned my dreams to dust.
>
> Never shall I forget these things, even if I am condemned to live as long as God Himself. Never.[2]

Wiesel's anguished testimony reflects an unresolved inner turmoil about God in light of the Holocaust; a turmoil common to many survivor accounts. Survivors and religious scholars—Jewish and non-Jewish—have attempted to resolve this conflict in multiple ways. Some have proposed the death of God, or posited that God never existed at all.[3] Others, such as Richard Rubenstein, have suggested that the only logical response is to reject a God that has not protected His people.[4] Rabbi and theologian Eliezer Berkovits asserted that humankind's free will was dependent upon God remaining hidden; were God

---

2   Elie Wiesel, *Night* (1960; London: Fontana, 1972), 45.

3   Gabriel Vahanian, *The Death of God: The Culture of Our Post-Christian Era* (1961; Oregon: Wipf & Stock, 2009).

4   Richard L. Rubenstein, *After Auschwitz: History, Theology and Contemporary Judaism* (Baltimore: John Hopkins Press, 1992).

to intervene to curb humankind's capacity for evil, it would nullify free will.[5] Harold Kushner and others have taken that concept further, identifying a God that is not omnipotent and thus unable to intervene.[6] Explanations of the Holocaust as a punishment for sin have been proposed but widely rejected. Yet there has been no satisfactory resolution to this theological conundrum; no explanation has proven acceptable to a majority.

Ultimately, religious leaders have recognised that perhaps resolution is impossible. Rabbi Menachem Mendel Schneerson, the former leader of the Chabad Lubavitch branch of Judaism, stated that there "is no rational explanation" and that religious texts could provide no elucidation for the devastation of the Holocaust.[7] Pope Benedict XVI, when visiting Auschwitz, reflected: "In a place like this, words fail; in the end, there can only be a dread silence—a silence which is itself a heartfelt cry to God: Why, Lord, did you remain silent? How could you tolerate all this?"[8] For survivors of genocide, this remains an urgent question, a question without resolution but one that must be explored. It is this question that the graphic novels discussed in this chapter address.

Graphic novels and genocide

Graphic novels are a relatively new genre. Will Eisner's *A Contract With God*, published in 1978, is often regarded as the first graphic novel. Eisner sought to take the medium of comics and imbue it with literary content. Interestingly, the eponymous story in this collection of four shorter stories is one in which the protagonist grapples with theological anguish after the premature death of his adopted daughter. The genre is a diverse one, but is typically characterised by "juxtaposed pictorial and other images in deliberate sequence, intended to convey information and/or to produce an aesthetic response in the viewer."[9] That is, the narrative of graphic novels unfolds through both text and images, rather than exclusively through text. In doing so, graphic novels "generate narrative effects not available to non-pictorial novels."[10] For example, they provide unique spaces to pictorially represent the unspeakable; to portray contradic-

---

5   Eliezer Berkovits, *Faith after the Holocaust* (New York: KTAV Publishing House, 1973).
6   Harold S. Kushner, *When Bad Things Happen to Good People* (1981; New York: Schocken Books, 1989).
7   Menachem Mendel Schneerson, *Sefer HaSihot 5751*, vol. 1 (Brooklyn: Kehot, 1992), 233–34.
8   Pope Benedict XVI, "Pastoral Visit of His Holiness Pope Benedict XVI in Poland: Address by the Holy Father: Visit to the Auschwitz Camp," May 28, 2006, http://w2.vatican.va/content/benedict-xvi/en/=speeches/2006/may/documents/hf_ben-xvi_spe_20060528_auschwitz-birkenau.html.
9   Scott McCloud, *Understanding Comics: The Invisible Art* (New York: HarperCollins Publishers, 1993), 9.
10 Liam Kruger, "Panels and Faces: Segmented Metaphors and Reconstituted Time in Art Spiegelman's *Maus*," *Critical Arts* 29, no. 3 (2015), 358.

tion and conflict through disagreement between the words and texts in a panel; and to provide the reader with insight into the thoughts and feelings of characters through the literal depiction of "thought bubbles." Like other new genres, however, graphic novels have struggled for legitimacy and literary recognition, particularly when grappling with serious topics such as trauma.

The publication of Art Spiegelman's groundbreaking Holocaust graphic novels, *Maus I, A Survivor's Tale: My Father Bleeds History* (1986) and *Maus II, A Survivor's Tale: And Here My Troubles Began* (1991) accorded a new space and legitimacy to graphic novels about genocide. Maus, recounting the tale of Spiegelman's father's experiences in Auschwitz, yet unsettling the reader through its illustration of its characters as mice, cats and pigs, won the Pulitzer Prize and identified the graphic novel as a new medium for the exploration of extreme violence. Like *Maus*, graphic novels about genocide have typically adopted a creative, rather than journalistic style, and that is true of those examined herein. *Maus*, however, almost completely refrained from theological reflection on the Holocaust. Only in one small scene, in Auschwitz, is there arguably a theological component. In this scene, the character Mandelbaum prays: "My God. Please God . . . help me find a piece of string and a shoe that fits."[11] In a caption at the bottom of the cell, Spiegelman informs us matter-of-factly: "But here God didn't come. We were all on our own."[12] The narrative continues briskly, leaving little opportunity to reflect as to whether this was just a mechanism to inform the reader that Mandelbaum had to struggle on without string or a shoe that fits, or whether Spiegelman was offering a broader theological statement.

Since the publication of *Maus*, there has been a very small yet growing number of graphic novels depicting genocide. Despite this, graphic novels attempting to portray the experience of genocide remain marginalised and viewed as a somewhat experimental format.[13] The subject matter is one often perceived as at the limits of representation, that is, one in which there are serious challenges to compellingly describing or representing such horrific events within the limits of expression. The unconventional format can be perceived as provocative in overlaying an additional challenge to mainstream notions of historical representation. Moreover, graphic novels are rarely the subject of critical analysis.[14] Interrogations of the limits of portrayal, of the relationship

---

11 Art Spiegelman, *The Complete Maus* (London: Penguin, 2003), 189.
12 Ibid.
13 Deborah Mayersen, "One Hundred Days of Horror: Portraying Genocide in Rwanda," *Rethinking History* 19, no. 3 (2015), 359.
14 Hugo Frey and Benjamin Noys, "Editorial: History in the Graphic Novel," *Rethinking History: The Journal of Theory and Practice* 6, no. 3 (2002), 255.

between literary representation and truth, and of that between meaning and history, have typically focused on the functions of language and text, not images.[15] Traditional historiographical notions of representations of history have been challenged in recent decades, but the privileging of text over images "has remained relatively unquestioned."[16] Images have been regarded as too ambiguous, too emotive, too distant from their subject matter.[17] In the graphic novel in particular, they compress the elements of a sequence of events within frozen panels, distorting time and space.[18]

Yet there are also opportunities for alternative conceptualisations of the graphic novel that embrace the strengths of the format.[19] The emotive nature of graphic novel depictions of genocide, for example, can be perceived as promoting reader engagement rather than detracting from parochial notions of the primacy of "objectivity." Images can tell a tale of their own, depicting a complex and multilayered scene with a richness that text alone cannot. Moreover, the experimental nature of graphic novels makes them "good sites for 'thinking' about history and memory in a creative fashion."[20] I suggest they also offer valuable sites for exploring the raw and emotional issue of faith after genocide. The sparse text facilitates a directness in communication that quickly informs the reader of the theological anguish of protagonists. Speech bubbles enable the reader to literally "read the mind" of characters as they beseech or berate their God. The reader is thus privileged to access the innermost thoughts of protagonists in a way unlikely to be expressed through external communication. Biblical imagery, and images of churches, priests and prayer books provide context for the reader far more efficiently than could be achieved solely through text. Moreover, the inherently fragmented and incomplete nature of depiction within a graphic novel provides an almost ideal space for the sometimes conflicting, confused and unresolved nature of attempts to theologically grapple with genocide. In some ways the graphic novel also has a unique capacity to resist the impetus of purely written forms to reach a neat resolution in the concluding chapters.

---

15   Frank Ankersmit, *Meaning, Truth, and Reference in Historical Representation* (Ithaca, NY: Cornell University Press, 2012), 117, 124.
16   Jan Baetens, "History Against the Grain? On the Relationship Between Visual Aesthetics and Historical Interpretation in the Contemporary Spanish Graphic Novel," *Rethinking History: The Journal of Theory and Practice* 6, no. 3 (2002), 346.
17   Ibid., 345–56.
18   Jonathan Walker, "Pistols! Murder! Treason!" *Rethinking History: The Journal of Theory and Practice* 7, no. 2 (2003), 146.
19   Baetens, "History Against the Grain?" 346.
20   Hugo Frey, "History and Memory in Franco-Belgian *Bande Dessinée (BD)*," *Rethinking History: The Journal of Theory and Practice* 6, no. 3 (2002), 302.

Faith in the aftermath of genocide

This essay explores theological responses to genocide through three very different, yet in some ways surprisingly similar, graphic novels. *We Are On Our Own* is a memoir written by accomplished graphic novelist, Miriam Katin. While it tells her own story of survival during the Holocaust, she remembers none of the events she depicts. She survived as a toddler, and the tale she records is her journey with her mother, as her mother recounted it. Within the narrative she is depicted as Lisa. Lisa and her mother, Esther, became caught up in the Holocaust as it reached Budapest in 1944. With fake documents, they went into hiding to avoid deportation. They survived precariously in the countryside, fleeing on foot from place to place, staying just a few steps ahead of the German soldiers. Miraculously, Lisa's father Ka'roly also survived the war fighting for the Hungarian army. After the war they reunite and rebuild their lives. Alongside and within the compelling narrative of survival, Katin devotes substantial space to her exploration of the issue of faith, and the presence or absence of God during the Holocaust.

Smile Through the Tears is also a non-fictional account of the fate of one family during genocide. Author Rupert Bazambanza is a survivor of the Rwandan genocide, but it is not his own story that he tells, rather that of close family friends, the Rwangas. The Rwanga family is a Tutsi family with a long history of experiencing discrimination and persecution. The graphic novel presents their story within a narrative that also provides a broader account of Rwandan history. The Rwangas are a deeply religious Catholic family, but when they are targeted during the genocide, the Church offers no safe haven, and neither the UN, nor the international community provide protection. Ultimately only the mother, Rose, survives the genocide, while her husband and three children are killed. As the Rwangas experience genocide, the corruption of the Church is revealed. Yet while their faith is challenged and questioned, it provides ongoing comfort for Rose after losing her family.

Deogratias differs from *We Are On Our Own* and Smile *Through the Tears* in that it is a fictional account of the Rwandan genocide, and was not written by a survivor. *Deogratias* tells the eponymous story of a teenage boy and the community in which he lives. Deogratias is Hutu, and despite liking a Tutsi girl, becomes a reluctant perpetrator of the genocide. The author oscillates between scenes before, during and after the genocide, deftly utilising colour and darkness to alert the reader to these scene changes. In the aftermath of the genocide, such is Deogratias' distress that he morphs between human and dog-like forms as he loses his sanity. Many scenes in the novel are violent and shocking, and it provokes both horror and a strange compassion for Deogratias. A major theme within the narrative is the corruption and complicity of the Catholic Church during the genocide. Yet it also goes beyond critical examination of the Church, directly questioning the role of God in the genocide.

In many respects, *We Are On Our Own* and *Deogratias* can be interpreted as having been written as theological statements about God and genocide. That is, a core purpose—if not the core purpose—of each, is to explore the theological anguish created by the Holocaust and the Rwandan genocide. This is immediately evident from the titles of each graphic novel. The title *We Are On Our Own* is taken from a scene towards the end of the book, when Lisa's parents, Esther and Ka'roly, are reunited after the war. Esther joyously proclaims "Thank God that we are alive and together again," but for Ka'roly "God has nothing to do with any of this."[21] He questions, "How can you give thanks to a deadly sky?"[22] While Esther is shocked at Ka'roly's sacrilege, he insists, "We are on our own, Esther. That's all there is," as a young Lisa looks on.[23] The title *Deogratias* is similarly explicit in defining the theological focus of the graphic novel, albeit through irony. *Deogratias* literally means "thanks be to God," and is used as a Catholic given name in the region. There are also additional layers of depth within this choice. The term *Deo Gratias* is used during mass, a liturgical formula repeated after readings from the scriptures, and after communion. Thus, it is repeated after parishioners receive something, becoming a statement of gratitude in response to a gift. Into the title *Deogratias*, therefore, we can perceive an even deeper layer of irony in the aftermath of genocide.

Katin goes even further to immediately locate *We Are On Our Own* within a theological framework. The opening panel, a full-page cell in black with only a small square of text in the centre, begins "In the beginning darkness was upon the face of the deep"—a condensed version of the opening sentences of the bible.[24] The biblical rendition continues with God creating light. A series of panels slowly zooms out from the Hebrew text of God's name to a page of the Hebrew bible, then to Esther teaching a young Lisa the story of creation as they sit at the family table together. On the next page, the scene changes seemingly innocuously, to the view of a Budapest street out the apartment window. Across six panels, however, the pleasant view of buildings and blue sky is obscured by the approaching of a Nazi flag, until in the final image the black of the swastika blots out the view from the window completely. Text, written between the panels, states simply "And then one day, God replaced the light with

---

21 Katin, *We Are*, 117.
22 Ibid., 118.
23 Ibid.
24 Ibid., 3.

the darkness."[25] This highly evocative scene, placed even before the reader meets the protagonists of the graphic novel, identifies the fundamental place of theological anguish within the memoir. To suggest that "God replaced the light with the darkness" is effectively to hold God responsible for all that follows in Katin's experience of the Holocaust. Yet this is not a clear theme that emerges consistently. Rather, there is an ongoing tension between an anger at God—as expressed in this statement of blame—and the assertion that God does not exist. Underlying this tension are additional themes of abandonment by God and oblique references to divine malevolence.

In the first half of the graphic novel, themes of anger and abandonment dominate. For Katin, however, anger cannot be expressed directly. Instead, a muted fury appears in repeated images of a broken God, an evil God; images that can only be regarded as blasphemous. The reader is shocked out of the narrative by these intense scenes. In the first, a young Lisa is delighted to meet a new "doggie" friend when Esther finds refuge at a vineyard in the Hungarian countryside.[26] The dog is starving, but without enough food even for the people, there is nothing to feed it. Esther gives the contents of a chamber pot Lisa has just used to the dog. As the dog eagerly eats her waste, Lisa reflects "I am helping my bestest friend to eat. I am the God of my doggie."[27] Just a few pages later, Lisa confuses God with a Nazi commander. The commander arrives at the vineyard in search of good wine, meeting Esther while appropriating a supply. Attracted to her, he soon returns with a box of chocolates and carnal desires. As Esther is forced to comply, Lisa enjoys the chocolates in a different room, musing "Mmm. So Good. Such a Nice man. Maybe he is God. The Chocolate God."[28]

As Lisa and Esther struggle to survive the war, these profane scenes continue. When they seek refuge from bombs in a wine cellar, it is not God that can provide comfort but the wine. "God's only truth is inside these barrels. Give some to the child," says the vintner, and as Lisa is calmed by the alcohol she muses, "God is red. God is in the glass. . . . God lives inside the big barreeellsss."[29] Later, it is a doll of Saint Anthony that provides comfort in a storm—a striking blasphemy for a Jewish child.

As *We Are On Our Own* progresses there is a subtle shift in its theological focus. Slowly, hesitantly, the author begins to explore the possibility that God

---

25   Katin, *We Are*, 5.
26   Ibid., 34. Her previous pet dog had been forcibly confiscated by the Nazis.
27   Ibid.
28   Ibid., 42.
29   Katin, *We Are*, 50.

does not exist. As Esther and Lisa flee the vineyard in a storm, they discover Lisa's "doggie" friend shot by the approaching Russian soldiers. Lisa, just a few years old, experiences the loss of a second beloved dog. As she mourns, her reflection takes us back to the opening scene of the novel: "And then, somehow she knew that God was not the light and God was not the darkness and not anybody at all. Maybe, God was not."[30] Several pages later, Katin returns to this theme in one of the occasional scenes that flash forward to Lisa's adulthood. In this scene—depicted in colour rather than the drab greys of the wartime narrative—Lisa is herself a mother with her toddler son. We join the family mid-discussion, as the child's father insists he must go to Hebrew school "to learn the bible and the prayers the way I did."[31] As father and son go outside to play though, Lisa replies to the empty room "And so did I. I prayed and I prayed."[32] But in the poignant final panel in the scene the reader sees a downcast Lisa opening a bottle of wine as she continues "God, He turned out to be residing in a wine barrel."[33] Lisa's desire for, yet inability to find, comfort in a belief in God, is strikingly portrayed in this redolent image. In the second half of *We Are On Our Own* this emerging conclusion of the non-existence of God comes to dominate. Indeed, in the epilogue Katin remarks, "I could not give this kind of comfort, a comfort of faith in the 'existence of God,' to my children. I was unable to lie."[34]

Smile Through the Tears, like *We Are On Our Own*, also has moments in which the faith of the protagonists is severely tested. When Rose's husband Charles and two sons Wilson and Degroot are taken away to a certain death during the genocide, Rose cries out "God! What sin did we commit to warrant this?"[35] Later in the genocide, when Rose's daughter Hyacinthe is shot in front of her, she beseeches "God in Heaven! Why have you abandoned me?"[36] Yet in *Smile Through the Tears*, these questions arise only during times of crisis. The narrative operates within a framework of faith and prayer, and there are many references to trust and comfort in God. Even as Rose buries Hyacinthe after the *interahamwe* (Hutu militia) leave, she prays "May you be with God, my child!"[37] After the genocide, she reflects: "God! You gave me angels for

---

30 Ibid., 69.
31 Ibid., 84.
32 Ibid.
33 Ibid.
34 Ibid., epilogue.
35 Rupert Bazambanza, *Smile Through the Tears: The Story of the Rwandan Genocide* (Montreal: Les Éditions Images, 2006), 50.
36 Ibid., 59.
37 Bazambanza, *Smile Through*, 60.

children. I returned them to you as I received them. Knowing that I've fulfilled my task and done it well is my sole happiness today."[38] In the closing scene of the graphic novel, Rose visits a mass gravesite where she has been told her husband and sons were buried. She finds a child there, calling out to his parents whom he believes were buried alive. She comforts him: "Your parents suffer no more. Their souls have left this grave and gone somewhere marvellous!"[39] For Rose Rwanga, genocide has robbed her of her entire family, but not the comfort of a loving God.

In *Smile Through the Tears*, it is not faith in God that is tested and found wanting, but faith in the Church. The corruption and complicity of the Catholic Church emerges as a major theme of the narrative. As the genocide approaches, the reader gets the first hint of the issue. Degroot, in a conversation with his brother about the dangers of the *interahamwe*, notes that the Church is unlikely to offer protection.[40] Its leadership is associated with the MRND, the increasingly extremist Hutu political party of Rwandan President Habyarimana.[41] At the outbreak of the genocide, the failure of the Church to offer protection rapidly becomes clear in a series of scenes that take place at the *Centre d'éducation de langues africaines* (CELA), a school run by the White Fathers, Catholic missionaries. Rose and Hyacinthe seek refuge at CELA. At first they are warmly welcomed and given assistance so that the rest of the family can seek refuge there too. Just as they are seemingly safe under the protection of the White Fathers, the reader learns: "At that moment inside the CELA, the White Fathers considered their position."[42] Belgian soldiers have arrived in Rwanda to evacuate their compatriots, including the White Fathers. In the following panel, a warm yellow light radiates from above, signifying the presence of God. As a White Father packs his suitcase, a voice emanating from the warmth intones: "The good shepherd stays with his sheep when the wolves come!"[43] Nevertheless, the White Father replies: "Lord! I hear your voice but the flesh is weak. We lack the strength to do as You wish."[44] The following day, "every last one of the White Fathers left."[45]

It is not just the weakness of the White Fathers that is highlighted in the narrative, but also the active complicity of many priests. After the White Fa-

---

38 Ibid., 61.
39 Ibid., 64.
40 Ibid., 37.
41 Ibid.
42 Ibid., 43.
43 Ibid.
44 Bazambanza, *Smile Through*, 43.
45 Ibid.

thers leave CELA, the Tutsi that had gathered there seeking protection attempt to defend themselves from the genocidal onslaught. When Tutsi resistance at CELA is crushed, Rose and Hyacinthe are transferred to the nearby Sainte-Famille Church. There they are welcomed by Father Munyeshyaka, but it quickly becomes apparent he is acting in league with the *interahamwe*.[46] Father Munyeshyaka offers Hyacinthe "favours" in exchange for sex. When Hyacinthe refuses, she is targeted by *interahamwe* but manages to hide. Later, in a desperate bid to stay alive, Rose and Hyacinthe again seek the protection of Father Munyeshyaka, this time at his private apartments. When Hyacinthe continues to refuse his sexual advances, she is cast out and dies shortly thereafter. The complicity of the Church in the deaths of the Rwanga family is clear.

In *Deogratias*, as in *Smile Through the Tears*, the malevolence of the Church is a key theme. Very quickly, the centrality of the Church within the narrative is established. Images of the church are repeatedly used to signify a change of scene (for example pages 3, 28, 49–50 and 67). Images of the cross are everywhere. Yet they are confronting, not comforting images, often juxtaposed with depravity. In a darkly coloured scene from after the genocide, for example, a filthy, decrepit Deogratias sits directly under a cross outside his local church.[47] In the next panel Deogratias—now in a bright, full-colour scene from before the genocide—is secretly examining a magazine featuring erotica, his back turned to the church behind him. In school, meanwhile, Deogratias is taught the racist attitudes that led to the genocide under the image of the cross.[48] In these ways, the reader is continually drawn back to the Church as a central reference point, but in a manner that can provide no comfort.

Two of the main characters within the narrative are Father Stanislas, a white priest that has lived in Rwanda for decades, and Brother Philip, a newly arrived Belgian missionary. From the first image of Father Stanislas the reader is cued to suspicion by his severe expressions and the bottle-end thick glasses that obscure his eyes. Before the reader even learns his name, they hear of the rumour of a previous mistress and illegitimate child Apollinaria—now a beautiful young lady.[49] Brother Philip is presented as naïve but well-meaning, but he too acts improperly. Shortly after his arrival he gets terribly drunk on the local beer, and he is unable to keep himself from ogling Apollinaria.[50]

It is when the genocide erupts that the reader sees the true depths of the

---

46 Ibid., 53.
47 Jean-Philippe Stassen, *Deogratias: A Tale of Rwanda*, trans. Alexis Siegel (New York: First Second, 2006), 13.
48 Ibid., 17-18.
49 Ibid., 12.
50 Ibid., 35.

behaviour of these missionaries. At first it seems honourable. At the outbreak of the genocide, Father Stanislas and Brother Philip are depicted defending the church from a gang of *interahamwe* who are armed with guns, machetes and clubs. Behind them, Tutsi cower in the church for protection.[51] In the next scene, however, the missionaries are fleeing Rwanda in a convoy. Stanislas justifies his behaviour: "We did what we could, Brother Philip. We have to go now. Staying any longer would be suicide."[52] Brother Philip counters: "We could at least have tried to take Apollinaria."[53] It becomes apparent that not only has Father Stanislas abandoned the Tutsi seeking the protection of the Church, but he has made no special effort to protect even his own daughter.[54] The immorality of Stanislas sinks even lower when Apollinaria's mother, Venetia, comes across them in the convoy. "Where is Apollinaria? She's not with you?" Venetia demands to know.[55] Stanislas responds: "We had to leave her in the church. These . . . people prevented us from taking anyone with us."[56] For once his glasses are off and eyes clearly visible in a seeming display of sincerity, but the reader knows this is a complete lie. When Venetia arrives at the church shortly thereafter, the double doors are ajar. On one side of the door is the cross, on the other a pool of congealing blood.

Beneath the narrative exploring the culpability of the Church, a further and more subtle narrative exploring the role of God in the genocide can be discerned. In the scene described above in which Father Stanislas and Brother Philip defend the church against the *interahamwe*, for example, Father Stanislas responds to the armed men: "My children, my children, you can't think of desecrating the house of God."[57] Yet the reply he receives is "You don't understand Father. We're working with God. God loves justice."[58] The scene abruptly shifts to the convoy fleeing Rwanda; the reader does not get the opportunity to hear the missionaries' reply. Following the genocide, Brother Philip returns to Rwanda, somehow still naïve to the reality of the violence. A broken Deogratias cryptically recounts his role in the genocide to him, to which Brother Philip declares he will pray to God to forgive him. But Deogra-

---

51   Ibid., 59.
52   Ibid., 60.
53   Ibid.
54   Ibid. Throughout the narrative Stanislas neither admits nor denies being Apollinaria's father, but the rumour of his paternity is presented multiple times. Moreover, in the next scene, Apollinaria's mother Venetia appears to indirectly confirm his paternity of Apollinaria through implying he holds a special responsibility towards her.
55   Ibid., 61.
56   Ibid.
57   Ibid., 59.
58   Stassen, *Deogratias*, 59.

tias replies, "I don't need your forgiveness! Or the mercy of your god! . . . It wasn't a confession!"[59] Faith is now only relevant to Brother Philip, safely removed from the genocide.

It is the final scene of *Deogratias* that most powerfully challenges the role of God in the Rwandan genocide. It is a complex scene that can be interpreted in multiple ways, depicted through multilayered allusion.[60] In a dark climax, Deogratias—taking on the form of a dog in his distress—tries to poison Brother Philip while recounting his role in the genocide. Fortuitously, he is prevented from doing so when police swoop in and arrest Deogratias for previously poisoning a French soldier. As Deogratias is led away, an officer asks the shocked Brother Philip, "Friend of yours, that madman?" A downcast Brother Philip replies, almost to himself, "He was a creature of God."[61] The final three wordless panels slowly zoom out, from the exterior of the hotel, to the beauty of the setting sun, to a vast image of the stars in a dark night sky. These wordless images and the opening vista invite the reader to reflect upon this final statement. Does Brother Philip, secure in his faith, believe Deogratias was "a creature of God" in that all beings are divine creations, even those who have somehow gone astray? Or perhaps the reader can ponder a more insidious interpretation. If a creature of God is capable of murder, indeed of genocide, does the creator himself bear responsibility for this evil? A clue to interpreting this scene may lie much earlier in the graphic novel. When Brother Philip's parents visit him in Rwanda before the genocide, Apollinaria joins the family as a guide for a museum visit. As they explore an exhibit, she explains of traditional Rwandans: "because they did not yet know our Lord Jesus Christ and the greatness of His love, they believed the spirits of the dead filled the underworld, where they schemed spitefully against the living; and at night they lit up the sky over Rwanda."[62] According to a traditional Rwandan interpretation, the reader is thus informed, the stars represent malevolent spirits. As the reader reflects on the starry night sky, Stassen's ambiguous conclusion may be suggestive of a malevolent divinity above.

The conclusion of *We Are On Our Own* is no less powerful. If, for Stassen, the God that allowed the Rwandan genocide is evil, for Katin her experience of the Holocaust is evidence that God does not exist. The final scene of *We Are On Our Own*, like that of *Deogratias*, is complex. The joyous reunion of Esther with her husband Ka'roly is tempered by Ka'roly's assertion that God

---

59 Ibid., 76.
60 This style is reminiscent of Nobel prizewinning author Shmuel Yosef Agnon.
61 Stassen, *Deogratias*, 78.
62 Ibid., 44.

does not exist, only "a deadly sky."[63] As a young Lisa plays at their feet during this reunion, she re-enacts some of her traumatic experiences and reflects upon her unanswered prayers for her beloved dog Rexy to return.[64] The final panel refers back to a scene near the opening of the novel. Esther, in preparation for going into hiding, burns all evidence of their Judaism. While throwing pages of a Hebrew prayer book onto the fire, however, she is secretly observed by Lisa, who misinterprets the scene. "You burned him! Yo [sic] burned God! I saw it! I saw it!" cries Lisa.[65] At the time her mother replies "Hush! You can't burn God silly. He will be with us everywhere helping us. You will see."[66] In the final panel of the novel, however, after Lisa reflects on all of her traumatic experiences, she asks "And what if Mommy burned that God after all?"[67]

The concluding reflections in *Smile Through the Tears* contrast starkly with those of *We Are On Our Own* and *Deogratias*, and yet the reader is again deeply moved. Rose visits the mass grave where her son Wilson is supposed to be buried, and she is accompanied by Wilson's girlfriend. Wilson's girlfriend reflects: "Before he died, Wilson asked me to embrace life. To live and be happy! He said this would help him live in Paradise."[68] Rose affirms, "None of our loved ones who are now dead would wish us to live our lives in mourning. . . . You young people, your mission is to restore harmony so that your children never know the meaning of the words 'racial discrimination.' "[69] For Rose, it is not God that is responsible for the Rwandan genocide, "But its own people [who] have sullied this Eden."[70] What humankind has destroyed, it must attempt to rebuild.

Conclusion

The three graphic novels explored in this chapter, *We Are On Our Own*, *Smile Through the Tears* and *Deogratias*, are all very different. They span different genocides, different generations, and they divide between fiction and non-fiction. Yet each has successfully utilised the format of the graphic novel to pose searing questions about theology and religion during and after genocide. *Smile Through the Tears* and *Deogratias* hold the Catholic Church to account for its

---

63   Katin, *We Are*, 118.
64   Ibid., 119-21.
65   Ibid., 23.
66   Ibid.
67   Ibid., 122.
68   Bazambanza, *Smile Through the Tears*, 63.
69   Ibid., 64.
70   Ibid., 64.

complicity with the genocide in Rwanda. All of the graphic novels hold God to account. In Deogratias, Stassen questions whether divine malevolence enabled the genocide; for Katin the tentative explanation is divine absence. Yet Rose Rwanga is able to retain her faith in *Smile Through the Tears*, despite losing her husband and three children. In each case, the reader is taken on a deeply emotive journey. The graphic novel format provides a compelling medium and a unique space to explore unresolved, and perhaps unresolvable questions, concerning the existence and role of God during genocide. The inherently incomplete and fragmented nature of the medium challenges the reader to reflect on these unanswered questions. The authors have the space and ability to conclude in a manner that invites ongoing theological reflection. As these three masterful works demonstrate, the graphic novel provides an extraordinarily powerful medium for exploring the impact of genocide.

CAN THE AMERICAN ALLIANCE STOP COLLUDING IN GENOCIDE?

Winton Higgins

Be careful. Legal at State was worried about this yesterday—Genocide finding could commit [the US government] to actually "do something"—Office of the US Secretary of Defence, secret discussion paper on the Rwandan genocide, 1994.

After 9/11, President Bush asked, "Why do they hate us?" From Iran (1953) to Iraq *(2003), the better question would be, "Why would they not?"*— Chalmers Johnson, 2010.

The concept of genocide, and outspoken abhorrence for what it stands for, have arisen over the last hundred years on the back of Western sensibilities and legal initiatives. Yet since the end of World War Two, Western countries have typically failed to take action against actual or impending genocides, in spite of the growth of explicit legal and moral obligations to do so. Some Western countries have even avoided denouncing genocidal regimes, and failed to withdraw their economic and diplomatic privileges from them. In some cases Western countries have colluded with these regimes in ways that go beyond bystanderism, even if bystanderism remains the most ubiquitous and effective form of collusion in virtually all historical genocides.

In this essay I probe this gap between pious recoil from genocide in the abstract on the one hand, and passive and active practical collusion in genocide on the other. I will extend the concept of active collusion to include self-interested (overt and covert) overseas incursions, ones that sow the seeds of genocide by unleashing mayhem on a grand scale, and subvert the long-term project of creating an international rule of law, of which the prevention of genocide forms an integral part. I look at the provenance of the contradiction between pious recoil and practical collusion, and at the challenge of closing the gap between sanctimonious self-preening and effective responses to genocide. Genocidaires commonly commit cognate crimes, such as starting wars, and crimes against humanity like routinised torture. I will treat these crimes as contextually significant in this analysis, as they take their place in the currently intense assault on the international rule of law as a whole.

Few Western countries enjoy the military and economic heft to unilaterally tackle genocidaires in distant lands. Thus, the main moral responsibility for Western failure to do so falls on the American alliance, which does possess ample capability, and claims a leadership role in the Western world (even though the alliance from time to time also includes non-Western countries). Membership of what I call "the American alliance" refers to substantial military or diplomatic co-ordination with the US, whether under the auspices of formal alliances such as NATO and ANZUS[1]; ongoing intimate military, intelligence and economic ties, such as those that bind Saudi Arabia, the Persian Gulf emirates, and Pakistan to the US; or ad hoc co-belligerencies such as the US, British and Australian invasion of Iraq in 2003.

The core members of the alliance, however, are the US, Britain and Australia—the latter two having played follow-my-leader in virtually all matters of diplomatic and military significance that relate to creating the preconditions for genocide, and subsequent inertia towards it. The focus of this inquiry falls on America itself, which sets the agenda for the alliance that bears its name. This focus in no way exonerates the other members of the alliance for their collusion in "the crime of crimes."

To ensure coherence and keep the essay within reasonable limits, I take this investigation through three stages, each represented by a major analyst. In the first stage, Samantha Power's monumental *"A Problem from Hell": America and the Age of Genocide* accounts for the manoeuvres whereby American decision-makers have almost always evaded their moral and treaty responsibilities to confront genocide.[2] (Power's analysis has added force given that she was the US ambassador to the UN between 2013 and 2017.)

As a prelude to the second and third stages, I briefly introduce Steven Pinker's hypothesis that links the suppression of violence (including genocide) to the consolidation of democratic governance.[3] Since the American alliance has convincingly bucked this trend to suppress violence, I ask whether its democratic pretensions are now just as hollow as its commitment to "prevent and punish" the crime of genocide under the terms of the 1948 Convention on the Prevention and Punishment of the Crime of Genocide ("the Genocide Convention"), which the US and all its allies have either ratified or acceded to. Thus,

---

1 North Atlantic Treaty Organisation; Australia, New Zealand, United States Security Treaty.
2 Samantha Power, *"A Problem from Hell": America and the Age of Genocide* (New York: Basic Books, 2007).
3 Steven Pinker, *The Better Angels of our Nature: The Decline of Violence in History and Its Causes* (London: Allen Lane, 2011), 194.

in the second stage of the investigation, I place these sins of omission in the wider context of America's robust real-world foreign relations, and the nature of its domestic polity today. Our preliminary guide here is the late Chalmers Johnson in his so-called "blowback trilogy" and its sequel.[4]

In the third stage, I invoke Colin Crouch's "post-democracy" thesis. It highlights currently profound but less obvious democratic deficits in the core members of the American alliance—deficits that obstruct the emergence of a political will to meet moral and legal obligations in the face of today's genocidal threats.[5]

The US and genocide since World War Two

During the years from 1941 to 1949, the US proved itself on the world stage, not just as a military leader in the struggle against tyranny, but also as a moral and jurisprudential pioneer of a new international order based on the rule of law—one with the criminalising of aggressive war, foreshadowed in the 1941 Atlantic Charter, as its centrepiece.[6] These years saw the development (in the Pentagon, under the auspices of the US Department of War) of the jurisprudence that underpinned the Nuremberg trials of 1945–1949—themselves American initiatives that essentially created modern international criminal law.[7]

Raphael Lemkin coined the word "genocide" as a refugee in the US in 1944. It gained its first official airing in the indictment of October 1945 that triggered the first Nuremberg trial of Nazi leaders, which began in the following month under international auspices. This trial established the crime of aggressive war and crimes against humanity in international law. It set a precedent that stripped state perpetrators and their underlings of the automatic impunity that the institution of national sovereignty had previously afforded them. The erstwhile "prophets unarmed" of human rights now held a potential weapon in their hands: offences against these rights were now justiciable

---

4   Chalmers Johnson, *Blowback: The Costs and Consequences of American Empire*, 2nd ed. (New York: Holt Paperbacks, 2004); Chalmers Johnson, *The Sorrows of Empire: Militarism, Secrecy, and the End of the Republic* (New York: Metropolitan Books, 2004); Chalmers Johnson, *Nemesis: The Last Days of the American Republic* (New York: Metropolitan Books, 2007); Chalmers Johnson, *Dismantling the Empire: America's Last Best Hope* (New York: Metropolitan Books, 2010).

5   Colin Crouch, *Post-Democracy* (Cambridge: Polity, 2004).

6   In paragraph eight of the charter, President Franklin Roosevelt and Prime Minister Winston Churchill declared that "all nations of the world . . . must come to the abandonment of the use of force." See Philippe Sands, *Lawless World: Making and Breaking Global Rules* (London: Penguin, 2006), 8–9. As he points out, the charter inspired the emergence of the nascent "united nations" on the Allied side during the war.

7   Telford Taylor, *The Anatomy of the Nuremberg Trials* (London: Bloomsbury, 1993), 21–42; Colin Tatz and Winton Higgins, *The Magnitude of Genocide* (Santa Barbara: Praeger, 2016), 174–77.

and punishable. Twelve follow-on trials in Nuremberg, under purely American auspices, cemented the precedent. The UN General Assembly affirmed the status of the "Nuremberg principles" in 1947 as part of international law, and tasked the International Law Commission to formulate them in precise legal terms, which the latter published in 1950.[8]

In May 1945, the US hosted the founding congress of the United Nations in San Francisco. Its charter's opening words declare the intention to save future generations from "the scourge of war" and to defend human rights. In the years immediately following, Eleanor Roosevelt chaired the fledgling UN Human Rights Commission and presided over the drafting of the Universal Declaration of Human Rights (UDHR) on the shores of Lake Success, New York.[9] It was duly adopted by the UN in 1948, together with the Genocide Convention, the first signatory of which was the US itself. The UDHR created rights that inhered in all human beings without exception, not as "gifts" that could be withdrawn by political authorities.[10]

Taken together, these American-led innovations laid the basis for an *international rule of law* that set its face against warmongering, genocide, and a host of other human rights abuses. For America itself, the 1940s set a benchmark in its contribution to a safer, more orderly world. This project brought together existing legal concepts that stretched back as far as the 1215 Magna Carta, which proscribed arbitrary imprisonment and prescribed access to fair courts of justice and the liberty of the subject (*habeas corpus*). The pre-existing elements also included international humanitarian law to be applied in wartime, such as the Hague Conventions that emerged from 1899.

In the years following the late 1940s, under UN auspices, new conventions and treaties kept up this momentum towards an international rule of law focused on universal human rights. "Universal" meant what it said: no individuals fell outside their ambit, and the rights themselves constrained the actions of states even beyond their sovereign territories.[11] The new provisions included the four Geneva Conventions of 1949, the International Convention on Civil and Political Rights (in force from 1976), the 1977 Geneva Protocol I, and the 1984 Convention against Torture. The elements of the new international rule of law spelled out the special rights of women, children, prisoners of war, refugees, and people with disabilities, as well as criminalising tor-

---

8   The text of the seven Nuremberg principles appears at http://deoxy.org/wc/wc-nurem.htm.
9   Mary Ann Glendon, *A World Made New: Eleanor Roosevelt and the Universal Declaration of Human Rights* (New York: Random House, 2001).
10 Sands, *Lawless World*, 152.
11 Ibid., *Lawless World*, 150-53.

ture.¹² The strengthening of this overall international legal framework seemed (and still seems) to offer the best hope of suppressing genocide.

From this vantage point, the US's subsequent relentless subversion of its own civilising project, the international rule of law, appears all the more startling. From 1949, American foreign relations began accelerating in the opposite direction, as if the Nuremberg trials, their jurisprudential achievements and later ramifications, had never seen the light of day (least of all in the Pentagon itself, where the Nuremberg principles were generated). I will have more to say on this about-face in the second section of this essay.

Having been the first country to *sign* the Genocide Convention, it took the US 40 years to *ratify* it. Even then it hedged its ratification with so many "RUDs" (reservations, understandings and declarations) that even the UK—along with 21 other Western countries—formally opposed them.[13] The RUDs rendered the Convention a dead letter in American law and policy formation from the start. But as we shall see, US abhorrence towards genocide was strictly rhetorical up to ratification, and remained so afterwards, with no echo in the practice of American foreign relations. Of the 18 subsequent international human rights conventions and protocols, the US has ratified or acceded to just five.[14]

The successful resistance from within the US to the accumulating international human rights provisions (including the Genocide Convention) has rested on a vociferous defence of national sovereignty, which its own Nuremberg legacy had subordinated to the international rule of law. As we shall see, the thrust of US foreign policy during and after the Cold War has been to assert US sovereignty at the expense of the international rule of law *and* the national sovereignty of other countries. It is the only Western country to spurn the International Criminal Court (ICC—the successor to the International Military Tribunal in Nuremberg in 1945–1946). In its first years, the GW Bush Administration vilified the ICC, even legislated to criminalise co-operation with the court's investigations, and empowered the President to take military action against the court if any US official is ever brought before it.[15]

---

12 Ibid., 146-53. Sands summarises the historical development of the relevant international law. As he points out on page 152, the Fifth Amendment (guaranteeing due process) to the US Constitution provided key terms in which the new rights were expressed, starting with articles 10 and 11 of the UDHR.

13 Power, *"A Problem,"* 163–69. Denmark, Estonia, Finland, Greece, Ireland, Italy, Mexico, the Netherlands, Norway, Spain and Sweden also lodged formal objections to the RUDs attached to the US ratification.

14 Office of the UN High Commissioner for Human Rights at http://indicators.ohchr.org. For instance, the US is the only member of the UN that has not ratified or acceded to the Convention on the Rights of the Child (in force since 1990).

15 The *American Service-members' Protection Act*, 2002, informally known as "The Hague Invasion Act." See Sands, *Lawless World*, 62–63; Tatz and Higgins, *The Magnitude*, 187. Power, *"A Problem,"* 491, gives pro-

American policy-makers' nonchalance towards what came to be known as genocide goes back a century, to 1915 when the Armenian Genocide began. The US Ambassador to the Ottoman Empire, Henry Morgenthau, kept his government well informed of the genocide's progress, yet the US refused to sign the joint British, French and Russian protest of May 1915 against "these crimes against humanity and civilisation." Under the doctrine of national sovereignty, US policy-makers reasoned, the Turks' slaughter of their own Armenian compatriots was no concern of other states, not least ones like the US that enjoyed good trading relations with the perpetrator state.

"America's nonresponse to the Turkish horrors established patterns that would be repeated," Power writes. "Time and again the U.S. government would be reluctant to cast aside its neutrality and formally denounce a fellow state for its atrocities."[16] Thus US backsliding from the 1950s constituted a return to the status quo ante (although, as we will see in the next section, there was more to it than that). However, the standard excuses did not apply during the Holocaust, when the US and Britain failed, in spite of vociferous lobbying, to bomb the death factory in Auschwitz- Birkenau and the railway leading thereto.[17]

Samantha Power presents us with the history of a protracted non-event—the US's and its allies' failure ever to "put boots on the ground" to stymie highly publicised and enormously destructive genocides in the second half of the twentieth century. Two of them—targeting non-Serbs in the former Yugoslavia, and Tutsis in Rwanda—occurred after the Cold War ended, when the US was the world's sole superpower facing no appreciable threats elsewhere. The bystander policy persisted despite the fact that the Indian army (in East Pakistan in 1971), the Vietnamese army (in Cambodia in 1979), and a Tutsi rebel militia, the Rwanda Patriotic Front (in 1994), had demonstrated how limited military action can stop major genocidaires in their tracks.[18]

US inertia is all the more astonishing when we consider the enormous relative size of the country's military establishment, which it has maintained since the Cold War began. Today America's military spending accounts for 39 per cent of global military expenditure. At 596 billion USD, annual US military expenditure exceeds the aggregated military expenditure of the seven next-largest military powers. Its armed forces (excluding reservists and the

---

tectiveness of national sovereignty as the reason for US refusal to join the ICC, but given the circumstances reviewed in the second part of this essay, a far stronger motive is the one that the 2002 Act indicates: (well-grounded) fear of US officials being indicted for gross infringements of international criminal law.

16 Power, *"A Problem,"* 13.
17 Tatz and Higgins, *The Magnitude*, 147–49.
18 Ibid., 100–02; Power, *"A Problem,"* 141.

"civilian" CIA) comprise over 1.3 million personnel, 666 overseas bases (just part of its 103,270 overseas "assets" that encircle the world).[19] Yet during the 1994 Rwandan genocide, this colossus even turned down a desperate request to use its technical capability to jam Radio Mille Collines, which was the main means used to incite and co-ordinate the genocide. US policy-makers saw this request as involving an unwarranted diversion of American resources.[20]

The Indian, Vietnamese and domestic Rwandan military actions remain our only post-war examples of troop deployments to stop genocide, apart from token UN peacekeeping missions. These aside, NATO (including US) bombers targeted genocidal Bosnian Serb forces for three weeks in 1995, long after their predicted and widely publicised atrocities in Srebrenica and other designated UN safe havens. NATO bombers raided Serbia itself, as well as its forces in Kosovo in 1999, when that country resumed genocidal attacks, this time against ethnic Albanians in the province in question.[21] These aerial campaigns exhaust the American alliance's record of anti-genocidal military actions, and were not complemented by troop deployments.

As noted above, bystanderism is a powerful—and indeed indispensable—form of collusion in genocide, one that emboldens actual and potential genocidaires. Their ilk has learned from experience in virtually all cases that they have nothing to fear from the American alliance, whatever the identity and party affiliation of the sitting US president.

But American collusion has sometimes tipped over into active support for genocidal regimes. In 1979–1980 the US government continued to provide the genocidal Khmer Rouge regime with diplomatic legitimation in the UN, long after its atrocities had become common knowledge, and even after the Vietnamese had ousted it from Cambodia itself. (Quite apart from the issue of arch-criminality, under longstanding international law a regime should not receive diplomatic recognition if it no longer controls the country it claims to represent.) In the 1980s the American government strenuously defended Saddam Hussein's regime in Iraq, armed it, and provided it with substantial economic credits, at the same time as the latter was gassing and massacring its Kurdish population (as well as using gas and chemical weapons against Iranian troops in the Iran-Iraq war).[22]

---

19 Figures taken from the Peter G. Peterson Foundation, and the US Defence Department's most recently available *Base Structure Report* for fiscal year 2012, 7–8. These figures probably grossly underestimate actual overseas US bases and assets, as they do not, for instance, include the CIA's secret establishments: see Johnson, *Nemesis*, 137. He found 737 US bases on foreign soil in 2006.
20 Power, *"A Problem,"* 371–72.
21 Ibid., 440, 448.
22 Ibid., 146–54, 171–243.

The American media had access to written and photographic evidence of all the genocides mentioned above in real time, and the progressive outlets at least did not stint in airing it. Commentators and op-ed writers often excoriated the US government for its collusion in genocide. For instance, during the US no-show while genocide was raging in Bosnia, Leon Wieselter wrote in *The New Republic*:

> The United States seems to be taking a sabbatical from historical seriousness, blinding itself to genocide and its consequences, fleeing the moral and practical imperatives of its own power. . . . The American president is an accomplice to genocide. . . . The president of the United States does not have the right to make the people of the United States seem as indecent as he is. He has the power, but he does not have the right.[23]

In light of such spirited criticism from at least part of the American fourth estate, we have to ask how the US government has retained legitimacy in the absence of decency.

In answer to this question we can briefly extrapolate five governmental ploys from Power's account. The first one—best illustrated by the government's non-response to the Cambodian, Iraqi and Rwandan genocides—is to simply ignore the genocide. Not acknowledge it, not summon meetings of senior advisors, not find any place for it on the policy agenda. The second ploy is to trivialise the genocide, or present it as intractable, or both. When the first ploy began to fail in the Rwandan case, and again in the Bosnian one, this second one came into its own. US officials deplored mass death as a "tragedy" due to "war" that arose out of "ancient tribal hatreds"; it was a question of perennial internecine strife that no third force could possibly ameliorate, let alone end. Perpetrators and victims were equally to blame.

The third ploy consists in discounting the evidence. The relevant genocides all commanded widespread media coverage, while the US government had its own lavish sources of intelligence, including (since the 1980s) high-resolution satellite imagery. Yet officials described all reports of genocide as "unconfirmed," or "lacking specific detail," and thus insufficient to trigger intervention. The fourth ploy is the populist self-referential argument that a genocide does not threaten America's "vital interests," so no such interest is served by initiatives to stop genocide.

But the fifth, most practised ploy has been to forbid US officials' use of the word "genocide" itself—the dreaded "g-word." In extremis, officials could

---

23 Quoted in Power, *"A Problem,"* 430–31.

use weasel formulations such as "acts of genocide" and "tantamount to genocide," all of which fall short of plain genocide, with all the moral and legal imperatives it would attract. Power notes that some junior officials chafed at these shabby word games, hence the State Department maintained an internal "dissent channel" through which they could vent their frustration into the silence of the upper echelons without jeopardising their careers. In 1999 that department endured its third "g-word" controversy in six years, and for the first time it authorised the "tentative use" of the g-word 10 days before NATO began bombing the Serbs. At the same time, in a first for the US presidency, Bill Clinton referred to "deliberate, systematic *efforts at* genocide."[24]

Samantha Power comes to the counterintuitive—but ineluctable—conclusion that US policy towards genocide has hardly proved a failure:

> Simply put, American leaders did not act because they did not want to. . . . One of the most important conclusions I have reached, therefore, is that the U.S. record is not one of failure. It is one of success. Troubling though it is to acknowledge, U.S. officials worked the system, and the system worked.[25]

This insight brings more questions into view. What purpose does this perennial collusive policy serve? What other reasons of state (*raisons d'état*) does it make room for? Is "the system" that Power refers to just institutionalised moral nihilism, or is it a sub-assembly in a more encompassing system? What is the US's gargantuan military establishment *for* (given that genocide prevention clearly lies outside its remit)? Under what conditions could the political will to prevent and punish genocide arise—thus reversing the current longstanding bystander policy?

To answer these questions we have to go beyond the narrow disciplinary confines of genocide studies, to consider the rationale of America's post-war relationship to the wider world, and the actual (as opposed to rhetorical) nature of its political culture and system.

Empire versus law and democracy

America's inertia in the face of genocide stands in stark contrast to its habit of intervening—frequently, brutally, and uninvited—in the affairs of many other

---

24 Power, "*A Problem*," 467–68. Quote on 468, emphasis added.
25 Ibid., 508.

countries in pursuit of its "vital interests." In the wider context of American foreign relations, these extremes—of inertia on the one hand, and multiple trespass on the other—constitute the two sides of the same imperial coin. As against the US's near-zero score for military operations to stop an ongoing genocide, between the end of World War Two and 9/11 in 2001 it mounted over 200 overseas military incursions—typically unprovoked,[26] usually from one or several of its hundreds of overseas military bases noted above. And since 9/11, the American alliance has invaded Afghanistan and Iraq, sparking still-ongoing wars, massive humanitarian crises, and genocidal risks that have drawn in several neighbouring countries, either as unwilling battlefields or willing participants. Thus, traditional US isolationism certainly does not explain that country's absence from the struggle against genocide.

In our recent book, *The Magnitude of Genocide*, Colin Tatz and I dedicate a chapter to pondering Steven Pinker's thesis that violence (including war and genocide) has tended to decline over the last five millennia, and that the decline in question has steepened in the modern era. Pinker plausibly considers the factors that have contributed to this trend, including democracy.[27] "The idea of democracy, once loosed upon the world, would turn out to be one of the greatest violence-reduction technologies since the appearance of government itself," he writes.[28] War has profound negative impacts on political communities that, if empowered through genuinely democratic representation, inhibit warmongering. Most if not all democratic polities recoil from genocide.

The core members of the American alliance conventionally pass for fully-fledged democracies, yet they demonstrably have no interest in meeting their moral, legal and treaty obligations to curb genocide. At the same time, they have repeatedly initiated war and disturbed the peace in other countries—in flagrant contravention of post- Nuremberg international criminal law—thus sowing the seeds of future genocides. If we assume for the sake of argument that Pinker's general claim for democracy holds water, we must now look more critically into the democratic credentials of the American alliance. I will turn to the travails of American democracy below, and to those of Western countries in general in the next section.

Self-evidently American democracy rests on its 1787 Constitution—the inspired work of framers steeped in Enlightenment thought (especially Montesquieu's), the history and constitution of the Roman Republic (509–27

---

26   Johnson, *Nemesis*, 2007, 18; Johnson, *Dismantling the Empire*, 56. And see the list of US military incursions at http://academic.evergreen.edu/g/grossmaz/interventions.html.
27   Tatz and Higgins, *The Magnitude*, 191–225; Pinker, *The Better Angels*, 2011.
28   Ibid., 194.

BCE), and the development of English common law with its reigning concept of the rule of law. The venerable civic-republican tradition united the Constitution's framers on the side of freedom understood as popular self-rule, as against tyranny understood as the capricious, hubristic rule of one individual or a closed cabal. The framers adopted Montesquieu's schema of the separation of powers—legislative executive, and judicial, *in that order*—to provide the checks and balances to prevent tyranny. The legislature in which "we the people" were represented was to take pride of place.

Acutely aware as the framers were of the historic link between tyranny and warmongering, they vested the power to declare war exclusively in the legislature. "Of all the enemies of true liberty, war is, perhaps, the most to be dreaded, because it comprises and develops the germ of every other," declared James Madison (sometimes dubbed "the Father of the Constitution") in 1795.[29] The framers insisted that all expenditure of public funds be publicly accounted for, as just one aspect of every citizen's essential right to know what public officials are doing, how and why. Without that knowledge, the public cannot make informed decisions and exercise popular sovereignty over those in positions of power. The framers bolstered the rule of law by insisting that treaties, once duly entered into, constitute part of the law of the land. The fourth amendment to the Constitution protects citizens' privacy from "unreasonable" searches and seizures by agents of the government, while the fifth guarantees due process.

At this point Chalmers Johnson's analysis becomes relevant. Apart from his long career as a prominent American political analyst, he served as a naval officer during the Korean War, and as a consultant to the CIA between 1967 and 1973. He identified with the US republican tradition and its constitutional basis, but entertained dire fears for American democracy and constitutional observance in the post-war era, not least since 9/11. I will briefly extrapolate the main arguments from his four relevant books.[30]

In the post-war period four factors have driven the US to develop its "empire of bases," the present colossal extent of which is sketched above. The first factor was "military Keynesianism"—the maintenance of high levels of military spending to stimulate manufacturing, general economic activity, and employment in the domestic economy.[31] The second factor was Cold War rivalry with the Soviet Union. Clearly, these two factors have reinforced each

---

29 Quoted in Johnson, *Nemesis*, 18. This sentiment foreshadows Pinker's thesis (mentioned above) that democratic governance constitutes an anti-violence "technology."

30 See note 4. Of these, the third book is perhaps the most comprehensive.

31 Johnson, *Nemesis*, 271–78.

other. The third factor was US dependence on imported oil, not least from the Middle East. Together these factors drove US military self-projection onto the world stage. They led to the hundreds of military incursions into foreign countries mentioned above, many of which were clandestine and kept secret from the American public—at least until well after the event.

This pattern led to a fourth, fateful imperial dynamic: "blowback." The CIA coined this term as a contribution to its own tradecraft in 1953, after one of its early staged coups against a democratic but inconvenient foreign government, that of Iran. The term arose from the insight that such gross trespass in the affairs of other countries could visit negative consequences on the US itself. Johnson elaborates the concept to extend it to its effects on US domestic politics. When the blowback comes, the American public is not able to put it into context, given the clandestine nature of the original American provocation, which it knows nothing about. Blowback—attacks on US military assets, embassies and citizens overseas, and eventually on the US itself on 9/11—thus appears to the American public as gratuitous aggression. It fuels popular mobilisation around hefty US retaliation, culminating in the invasions of Afghanistan and Iraq in 2001 and 2003 respectively, and the heady warlike mood at home.[32] Seen in this light, blowback is not simply a question of one-off events, but a vicious circle that puts the US and its core allies on a more or less permanent war footing against a growing list of sworn enemies. The President's role as the executive of a constitutional democracy gives way to his status as Commander-in-Chief of the armed forces in (real or rhetorical) wartime—a commander in whose office the twin phenomena of empire and militarism converge.

James Madison's "dread" of war as a threat to the republican order was thus prophetic. In the latter half of the twentieth century and in the current one, a republican presidency has morphed into an "imperial presidency" that comprehensively denies the citizens' right to information, and overrules the legislature, the rule of law, and the judiciary.[33] All the features of the Constitution mentioned above have been effectively curtailed, its checks and balances now little more than ritualistic relics. Government has sunk ever more deeply into illegality, such as holding prisoners indefinitely without trial

---

32 Johnson, *Nemesis*, 278.
33 The US presidency has developed the practice—energetically deployed by GW Bush—of issuing "signing statements" when signing congressional bills into law. In these documents, the President purports to suspend or modify the effect of the bill. This mechanism means that he can frustrate the legislature's intent without issuing a formal veto, which could in turn be overruled by a two-thirds majority in Congress: Johnson, *Nemesis*, 248, 257–60. The practice quashes the fundamental point in the Constitution (Article 1), that Congress shall have exclusive power over legislation.

under grotesquely inhumane conditions; routine, officially sanctioned kidnapping and torture; and spying on the American citizenry—again flouting the Constitution, treaties duly entered into, and domestic law.[34]

The main cause (as well as effect and beneficiary) of this fall from legal and democratic grace has been the CIA itself. It began life in 1947, as a replacement for the Office of Strategic Services, which had played a progressive role, for instance, in servicing the American prosecution in the first Nuremberg trial of 1945–1946. In contrast, the CIA has been set up to serve the President only, by supplying intelligence and assessments of threats to US security, and undertaking subsidiary "operations." It soon became (in Johnson's term) the President's secret private army, as its "operational" functions overtook its intelligence-gathering ones.[35] No president has been able to resist using it as a private army. In the year of its establishment it interfered in Italian politics. Two years later it toppled the democratic government of Syria (destroying that ill-fated country's first and arguably last chance of attaining stable, peaceful democratic government) in order to advance the interests of the Arabian American Oil Company (Aramco).[36]

The CIA's orientation and main modus operandi were now set. It has directly or indirectly unseated a long list of democratic governments, replacing them with brutal despotisms, among other places in Iran (as noted), Guatemala (1954), Indonesia (1957–1958), Brazil and South Korea (both in 1961), Greece (1964), Ghana (1966), the Philippines (on multiple occasions), and Chile (1973). The CIA's obsession with regime change has rubbed off onto senior US policy-makers in general: it was the main motive behind the invasion of Iraq in 2003. The agency mounted the abortive 1961 invasion of the Bay of Pigs in Cuba, and made several attempts to assassinate Fidel Castro. Its secretiveness confers unaccountability and "plausible deniability" for all its transgressions on its one and only client—the US President.[37] As Johnson comments:

> The CIA remains the main executive-branch department in charge of over-

---

34 Johnson, *Nemesis*, 204–05, 254–45, 258–89. See also US Senate Select Committee on Intelligence, *Committee Study of the Central Intelligence Agency's Detention and Interrogation Program: Findings, Conclusions and Executive Summary* (Washington: US Senate, 2014); Sands, *Lawless World*, 205–23; Michael Hayden, *Playing to the Edge: American Intelligence in the Age of Terror* (New York: Penguin, 2016).

35 Johnson, *Nemesis*, 92–93.

36 Charles Glass, *Syria Burning: A Short History of a Catastrophe*, 2nd ed. (London: Verso, 2016), 20–23.

37 The authoritative history of the CIA is Tim Weiner, *Legacy of Ashes: The History of the CIA* (New York: Anchor Books, 2008)—the fruit of 20 years of research.

throwing foreign governments, promoting regimes of state terrorism, kidnapping people of interest to the administration and sending them to friendly foreign countries to be tortured and/or killed, assassination and torture of prisoners in violation of international and domestic law, and numerous "wet" exercises that both the president and the country in which they are executed want to be able to deny.[38]

In direct contravention of the Constitution, its entire budget (14.7 billion USD in 2013) is kept secret from the public and immune to congressional oversight—along with about 40 per cent of the overall US military budget.[39]

Long before 9/11—and as the essential precondition thereto—the CIA (in league with its British counterpart, MI6) launched its most fateful operation, in Afghanistan in July 1979. It armed and encouraged jihadi extremists, the *mujahideen*, to revolt against the secular, modernising pro-Soviet government that sought, among other things, to provide girls with schooling, which the extremists abhorred. The CIA aimed to lure the Soviet Union to come to the Afghani government's aid, whereupon the Soviets would bog down in a counter-insurgency and so get their own " Vietnam."[40]

The Soviet Union duly took the lure six months later, and the CIA and MI6 ramped up their aid to the *mujahideen*. The CIA's chief of station in Pakistan from May 1981, Howard Hart, took charge of clandestine operations in Afghanistan. As he himself paraphrased his superiors' orders, they were: "Here's your bag of money, go raise hell. Don't fuck it up, just go out there and kill Soviets, and take care of the Pakistanis and make them do whatever you need to make them do."[41] Among the beneficiaries of the CIA's tutelage and largesse was a promising young Saudi fanatic called Osama bin Laden: the CIA built him and his followers (al Qaeda) a base in Khost province in eastern Afghanistan.[42]

The sequel is well known: the Soviet Union suffered 15,000 war dead, and withdrew from Afghanistan in 1989, only to collapse in 1991. Mission accomplished, then. In the process, 1.8 million Afghanis were killed in the CIA-staged civil war, and 2.6 million became refugees. One jihadi element,

---

38   Johnson, *Nemesis*, 102.
39   We only know the size of the CIA budget thanks to the leaker Edward Snowden and the *Washington Post*. The US fields 16 intelligence services, which share 52.6 billion USD between them: http://www.bbc.com/news/world-us-canada-23903310. See also Johnson, *Nemesis*, 9.
40   Johnson, *Nemesis*, 110–11.
41   Steve Coll, *Ghost Wars: The Secret History of the CIA, Afghanistan, and Bin Laden, From the Soviet Invasion to September 10, 2001* (New York: Penguin, 2004), 33–35. Quote (from interviews with Hart) on 35.
42   Coll, *Ghost Wars*, 156–57.

the Taliban, seized control of Kabul in 1996, while another, al Qaeda, turned its attention (and CIA-sourced skills and weaponry) on the US itself.[43] Such is the backstory to 9/11 and today's ongoing wars in Afghanistan and Iraq.

Presidential fury and hubris after 9/11 unleashed the CIA from the few legal and moral restraints on it. As Commander-in-Chief in "wartime"—so designated by his "war on terror" slogan—President Bush claimed exemption from legal and constitutional compliance. As Philippe Sands argues, the administration's "war on terror" implied a "war on law"; it made "a conscious decision . . . to propel its assault on global rules."[44] Tyranny breeds lawlessness at home, too.[45] Kidnap and torture, which had hitherto been a small and furtive part of the CIA's operations, now became a major part of it, with the President's written approval. The US is a party to the 1984 UN Convention against Torture that (under the US Constitution) makes it part of the law of the land, so this entire programme was felonious even in American domestic law.

Nonetheless, the CIA began kidnapping large numbers of people from North America, Western Europe and the Middle East, and sending them to torture-friendly allied countries (Egypt and Syria in the main), and to its own "black sites" around the world, including its larger facilities such as Abu Ghraib, Bagram air base, and Guantánamo Bay. Bush declared the victims to be "bad people" and "unlawful combatants" to whom no legal protections whatever applied. They occupied (in Sands' term) a "legal black hole" that negated all applicable legal developments from Magna Carta to the present day.[46] Photographic, video and written accounts of the sadistic practices inflicted in this black hole flooded the world media. In all the facilities mentioned, the CIA oversaw the torturing of its captives to extract "intelligence."[47] (In a rare moment of self-assertion, the US Senate inquired into this "extraordinary rendition program" and found it to have been ill-conceived, poorly managed, and fruitless. But the public is still not allowed to see the Inquiry's full report, only a comparatively short summary.)[48]

---

43   Coll relates in 588-page detail the history of the US-led imbroglio in Afghanistan, and lays bare the CIA's brutality and incompetence therein.
44   Sands, *Lawless World*, xii, 153.
45   See Naomi Wolf, *The End of America: Letter of Warning to a Young Patriot* (Burlington, VT: Chelsea Green Publishing, 2007).
46   Sands, *Lawless World*, 143–73.
47   See Philippe Sands, *Torture Team: Deception, Cruelty and the Compromise of Law* (London: Penguin, 2008).
48   Two NATO members—Italy in 2005 and Germany in 2007—issued arrest warrants and extradition requests for 22 and 13 CIA agents respectively, for involvement in kidnap-and-torture operations within their jurisdictions: Johnson, *Nemesis*, 131–15; Matthias Gebauer, "Germany Issues Arrest Warrants for 13 CIA Agents in El-Masri Case," *Der Spiegel*, January 31, 2007, http://www.spiegel.de/international/el-masri-kidnapping-case-germany-issues-arrest-warrants-for-13-cia-agents-in-el-masri-case-a-463385.html. Readers with a taste for

The framers of the 1787 US Constitution would have recognised this pattern of constitutional, legal and democratic eclipse. They were acutely aware of the fate that overtook the Roman Republic that they so greatly admired. Having over-committed to territorial expansion and the militarism it entailed, the Republic signed its own death warrant by appointing Julius Caesar, a populist military hero, dictator for the years 49–44 BCE, and then dictator for life. The stage was then set for the long-lived imperial absolutism first exercised by Caesar's grandnephew, Augustus. This return to tyranny was precisely the fate that the framers sought to spare their new American republic. "The collapse of the Roman Republic offers a perfect case study of how imperialism and militarism can undermine even the best defenses of a democracy," Johnson comments.[49]

Just as the Caesars enjoyed pseudo-legal backing for their despotism, so too the US imperial presidency found support in a neoconservative contribution to jurisprudence called "the unitary executive theory of the presidency." Among other things, it asserts the President's supremacy in all matter relating even indirectly to foreign relations and war, thus overriding all existing laws (including on due process and torture) that might otherwise have countermanded his executive orders.[50] Resort to the doctrine violates the Constitution's central principle—the sovereignty of "we the people" as exercised by elected law-making representatives in congress. This neocon principle chimes with the Nazi jurisprudence based on the *Führerprinzip* (leadership principle), which declares it impossible for the Führer to break any law because his will *is* the law. The doctrine formed part of the neocons' mission to create a whole "new legal regime,"[51] one based on a single, simple principle: *force majeure*. It compromises the integrity of the whole international rule of law on which the struggle against genocide depends.

---

gallows humour can visit the CIA's statement of its "vision, mission, ethos, and challenges" on its official website. Under the rubric "Integrity" it reads: "We uphold the highest standards of lawful conduct. . . . We maintain the Nation's trust through accountability and oversight." This claim competes with Heinrich Himmler's constant insistence on the *Anständigkeit* (decency) of his SS mass-murderers: see Yitzhak Arad, Yisrael Gutman and Abraham Margoliot, eds., *Documents of the Holocaust: Selected Sources on the Destruction of the Jews of Germany and Austria, Poland and the Soviet Union* (Jerusalem: Yad Vashem, with the Anti-Defamation League and Ktav Publishing House, 1981), 344.

49   Johnson, *Nemesis*, 55.

50   Johnson, *Nemesis*, 253. As he relates, Bush appointed two proponents of the new jurisprudence to the bench of the US Supreme Court in 2006. Much earlier, another justice thereof, Robert Jackson—the legendary US chief prosecutor in the first Nuremberg trial—delivered a judgment in 1952 that explicitly denied that the President had any special powers in wartime; even then his power "is subject to limitations consistent with a constitutional Republic whose law and policy-making branch is a representative Congress."

51   John Yoo, US Deputy Assistant Attorney General, announced this as the Bush Administration's intention in 2002. See Sands, *Lawless World*, 153–34. "We're an empire now, and when we act, we create our own reality," Yoo's fellow neocon, Karl Rove, famously asserted. See Richard Flanagan, "Does Writing Matter?" *The Monthly*, October (2016), 23. The "new legal regime" took its place in that created reality.

Johnson insists—and this is his central point—that democracy and the rule of law on the one hand, and imperialism on the other, are irreconcilable, because the maintenance of empire abroad in the long run demands tyranny at home. One or the other must give way. In Rome it was democracy and law that foundered. Following Hannah Arendt in *The Origins of Totalitarianism*, Johnson cites a counter-example—the British Empire. In this case the empire was dismantled (albeit often with the robust encouragement of the colonised) to eradicate its threat to the democratic and law-bound order at home.[52] On this argument, the US must choose between the " Roman" and "British" options.[53]

If the US continues down the present "Roman" path, Johnson wrote, it faces "a devastating trio of consequences: imperial overstretch, perpetual war, and insolvency, leading to a likely collapse similar to that of the Soviet Union."[54] At the time of writing, the US national debt (duly engorged by the lavish military budget) comes to 19.34 trillion USD, or 106 per cent of GDP.[55] *The Last Days of the American Republic*—the sub-title of Johnson's *Nemesis*—thus refers not just to the country's democratic and constitutional implosion,[56] but also to its current fiscal frailty as a nation-state.

If the US were to choose the "British" path, it would dismantle its empire of bases, starting with the abolition of the CIA,[57] and then be in a position to return to its American first principles—restore its constitutional, democratic and legal order. It might then resume the path it was treading in the 1940s when it was promoting an international rule of law, one antithetical to aggressive war and genocide, among other humanitarian violations. Unfortunately, few signs point to such a return. Obama's presidency saw the US faltering in its slide into tyranny, but not going into reverse. It did not distance itself from the criminality and lawlessness of its predecessor, let alone apologise or offer restitution to those wronged. The wars in Afghanistan and Iraq continue, and have metastasised into Libya, Syria and Yemen. The CIA endures, as does its "extraordinary rendition" programme, as does the Guantánamo hellhole[58]—all powerful symbols of the "Roman" path, and perhaps harbingers of the "Soviet" fate. In the next section I will disclose more sources of resistance

---

52 Johnson, *Nemesis*, 88.
53 Johnson, *Dismantling the Empire*, 29.
54 Ibid., 183. Oddly, he fails to cite the case of the French First Republic (1792–1804) that morphed into the ill-fated (Napoleonic) First Empire.
55 http://www.usdebtclock.org/.
56 In this context, see Naomi Wolf, *The End*.
57 Johnson, *Dismantling the Empire*, 28, 82.
58 Jonathan Hafetz, ed., *Obama's Guantánamo: Stories from an Enduring Prison* (New York: New York University Press, 2016).

to a democratic revival, ones not specific (but still applicable) to the American case.

Before I turn to them, I will raise one more connection between the imperialism/militarism couple and collusion in genocide. As Colin Tatz and I have argued, today's genocidal threats are largely concentrated in the Middle East and North Africa. Most of them take the form of ISIS, its allies, and its fervid jihadi imitators. US-led aggression and subsequent military bungling from July 1979, and especially in the wake of 9/11, let this "horde of genies" out of their bottles and have provided them with four major failed states (Afghanistan, Iraq, Syria and Yemen) in which to spread genocidal mayhem.[59] When we connect the causal dots, we lay bare the link between hubristic and impulsive decision-making—the hallmarks of tyranny—in the US on the one hand, and potentiating genocide elsewhere on the other. This link represents the converse of Pinker's thesis about democracy's efficacy as a violence dampener, and points up the third aspect of the American alliance's collusion in genocide mentioned in my introduction.

Post-democracy, bread and circuses

How might Western powers thwart today's principal genocidal threats in the Middle Eastern cauldron—ones that core members of the American alliance have conjured forth since 1979, and especially since 9/11? The military and intelligence specialist David Kilcullen concludes his analysis of the problems and options here on a challenging note: the *central* resource we need to tap into in this struggle is *political will*:

> This—political will, not troops, not money, not time, not technology—this is the scarcest resource, and without that political will *at the level of entire nations*, nothing else we do will work. Preserving and strengthening the political will of our societies, the will to continue this struggle without giving

---

59 Tatz and Higgins, *The Magnitude*, 227–41. "Horde of genies" is David Kilcullen's expression; we made extensive use of his shrewd analysis in our discussion. Inter alia, he reinforces the general view that the 2003 invasion of Iraq was not only illegal, but a catastrophic misstep: "the greatest strategic screw-up since Hitler's invasion of Russia." See David Kilcullen, "Blood Year: Terror and the Islamic State," *Quarterly Essay* 58 (2015), 11. The UK government's Iraq inquiry, headed by Sir John Chilcot, reported in July 2016 and came to much the same conclusion. It spells out the deceit, chicanery and recklessness that underpinned the British decision to join in the US-led invasion. But even this report pulled its punches on key points, such as on the sheer illegality of the invasion: see Philippe Sands, "A Grand and Disastrous Deceit," *London Review of Books* 38, no. 15 (2016), 9–11. Australia's more denialist political culture will probably preclude any such independent inquiry into its own government's decision to join in the 2003 invasion; were such an inquiry to come to pass, however, its findings would probably replicate Chilcot's.

in to a horrific adversary, but also *without surrendering our civil liberties or betraying our ethics,* is not an adjunct to the strategy—it *is* the strategy.[60]

As he makes clear, this struggle will be long and gruelling. By "political will," then, he does not mean fleeting popular assent to something like the catastrophic 2003 invasion of Iraq, which then US Defence Secretary Donald Rumsfeld sold to the public as a sure-fire quick-fix "cakewalk" (now a war in its fourteenth year). Rather, the "political will at the level of entire nations" needed to bring today's genocidaires to ground has to replicate the sustained, encompassing kind that galvanised the Allied home fronts during World War Two, even if the present conflict itself is not on that scale. Only substantive democratic processes can engender such durable mobilisation, as they did then.

In addition to the obstacles already canvassed—the ongoing, genocide-collusive thrust of the American alliance's foreign relations since 1949, and the corrosion of constitutional government and the rule of law in the US itself—several writers point to other travails of democratic governance in today's West that militate against the formation of a durable democratic will of the kind required. I will briefly introduce one influential strand in this literature, again focusing on the work of its main proponent.

In his book *Post-Democracy*, Colin Crouch sets up two ideal types of formally democratic government over the past century. The first, "democracy" as such,

> thrives when there are major opportunities for the mass of ordinary people actively to participate, through discussion and autonomous organizations, in shaping the agenda of public life, and when they are actively using these opportunities.[61]

In the core countries of today's American alliance, democracy's high tide arrived in the mid-twentieth century,[62] and they came at least a fair way to achieving this ideal.

A half-century later, though, a new model—post-democracy—has supplanted it:

> Under this model, while elections certainly exist and can change governments, public electoral debate is a tightly controlled spectacle, managed

---

60 Kilcullen, "Blood Year," 87. Emphasis added in the first two italicised phrases.
61 Crouch, *Post-Democracy*, 2.
62 Ibid., 7.

by rival teams of professional experts in the techniques of persuasion, and considering a small range of issues selected by those teams. The mass of citizens plays a passive, quiescent, even apathetic part, responding only to the signals given them. Behind this spectacle of the electoral game, politics is really shaped by private interaction between elected governments and elites that overwhelmingly represent business interests.[63]

The trend towards post-democracy gained its impetus from the overlapping Reagan and Thatcher years in the 1970s, when progressive politics in the West foundered in the oil crisis and concomitant stagflation. Neoliberal ideology then began its rapid rise to ascendancy, Crouch argues, to the point where Margaret Thatcher could notoriously claim, "there is no alternative." There has certainly been no alternative to neoliberalism in the mainstream electoral lives of the American alliance's core members since at least the 1980s, hence the narrow compass and impoverishment of political contestation to this day.

Post-democracy, far from mobilising and crystallising the political will of "we the people," empowers a new political class made up of corporate elites (including media moguls), professional lobbyists, and politicians' career staffers, minders, spin-doctors, brand- and image-controllers, perception-managers, and focus-group ringmasters—all united around neoliberal nostrums. In this scenario, Crouch writes, citizens "have been reduced to the role of manipulated, passive, rare participants," while "the content of party programmes and the character of party rivalry become ever more bland and vapid."[64] The closer the core members of the American alliance gravitate towards this model of political life, the more remote becomes the prospect of generating an anti-genocidal "political will at the level of entire nations."

Indeed, "we the people" find ourselves denied access to our supposed representatives—shouldered aside by corporate donors and professional lobbyists representing well-heeled clients under the terms of the cash-for-access system. "We the people" also experience increasing difficulty in finding the vocabulary and syntax with which to express any political will at all, given the current corruption of public language. Post-democracy imposes an idiom drawn from the professional manipulators of the advertising industry, and "advertising is not a form of rational dialogue," as Crouch drily observes.[65] It coaches politicians and other members of the political class into uttering "sound bites"—or

---

63 Ibid., 4. On the role of (and benefits to) business interests in the alliance's military adventures, see Naomi Klein, *The Shock Doctrine: The Rise of Disaster Capitalism* (New York: Allen Lane, 2007).
64 Ibid., 21.
65 Ibid., 26.

performing more drawn-out speech-acts—that do not resemble normal speech, but rather comprise Orwellian sequences of boiler-plate phrases, slogans, cant and weasel words that "articulate a vague and incoherent set of policies."[66] This corruption of language, exemplified by today's "retail politicians," is another hallmark of the tyranny that betokens democracy's malaise.

In the absence of rational public dialogue, "we the people" are diverted into choreographed rituals, hoop-la, and political spectacles that offer a mere simulacrum of political participation (but supposedly display our countries' democratic credentials). In reality they are little more than "media events"—advertising platforms for self-selecting elements of the political class, and therewith festivals of sloganising, posturing and cant.[67] All of this falls well short of Crouch's desiderata for democracy quoted above.

The American primaries in the run-up to the November 2016 presidential election made this point plainly enough: they constituted show business, not democratic conversations.[68] The campaign itself also illustrated a related but even more hazardous side of post-democracy: its propensity to reduce large segments of the citizenry to blind resentment at their socio-economic exclusion and insecurity under neoliberal policy regimes,[69] and their political exclusion at the hands of the political class. These segments can then fall in behind disreputable chancers who foment atavistic prejudices and entirely lack experience in public office. This scenario invites comparison with the fall of the German Weimar Republic in 1933 and its genocidal aftermath. We have certainly come a long way from the preconditions for an anti-genocidal political will at the level of whole nations.

Finally, the national governments and political elites of the American alliance rely on greater and greater secrecy to disempower their supposedly fully informed democratic constituencies—something that James Madison also foresaw as aiding the "gradual and silent encroachments of those in power."[70] Earlier I referred to the secrecy surrounding vital elements of Amer-

---

66   Ibid., 27. Much of this "cant, gibberish and jargon," as Don Watson calls it, also comes from contemporary management argot. Watson's mockery of contemporary political language serves a serious point in showing how much is lost in "the decay of public language." See Don Watson, *Death Sentence: The Decay of Public Language* (Sydney: Knopf, 2003); Don Watson, *Watson's Dictionary of Weasel Words: Contemporary Clichés, Cant and Management Jargon* (Sydney: Vintage, 2005); Don Watson, *Worst Words: A Compendium of Contemporary Cant, Gibberish and Jargon* (Sydney: Vintage, 2015).

67   Daniel Dayan and Elihu Katz, *Media Events: The Live Broadcasting of History* (Cambridge MA: Harvard University Press, 1992); Maria Wendt, *Politik som spektakel: Almedalen, mediemakten och den svenska demokratin* (Stockholm: Atlas Akademi, 2012).

68   Eliot Weinberger, "It Was Everything," *London Review of Books* 38, no. 16 (2016), 3–8; Christian Lorentzen, "Diary," *London Review of Books* 38, no. 16 (2016), 4.

69   See Crouch, *Post-Democracy*.

70   Speech delivered on June 6, 1788, at the Virginia Convention to ratify the Federal Constitution.

ican foreign relations, military excursions, and covert operations. In each of the core countries, applications for official documents made under freedom-of-information legislation have long met with ever-stiffer resistance motivated by vague references to "national security" or "national interests." When documents are released, they are often "redacted" to the point of deliberate unintelligibility. "Welcome to Peak Secrecy," the Australian journalist Sarah Gill comments—thus pinpointing another integral feature of post-democracy.[71]

Conclusion

Colin Tatz and I ended our recent book on genocide with this sentence: "The prevention of genocide is every citizen's business."[72] To a large extent, the genocidal risks that the world faces today arise from the political dysfunctions and imperial overstretch of the US and its closest allies, and their catastrophic long-run outcomes in the Middle East and North Africa. Thus for the citizens of the core members of the American alliance, the business of preventing genocide begins at home.

It begins by challenging our political and policy-making elites—their long-standing, institutionalised moral indifference to genocide; their brazen assault on the international rule of law on which the struggle against genocide depends; their subversion of domestic law; their inured imperial mind-sets; and their debauching of democratic rule at home. The task of building a political will to prevent genocide at the level of whole nations demands nothing less than reinstating our Western democratic politico-legal heritage so limpidly expressed in the 1787 US Constitution, and implicit in the Constitutions of the UK and Australia. It also requires a retrieval of the political culture of the 1940s, when our countries were truly democratic, belonged in the mainstream of Western civilisation, and energetically sought to nurture an international rule of law that would suppress war and genocide, and promote human rights.

Can the American alliance stop colluding in genocide? We stand at a crossroads much like the one where the classical sociologist Max Weber located the "iron cage" of capitalist society over a century ago in *The Protestant Ethic and the Spirit of Capitalism*:

No one knows who will live in this cage in the future, or whether at the end

---

71 Sarah Gill, "We've Reached Peak Secrecy, In a New Low Point for Transparency and Openness," *Sydney Morning Herald*, October 27, 2016. A draconian case in point is s.42 of the 2015 *Australian Border Force Act* that threatens members of the caring professions with imprisonment for disclosing the conditions under which imprisoned asylum seekers suffer.

72 Tatz and Higgins, *The Magnitude*, 249.

of this tremendous development entirely new prophets will arise, or there will be a great rebirth of old ideas and ideals, or, if neither, mechanized petrification, embellished with a sort of convulsive self-importance.[73]

We citizens of American-alliance countries face well-entrenched and well-resourced resistance to any attempt to recover our politico-legal patrimony in our own homelands. But the stakes could hardly be higher: not only our own civilisation and way of life, but also the lives of millions of potential genocide victims far beyond our national borders.

---

73 Max Weber, *The Protestant Ethic and the Spirit of Capitalism*, trans. Talcott Parsons (1905; London: Routledge, 1992), 124.

TEACHING ABOUT GENOCIDE

Colin Tatz

Researching and writing about genocide is easier than teaching it. An art and a craft, teaching young people and adults about the gruesome and grotesque has particular problems. Generally speaking, while younger audiences may be more inured to virtual violence, older listeners prefer good rather than bad endings.

There are the faltering moments when students cannot handle the material, cry, or rush from the room. This often occurs when viewing "Genocide," episode 20 of the 1974 Thames Television series *The World at War*. A few are transfixed by the morbidity of it all. This documentary is replete with mass shootings at the rims of pits, bulldozed corpses, and skeletal figures hanging off electrified camp wire. It is meant to shock, and it does. By contrast, Claude Lanzmann's brilliant pastel-coloured marathon documentary, *Shoah* (1985), sets out to unravel the bizarre and, in its educative way, it is far more compelling and evocative than the shock-horror presentations.

Once under way, students not only engage but become curious, even enthralled by the case studies. They like unravelling what seems so incomprehensible, demystifying what is so surreal. Often there is zest in their studies and assignments, as if on the road to making fresh discoveries about humankind, about good and evil, righteous and not so righteous behaviour, the machinations of bureaucracy, the meanings of accountability and responsibility, the nature of crime and punishment, the politics of apology, the nature and value of reparations, the vexed problem of wilful amnesia and outright denialism, the legacies for the victim communities—and much else as it becomes an intellectual pursuit.

Inevitably, awkward and often unanswerable questions arise. How would I have behaved if conscripted into something like the Hitler Youth? Would I have hidden a family at such danger to myself and my family? Would I have disobeyed an order from above? Could "my kind of people" have performed such deeds? Or if "my people" did do such things, how and why am I different? It is important to convince students of the hypothetical nature of such questions: that this is now, not then, and they are here, not there.

Crucially, audiences learn that genocide is never spontaneous combustion, a sudden and totally unexpected eruption into mass violence as seemingly happened in Rwanda in 1994. Every genocide trails history, and each builds up, aggregates, in a succession of "building blocks" or an assembling of "engine parts." Whichever metaphor one uses, genocide is evolutionary, not revolutionary. A holistic approach is needed, one that embraces anthropology, biology, cultural studies, geography, history, law, philosophy, sociology, studies of religion, and more. Most teenagers are not conversant or comfortable with that combination of concepts and the vocabularies involved. A different kind of educative process is required that involves teaching students how to confront some very large canvasses.

Some teachers use what I call the science-fiction movie approach—a group of bad guys descended from an alien spaceship in 1933, wrought evil upon the world and were then vanquished forever by the allied good guys a dozen years later. What is sometimes called "slice-history" does not work for the Holocaust or for any genocide. In the former case, it leads to ideas about a totally new kind of event, something meta-historical or even meta-physical. The Holocaust was many things: it is the central case in teaching, the tremendum of modern times certainly, but always a genocide and therefore examinable in the historical context of genocides.

What is regrettable is the lasting influence of American psychologist Gordon Allport who, in 1954, wrote *The Nature of Prejudice*. He posited a syndrome, something directly connected, running together, and sequential:

1. Antilocution—bad-mouthing an ethnicity, a race, a people;
2. Then the social exclusion of such people;
3. Followed by physical attacks on the target groups, such as lynching, desecration of tombstones;
4. Next, geographic exclusion of the targeted group from neighbourhoods, regions, nations;
5. Finally, their proposed, attempted or actual extermination.

American scholar Gregory Stanton has outlined 10 sequential stages of genocide, and Winton Higgins and I have established a similar set of demonstrable, connected steps—from formulation of the very idea to its actual implementation and aftermath.[1] Yet the Allport "syndrome" was, and remains, historical and empirical nonsense. These actions assuredly exist, but there is not any science of syndrome, no sequence of indelible connectedness. Most societies have had salon and literary antilocutions and yet have neither physically at-

---

1 Colin Tatz and Winton Higgins, *The Magnitude of Genocide* (Santa Barbara: Praeger, 2016), 112–13.

tacked Jews, nor killed them. Jews have been socially and geographically excluded from clubs, suburbs, schools and universities, yet not only survived, but thrived. Many communities, including Jews in Australia, have had tombstones shattered and synagogues set on fire without ensuing trade boycotts, bannings from the public service, roundups, deportations and gassings. The seemingly unshakeable problem is that so many believe "it has to start somewhere"—in the manner of Allport's antilocution—and point to either radio shock jock language, *The Merchant of Venice*, *Oliver Twist*, or to golf club exclusions. They are not the passageways to genocide, and that is not the way to teach about genocide.

Let me share some personal thoughts about teaching (and thinking) about genocide, developed over the past 30 years. My approach is not that of an instruction manual, nor is it set in stone, but it has worked for my audiences over the years, and for a number of former students who in turn have become teachers of the subject.

Here I address some of the approaches that work well in unravelling the "crime of crimes," among others, the value of a broad and holistic opening, a need to distinguish genocide from related crimes, the essential focus on the Holocaust, the ways of coming to grips with the actors involved in the phenomenon, and the ingredients common to most genocides.

The overview

Whatever it was called before Raphael Lemkin gave us the word genocide in 1944, there was, all too commonly, attempted or actual extermination of peoples in classical antiquity (roughly 800 BCE to 500 CE), the middle ages (500 to late 1500 CE), and the modern era (1600 to the present). Genocide is not simply a twentieth century horror story: there is a magnitude to genocide in and across world history.[2] The twentieth century warrants especial attention, but for maximum effect students need to approach genocide from the events in German South-West Africa [now Namibia] in 1904–1906, through to the Ottoman Turk genocides of Armenians, Assyrians and Greeks from 1915 to 1923, through to the Holocaust era starting in 1933. Then separately, traverse the dozens of genocidal episodes since the placard in the Buchenwald camp proclaimed (in 1945) the now empty catchcry of "Never Again." These should include Bangladesh, Burundi,

---

2 See Mark Levene, *Genocide in the Age of the Nation State* (London: I.B. Taurus, 2005); Ben Kiernan, *Blood and Soil: A World History of Genocide and Extermination from Sparta to Darfur* (New Haven: Yale University Press, 2007); Tatz and Higgins, *The Magnitude*.

Cambodia, Darfur, Guatemala, Bosnia, Kosovo, Rwanda, Chechnya, East Timor, Liberia, Sri Lanka, the Democratic Republic of Congo and the current genocidal jihadism of ISIS.

Gradations of genocide

Not all cases of genocide are alike, let alone the same. We need a measuring rod—and that can only come from explaining that the only judiciable and actionable instrument we have is the 1948 United Nations Convention on the Prevention and Punishment of the Crime of Genocide ("the Genocide Convention"), flawed as it is. There is no point going over the many definitions, even the improved ones that have come from scholars since 1948. The Genocide Convention sets out five somewhat divergent acts that constitute the crime of genocide, ranging from Article II (a) the physical killing of people because they are those people, to Article II (e) forcibly removing their children from their group to another group membership. And it relates to only four categories of people: racial, ethnic, religious, or national. Therein lies a problem in teaching about genocide: there are five essentially differing actions defined, with rape now added by the courts as a genocidal act. In spite of clear-cut differences, the five are co-equated and each can be ruled genocide. The equating of child removal, a form of social and cultural death, with physical death, presents a problem for many. Each is heinous but the Convention allows no gradations between them. That is how international law defines it and that is what we will have to abide by for many years to come.[3]

We need a metaphorical way of measuring, or at least appreciating the intensity and the gradations of genocidal events. Inevitably, there are differences in intent, motive, time-frame, scale, methods used, rescue and intervention efforts, outcomes, impacts on victim groups, legacies, trials and accountability, apologies, reparations, levels of denial, memorialisation, and so on. (Sometimes a nasty element intrudes: "my genocide" was bigger than or superior to yours—a league table of horror, what historian Michael Berenbaum excoriated as "a calculus of calamity" or a "suffering Olympics".)[4] In Rwanda in 1994, 800,000 people were killed in 100 days. In Australia, physical murder of Aboriginal people and child removal spanned almost 124 years, with killings in

---

3 The statute of the International Criminal Court in 2002 adopted *verbatim* the Genocide Convention definition.

4 Michael Berenbaum, *A Mosaic of Victims: Non-Jews Persecuted and Murdered by the Nazis* (New York: New York University Press, 1990).

sporadic "hunting party" attacks over weekends accounting for some 30,000 to 50,000 people, and child removal starting in late 1839 and ending in the late 1980s, involving perhaps 30,000 children.[5] Very different experiences, yet both were cases of genocide.

A hierarchy of crimes

Confusion often arises between genocide, genocidal massacres, massacres, pogroms, atrocities, war crimes, crimes against humanity and crimes against peace. There is no shortage of case studies to help illustrate the distinctions between them. Audiences are helped by examining events as seemingly remote as the Chmielniki massacre of Jews in the Polish-Lithuanian Commonwealth (now Ukraine) in 1648. Some 100,000 Jews perished in this Cossack rebellion, but the aims were political against the ruling regime rather than the intended elimination of most or all Jews. The scale of the events make it more of a genocidal massacre. The term for such events is the Yiddish word pogrom—an orchestrated attack on people and property as a warning, reprisal, or a chance for booty. (There was, and is, a homicidal tenor to pogroms, hence the adjective "genocidal".) What Lieutenant William Calley did at the village of My Lai in Vietnam in March 1968 was an atrocity and a massacre (of some 500 men, women and children), not an action to eliminate all Vietnamese. What the Nazis did to Jews in Poland was genocide, the extirpation of both a people and the very idea of such a people; what it did to Poland was a series of war crimes not to eliminate Poles but to dismantle the political entity of the Polish state, and enslave the inferior Slavic peoples.[6]

Unlike the allied behaviours mentioned above, genocide is a specific crime comprising the five acts specified in the Genocide Convention. The specificity of the crime is important because of a popular penchant of people to reach for the word "genocide" whenever they want to attract attention to a particularly heinous event.

The actors

Holocaust teachers most often use a triangle to portray the actors and factors involved in that crime: the perpetrators (on top), the victims, and the bystanders whose indifference or acquiescence allows the actions to unfold,

---

5   Colin Tatz, *Genocide in Australia: By Accident or Design?* (Melbourne: Monash Indigenous Centre and Castan Centre for Human Rights Law, 2011).
6   For a discussion of definitions, see Tatz and Higgins, *The Magnitude*, chap. 2.

unhindered. I use a hexagon, sometimes a heptagon, including perpetrators, victims, bystanders, beneficiaries, rescuers, denialists, and (on not too many occasions) the punishers. These are the common actors in modern genocidal events, each needing analysis and discussion.

The beneficiaries are little discussed and it is worth taking students through some examples of profitable "neutrality" during World War Two—as with Sweden, Switzerland and Spain. Sweden supplied Germany with steel and machinery for war; Switzerland provided war materials and acted as a banker for Jewish assets looted by the Nazis; Spain contributed thousands of men to the Nazi military and supplied rare minerals to Germany.

The rescuers include not only individuals designated as the Righteous Among the Nations, but organisations like the Polish Catholic *Zegota* (Council for Aid to Jews), whole towns like Le Chambon in France and Niewiande in Holland, and such nation-states as Bulgaria and even Italy in World War Two. They contrast sharply with those nations that did nothing, refused to do anything, averted their eyes, or chose (and choose now) to ignore genocide as it was (or is) occurring for fear of having to become involved.

However small rescue looms in genocide history, it is important for audiences to have a glimmer of optimism to offset the blackness and nihilism. Rescue is a form of intervention and students need introduction to the few efforts to intervene physically to stop a genocide. Declaring a no-fly zone (NFZ) in 1991–1992 to stop Saddam Hussein dropping chemical weapons on Kurds in northern Iraq, and later, similar NFZs in Bosnia and Libya, are among the few examples. A distinction must be made between intervention and prevention. We have yet to see a successful attempt to prevent what is a clearly foreseeable genocide, such as in the Nuba Hills region of Sudan today.

Accessing the actors

How do we get to these participants, these actors? Even with libraries of scholarly books, journals, as well as internet materials, the most effective teaching is to have students examine original material such as documents, archival materials, newsreel films, documentaries; and either to listen to a survivor or read what would have been contemporary eyewitness accounts. Post-event memories and memoirs are valuable but are at times corrupted by memory loss, appropriation of other testimonies and historical accounts, and by sheer time.

Holocaust documents are a start. They do not tell the whole story, but sufficient thereof. *The Documents of the Holocaust* is a good volume from which to work.[7] Students may find it easier to get to grips with actors from a somewhat surreal collection by historian Raul Hilberg, titled *Documents of Destruction*.[8] They can pick a short document for analysis: for example, an order placed from Poland to Berlin for so many pounds of bread and marmalade to induce Warsaw ghetto dwellers to "volunteer" for deportation; another for a huge quantity of nuts, bolts and tools (for gas chambers); another showing a railway timetable with loaded trains going to a destination (Auschwitz) and coming back empty and needing to be cleaned (having been paid for by the Jews).

Most local Holocaust museums will have documents or facsimiles on display or in their archives. Accessing material online is now possible from institutions like Yad Vashem in Jerusalem, the US Holocaust Memorial Museum in Washington, the Imperial War Museum in London, and the massive resources held at Bad Arolsen in Germany. The Armenian Genocide Museum-Institute in Yerevan is fast developing into a key resource. The Tuol Sleng Genocide Museum in Cambodia's Phnom Penh has become a "must" on visits there and provides internet material. Australia's National Archive in Canberra holds important material on the Aboriginal Stolen Generations.

Transcripts of trials and judgments by courts are an excellent resource. There is nothing quite like the spotlight of a forensic arena, under tight rules of evidence, to provide insight into an event and the dramatis personae. The Myall Creek Massacre in New South Wales in 1838, and the subsequent trials and executions of those who had killed local Aboriginal people, tell us a great deal about frontier society.[9] Trials of Nazis, Serbians, Rwandans teach us that "something happened" and what the something was—they are more than simply about crime and punishment. The Nuremberg trials, the doctors' trials and that of the *Einsatzgruppen* tell their own terrifying tales. An important trial in more recent times was the Akayesu case in Rwanda.[10] The International Criminal Tribunal for Rwanda (ICTR) established that direct and overt evidence is not always needed to establish that something happened and that someone was guilty: the context, preceding and surrounding history and circumstances can as readily establish that genocide was not only intended but occurred.

Valuable lessons lie in looking at statutes, decrees, and regulations. Again, the Holocaust era provides numerous examples of the Nazi rush to legislation

---

7   Yitzhak Arad, Yisrael Gutman and Abraham Margoliot, eds., *The Documents of the Holocaust: Selected Sources on the Destruction of the Jews of Germany and Austria, Poland and the Soviet Union* (Jerusalem: Yad Vashem, with the Anti-Defamation League and Ktav Publishing House, 1981).

8   Raul Hilberg, *Documents of Destruction: Germany and Jewry, 1933–1945* (Chicago: Quadrangle Books, 1971).

9   The Myall Creek Memorial Site was unveiled in 2000. It is vandalised regularly.

10 *The Prosecutor v. Jean-Paul Akayesu* (1998) ICTR-96-4-T (Aust.).

immediately after coming to power in 1933. There are several Ottoman statutes that legalised and legitimated deportations and confiscation of Armenian property before the genocide began in 1915. Going to original sources enables students to start thinking for themselves rather than being told what to conclude from scholarly commentaries.

Finding a genocide survivor may be difficult. Ageing and diminished memory do not detract from the excruciating experiences that unfold, but their sense of general history is not always accurate. Eyewitness accounts are now becoming common. (Social media technology provides images of events as they happen.) Samuel Totten's numerous volumes provide critical essays, guides to the literature, and some startling witness accounts recorded at the time.[11]

Film attracts attention. Segments of Lanzmann's compelling and memorable *Shoah* documentary convey the genocidal process without once resorting to footage of killing or camp liberation. Part two of the 2007 series *Racism in History* is "The Fatal Impact" and is essential viewing. The best and most lurid of Nazi propaganda films is *Der Ewige Jude* (*The Eternal Jew*), a 1940 "masterpiece" of new film techniques and crudities. The 2010 documentary *Einsatzgruppen: The Death Brigades* brings the viewer as close as one can get to "the action."

A vexing question arises when it comes to fiction, poetry, theatre, painting and movies depicting genocide. Apart from the art versus reality debate, the question is whether these art forms capture the reality of the time and achieve impact on those who were not there. Even a movie like *Schindler's List* (1993) insists on a redemptive (happy or "happier") ending. The Kramer Nuremberg film, mentioned below, is a more accurate account, and more dramatic for its sense of authenticity. László Nemes' 2015 movie, *Son of Saul*, depicting a day-and-a-half in the lives of the *Sonderkommando*, the Jewish prisoners in Auschwitz forced to dispose of the corpses, is considered one of the best films of all time.

The professions

The popular image of genocide is of a despotic regime in which the ruler orders "mechanics," the "field" thugs and guards, to go about the business of punishing, pillaging, killing. Imagery lingers of hard-core prisoners in Turkey, usually murderous Circassians, released on condition they kill Armenians on

---

[11] See, among others, Samuel Totten and Robert K. Hitchcock, eds., *Genocide of Indigenous Peoples: A Critical Bibliographic Review* (New Brunswick, NJ: Transaction Publishers, 2011).

death marches, and of Brown Shirts (the SA) in Germany cutting off rabbinical beards and burning books, seemingly at random and self-motivated.

The planning and specificity of gathering targeted populations, of relocations to labour camps, concentration camps, or death factories, required bureaucratic efficiency. Most of that came from the professions: architecture, accountancy, biology, chemistry, education, engineering, law, medicine, pharmacy, physics and zoology. Students are fascinated by this phenomenon and disbelief soon enough becomes acceptance as they tackle projects such as genocide and the law, medical ethics in the shadows of the Holocaust, and so on. A riveting text for them is Stanley Kramer's 1961 masterly *Judgment at Nuremberg*, based on Abby Mann's scripted account of the last of the Nuremberg trials, that of Nazi judges.

Books on the professions are not that plentiful, but Max Weinreich's classic *Hitler's Professors*,[12] written in 1946, and another immediate post-war account by Alexander Mitscherlich and Fred Mielke, *The Death Doctors*,[13] are crucial. Richard Grunberger's 1971 *Social History of the Third Reich* examines the rush to join the Nazi movement by doctors and teachers in particular.[14] In the 1990s, Konrad Jarausch probed the legal, educational and engineering professions.[15] Even the seemingly innocuous profession of accountancy was heavily involved in keeping the ledgers of genocide.[16]

The centrality of the Holocaust

Holocaust studies overwhelm—in canvas, breadth, depth, scope, meticulous detail. For any other single case study, there are at least a thousand Holocaust items. The templates are there, the analytical tools are there, the over-researched and the under-researched matters are there, the atlases, encyclopaedias, bibliographies are all there as models and paradigms. The trailer or prequel of the Armenian Genocide is there and needs to be taught in its own right of course, but also because of the precedent and prelude it set for the Holocaust: the deportations and "relocations" of population, confiscation of property, rounding-up of men for slave labour and death, medical experiments

---

12 Max Weinreich, *Hitler's Professors: The Part of Scholarship in Germany's Crimes Against the Jewish People* (1946; New Haven: Yale University Press, 2005).
13 Alexander Mitscherlich and Fred Mielke, *The Death Doctors* (1949; London: Elek Books, 1962).
14 Richard Grunberger, *A Social History of the Third Reich* (1971; London: Phoenix, 2005).
15 Konrad Jarausch, *The Unfree Professions: German Lawyers, Teachers, and Engineers 1900–1950* (New York: Oxford University Press, 1990).
16 Edwin Black, *IBM and the Holocaust: The Strategic Alliance between Nazi Germany and America's Most Powerful Corporation* (London: Little, Brown and Company, 2001).

in hospitals, elementary gas chambers and the final death marches into Syria. The Nazi regime learned much from the Young Turks. As Stefan Ihrig has reminded us, Kemal Atatürk loomed large in the Nazi imagination.[17]

Some genocide scholars seem to want to bypass the Holocaust, to engage in a chosen case study strictly avoiding not just the substance of the Holocaust but its echoes, shadows, metaphors and analogies. Hardly professional or academic, it is an approach unbecoming of scholarship. As noted above, the templates and frameworks of analysis by eminent and acclaimed scholars over the past 70 years are ever-present. Some scholars assert that the Holocaust drowns or eclipses other cases: it may well do so, but the established and tested templates are unassailable and cannot be swept aside merely in pursuit of "new" lenses. The Holocaust perspectives have yet to be found wanting or inappropriate.

Genocide and language

Inevitably, there is a flipside to these documented instructions and actions: the unstated, unspoken orders to round up, deport, loot, kill. In many cases, genocidaires invent new language, as with the Nazi euphemisms.[18] Resettlement, special treatment, and relocation "solutions" are but masks for the killing fields and methods of death. Part and parcel of this attempt to hide reality is the dehumanisation, animalisation and insectification of victims as bacilli, viruses (Jews), pests and vermin (Roma), cockroaches (Tutsi). Rowan Savage has analysed the language of dehumanisation: the sub-humans, fauna, wild beasts, vermin, rodents, insects, birds, pigs, monkeys, snakes.[19]

Not all genocides are acts of commission: at times, genocide is an act of omission, a deliberate failure to feed and water people for example. Again, there are degrees and gradations of criminal intent, or gross negligence involved—as in Ukraine in the 1920s and 1930s, the deliberately low rations for Jews in the Nazi era, some less than ambiguous agrarian practices in China, Ethiopia and North Korea in more recent times.

---

17 Stefan Ihrig, *Atatürk in the Nazi Imagination* (Cambridge, MA: Belknap, 2014). His new book, *Justifying Genocide* looks at the connections between both cases more comprehensively.

18 Shaul Esch, "Words and Meanings: Twenty-Five Examples of Nazi Idiom," *Yad Vashem Studies* 5 (1963), 133–67.

19 Rowan Savage, " 'Vermin to be Cleared Off the Face of the Earth': Perpetrator Representations of Genocide Victims as Animals," *Genocide Perspectives III: Essays on the Holocaust and Other Genocides*, eds. Colin Tatz, Peter Arnold and Sandra Tatz (Blackheath, NSW: Brandl & Schlesinger, 2006), 17–53.

Disciplinary approaches

The most appropriate discipline for teaching genocide is history. There is now strong attention from sociology, political science, law and more recently, anthropology, philosophy, and two somewhat fuzzy subsets labelled human rights and, increasingly, peace and conflict studies. "Human rights" is a term now (fashionably) attached to studies of atrocities, mass death, and genocide. It is an amalgam of many things: philosophical, religious, ethical, moral, legal. The problem is not that particular admixture but the haphazard way in which it is used as a mantra to cover a multitude of behaviours that co-equate issues like poverty, poor education, exclusion from voting, ill health and life's inequities with purposeful killings in Rwanda, Bosnia and Cambodia. The spectrum becomes so broad as to be meaningless.

Rarely used is political geography. It is highly effective, especially with the use of computer-generated maps. Thus, one can present a political map of Africa in 1939 and then another of that continent by 1970. In 30 short years, boundaries changed, new states emerged, and long-term colonial regimes that were there have vanished. Some 30 genocidal events have occurred in Africa as a result of colonial practices, and even more calamitous outcomes from ill-considered decolonisation procedures. Or, one can show graphically and demographically that Europe had 10 million Jews in 1939 and less than 2 million 50 years later—and ask how and why?

Ethnic cleansing—so historian Norman Naimark tells us[20]—inevitably bleeds into genocide. This is well illustrated by the cases of the Greeks, Assyrians and Armenians in Turkey, the Soviet deportations of Chechens, Ingush and Crimean Tatars, and the more recent Wars of Yugoslav Succession. The present-day crises in Afghanistan, Iraq, Yemen and Syria, and the plight of Kurdish peoples generally, lend themselves to the lens of political geography.

The race factor

Unfortunately, racism is the only single, flat word we have to cover a multitude of attitudes and actions. Since earliest history distinctions have been made between "them" and "us" on the basis of tribal affiliation, kin membership, skin colour, body form, ethnicity, religion, material culture, custom, language, and geographic domain. Race-ism has to cover all such different attitudes and actions. Essentially, racism refers to real (or imagined) beliefs that a specific characteristic, such as colour, language or religious belief, gives rise to cer-

---

20 Norman Naimark, *Fires of Hatred: Ethnic Cleansing in Twentieth-Century Europe* (Cambridge, MA: Harvard University Press, 2001).

tain undesirable social characteristics—and one can therefore legitimately take action against such a target group. Thus, in shorthand, blacks were slaves because they were black, or corporeal Jews were invisible and dangerous viruses to be eradicated.

Rare indeed is the genocide in history where race, in this sense, has not been a key factor. Much of the Atlantic slave trade led to the destruction of African and Caribbean family and ethnic life. Racism underlay the fate of Nama and Herero peoples in South-West Africa, the Congo Free State, and Native Americans. Similarly, the linguistically and religiously different Armenians in Turkey; the Bengali-speakers of East Pakistan; the Christian tribes of Darfur; the Chinese in Nanking at the hands of the Japanese; the Jews; the Tutsi in Rwanda; the Vietnamese and Muslim Cham in Cambodia; Bosniaks in the former Yugoslavia. And so many more.

The "science" factor

Appreciating the race factor also requires going through the growth of "scientistic racism," that is, the works of anatomists and physical anthropologists who began to examine and compare the human form and then started to attribute social characteristics to the physical ones. When physical forms as such could not establish a "suitable" hierarchy of races, they turned to measurements of "intelligence," using craniology (skull measurement) as the ultimate criterion. Researchers concluded that Caucasians—named after what was thought to be the perfect ("white") skull found in the Caucasus mountains in Russia—had the largest brain casing (87 cubic inches), according to physician Samuel Morton in his *Crania Americana* (1839). Native Americans had a mean volume of 82 cubic inches (measured using mustard seed) that, Morton deduced, made them slow of thought, averse to agriculture, vengeful, and lovers of warfare. Ethiopian and black skulls held an even smaller quantity of seed (78 cubic inches) but their owners' bodies were the more muscular. Thus laboratories spawned the brain versus brawn (or white versus black) dichotomy that is still prevalent in many circles. Australia's Indigenous people ("Australoids") had less skull volume than any other people, and were ascribed as having even more reduced capacities—a furphy propagated in Australian school texts until the 1980s.

Craniology, sometimes called craniometry, fell from favour at the turn of the twentieth century. That scientific nonsense gave way to another form of "brain power," the Stanford-Binet test of intelligence, the modern IQ test, still in use, or misuse, today for streaming children into different levels of education, for separating classes of people, the bright from the simple, and so on.

(No matter what spin one puts on modern IQ testing, it remains of the same genre and "scientific" validity as skull measuring.)[21]

Hand in hand with these developments was the emergence of eugenics, a veterinary term, a "science" that intended turning society into a social laboratory in which nations and "races" could be regulated biologically to produce desired citizens and breed out or otherwise exclude undesirable ones, like Roma (even as this is being written). Eugenics was hardly a Nazi fantasy. The United States had powerful elements that wanted nothing more than a white, Protestant America—to the detriment and, preferably, the exclusion of all who did not fit: Blacks, Catholics, Jews, Hispanics.[22]

There was another significant point about eugenics and "racial hygiene." Rulers no longer had to rely on religious canon to justify superior over inferior, slavery, "the white man's burden," imperial destiny and the like; science, with men in white lab coats and academic gowns, could now "prove" the fitness of the fittest to rule.

The governance factor

Two eminent scholars—Yehuda Bauer in Israel and Richard Dekmejian in the United States—have listed what they see as the prerequisites of twentieth century genocide: an ancient hatred or similar ideological imperative; a brutal dictatorship; a war setting; a compliant bureaucracy; and a use of some form of technology.[23] That template may well fit the Armenian and Jewish experiences, but it does not have universal application. Some genocides have occurred in (international) peacetime. But the main issue to convey to students is that genocide is not the sole domain of brutal dictatorships. Democracies are as capable of genocide in their way. One can point to Wilhelmine Germany at the start of the twentieth century, to Belgium in the Congo's history and that of both Burundi and Rwanda, to French behaviour in territories like Algeria, to some dubious British behaviour in the Empire's heyday, to Canada, the United States, and Australia in their frontier and later eras.

Following the Genocide Convention, one has to look at child removal practices in Canada and the United States, with children taken from families and sent to compulsory residential boarding schools for up to 12 years, denied va-

---

21 Leon Kamin, *The Science and Politics of I.Q.* (London: Penguin Books, 1974).
22 See Stephen Jay Gould, *The Mismeasure of Man* (New York: Norton, 1981); Leila Zenderland, *Measuring Minds: Henry Herbert Goddard and the Origins of American Intelligence Testing* (Cambridge, UK: Cambridge University Press, 2001).
23 Tatz and Higgins, *The Magnitude*, chap. 4.

cation time with kin, in the hope that their "Indian-ness" would be eradicated at the end of that time.

A much starker case of "decent democrats" committing the crime is Australia, with both a physical killing era and, later, massive and wholesale child removal practices. Under a Westminster system of constitutional governance, with reverence for the rule of law, with claims about a remarkable record of according and affording human rights, contrived—from 1896 to approximately 1985 (in Queensland)—to have Aboriginal people live under separate and special statutes that granted not one right in the amalgam we call human rights. They were "citizens" but could not enter or leave a reserve without permission, could not sell their labour on the open market, earn the national basic wage, marry non-Indigenous people without permission, have sex across the colour line, vote, drink, go within stipulated distances of licensed premises, carry firearms, join trade unions, own land or property, make wills, have legal guardianship of their children, apply for passports, or give evidence on oath in court. In several jurisdictions, they could be jailed by local administrators and missionaries (quite outside the domain of the national criminal justice system) for offences that only they could commit, like playing cards, being cheeky, being idle, refusing to work, or committing adultery.[24]

Dealing with denialism

People have difficulty dealing with denialism, especially of the Armenian and Jewish events. Students (and lay people) need to learn that the onus is not on them to prove that certain things happened, but that the burden lies on the denialist to show that they did not happen. For example: give the students a copy of the SS Statistics on the "Final Solution of the Jewish Question" March 23, 1943.[25] Let them confront a denialist and insist on being shown how and in what way that document was a forgery, who did the forging, on what paper and with what inks and typewriters and official stamps. Students need to appreciate that denialists never offer proof but simply assert; and that these are not debatable issues on which there are alternative views. Turkish denialism is much harder to deal with, given that the whole apparatus of the Republic of Turkey dedicates itself to denying the events of 1915 to 1923. Nevertheless, students need to know that some 23 nation states have recognised that genocide, as have some 48 American states, two Australian parliaments, the European Parliament, the Council of Europe, and the Vatican, among others. The onus is on

---

24 Colin Tatz, *Australia's Unthinkable Genocide* (Bloomington: Xlibris, 2017).
25 In Arad et al., *The Documents*, 332–34.

the denialists to show why it is that there has been such widespread "conspiracy" among reputable people and organisations to besmirch Turkish honour.

Conclusion

The social sciences engage in advocacies, with differing and even antithetical viewpoints. Genocide is unique: there cannot be a (legitimate) "pro-genocide" stance and there can be no alternative point of view as to its "merits." It is rare indeed to have a subject that does not have another "side"—except perhaps in today's upside-down world of ISIS and its confident claims that the killing of all infidels worldwide is warranted, no, commanded by the Quran.

There have been some lame attempts at justification of genocidal practices, notably the North American system of compulsory residential boarding schools, and Australia's forcible removal of children, both claiming this was "in their best interests." While the Genocide Convention conveys, from its 1948 context, that "with intent to destroy" meant to destroy with malice and *male fides*, there is no definition (or court interpretation) of the nature of "intent." Arguing that the intent was "good" is to trivialise and relativise the action. Australian philosopher Raimond Gaita has pinned down the matter: "the concept of good intention cannot be relativised indefinitely to an agent's perception of it as good." If we could, Gaita writes, then we must say that Nazi murderers had good, but radically benighted intentions, because most of them believed they had a sacred duty to the world to rid the planet of the race that polluted it.[26]

We have a sense of universalism about genocide, its perpetrators, its nature, horrors, outcomes, and legacies. The conundrum remains: why then do so many nations, governments, institutions and agencies look the other way, pretend it is not happening, ponder or dither over intervention when prevention and pre-emptive action was well warranted? There is no shortage of signposts, of some obvious "at-risk" factors when one examines—as intelligence agencies undoubtedly do daily—gross poverty, scarcity of resources, historical animosities, geographic and geopolitical conflicts, internecine and religious wars, territorial claims, and a sequential set of circumstances clearly suggesting prior or imminent attacks on targeted groups. Indifference is said to be a major, if not the major factor in genocide—that without the indifferent bystanders the event cannot take place.

Yehuda Bauer teaches that there is often an adjective involved: hostile in-

---

26 Raimond Gaita, "Genocide and Pedantry," *Quadrant*, July–August 1997, 41–45; Raimond Gaita, "Genocide: The Holocaust and the Aborigines," *Quadrant*, November 1997, 17–22.

difference. A tautology on the face of it, nevertheless there is a real sense in which averting the eyes is more than just "not wanting to be involved": it emanates a sense of not considering the victims as worthy people.

Many years ago, when Elie Wiesel— survivor of Auschwitz and Nobel Laureate for Literature—was asked about what anyone could do about the Holocaust, he replied that one must teach, and teach again. Teaching, of course, will not prevent genocide, but it will lay bare the essences of that behaviour. And so my contribution is to teach and to talk, even to preach.

Biographies

Jennifer Balint

Jennifer Balint is Senior Lecturer in Socio-Legal Studies in the Discipline of Criminology, School of Social and Political Sciences at the University of Melbourne. Her work considers the constitutive role of law, with a focus on genocide and state crime. Jennifer is the author of *Genocide, State Crime and the Law: In the Name of the State* (2012) and co-researcher on the *Minutes of Evidence Project*.

Tony Barta

Tony Barta is an Honorary Research Associate within the History Programme at LaTrobe University. His research interests include 20th century German history, especially relations between social life, culture and ideology; genocide in colonial societies; and history media.

Douglas Booth

Douglas Booth is Professor of Sport Studies and Dean of the School of Physical Education, Sport and Exercise Sciences at the University of Otago, New Zealand. His research includes historiography; and sport, politics and race. He incorporates aspects of the Holocaust into his teaching on racial ideology and sport.

Anna Haebich

Anna Haebich is a John Curtin Distinguished Professor and Research Professor in the Faculty of Humanities at Curtin University. She was Foundation Director of the Centre for Public Culture and Ideas at Griffith University. Anna's historical research is multi-disciplinary and transcultural, and addresses histories of Indigenous peoples, migration, the body, environment, visual and performing arts, museums, representations of the past, and crime and gender.

Winton Higgins

Winton Higgins has taught and published in genocide studies, political theory, political economy, organisational studies, and Swedish political history. He was a senior member of the Politics discipline at Macquarie University, Sydney; he is currently an associate of the School of International Studies at the University of Technology Sydney, and a director of the Australian Institute for Holocaust and Genocide Studies. With Colin Tatz, Winton co-authored *The Magnitude of Genocide* (2016), and in the same year published *The Rule of Law*, a novel based on the first Nuremberg trial.

The Honourable Michael Kirby AC CMG

Michael Kirby was a Justice of the High Court of Australia 1996–2009. Prior to that he held several high judicial positions in Australia and overseas. Since his retirement from the High Court of Australia Michael has been engaged in many international activities including his work as chair of the UN Commission of Inquiry to investigate and report on human rights abuses and crimes against humanity in the Democratic People's Republic of Korea. Michael was recently admitted as an Honorary Fellow of the Australian Institute of International Affairs.

Konrad Kwiet

Konrad Kwiet retired in 2014 as Pratt Foundation Professor in Modern Jewish History and Holocaust Studies, University of Sydney, but continues to lecture on a casual basis, and remains Resident Historian at the Sydney Jewish Museum. In his career, Konrad has held a number of senior posts including at the University of New South Wales and Macquarie University, the Australian War Crimes Commission and institutes overseas. Konrad's areas of research covers modern Jewish history and German history, antisemitism, the Holocaust and war crimes.

Edwina Light

Edwina Light is a postdoctoral Research Fellow based at the Centre for Values, Ethics and the Law in Medicine, University of Sydney, and a Visiting Fellow of the Sydney Jewish Museum. She has published on psychiatry and the Holocaust and her work is focused on mental health ethics and policy, and the use of qualitative methodologies.

Wendy Lipworth

Wendy Lipworth is a medically trained bioethicist and health social scientist, based at the Centre for Values, Ethics and the Law in Medicine, University of Sydney. Her work focuses on the values underpinning biomedicine, with a particular focus on biomedical research and innovation.

Nikki Marczak

Nikki Marczak is a genocide scholar with a research focus on women's experiences during genocide. She is a member of the Australian Institute for Holocaust and Genocide Studies and was the 2016 Lemkin Scholar with the Armenian Genocide Museum-Institute. Nikki's research on ISIS's genocides led to her current work as Australian Director of international Yazidi organisation, Yazda, and Deputy Director of Yazidi advocate, Nadia Murad's campaign.

Deborah Mayersen

Deborah Mayersen is an historian based at the University of Wollongong, Australia. Her research expertise is in comparative genocide studies, including the Armenian genocide, Rwandan genocide and genocide prevention. Her most recent publications include *On the Path to Genocide: Armenia and Rwanda Reexamined* (2014/6), and the edited volumes *The* United Nations *and Genocide* (2016) and *Genocide and Mass Atrocities in Asia: Legacies and Prevention* (with Annie Pohlman, 2013).

John Maynard

John Maynard is a Worimi Aboriginal man. He is Chair of Aboriginal History at the University of Newcastle and Director of the Purai Global Indigenous and Diaspora Research Studies Centre. As well as the recipient of numerous awards and fellowships, John is the author of several books concentrating on the intersections of Aboriginal political and social history, and the history of Australian race relations.

Annie Pohlman

Annie Pohlman is Lecturer in Indonesian Studies in the School of Languages and Cultures at the University of Queensland. She is author of *Women, Sexual Violence and the Indonesian Killings of 1965–1966* (2015) and co-editor of *Genocide and Mass Atrocities in Asia: Legacies and Prevention* (2013). Annie's research interests include comparative genocide studies, Indonesian history, gendered experiences of violence, and torture.

Geoffrey Robertson QC

Geoffrey Robertson QC is founder and joint head of Doughty Street Chambers. He has had a distinguished career as a trial and appellate counsel, an international judge, and author of leading textbooks. He is a major advocate for recognition of the Armenian genocide, with a 2015 book titled *An Inconvenient Genocide: Who Now Remembers the Armenians?*

Michael Robertson

Michael Robertson is a Clinical Associate Professor of Mental Health Ethics at the University of Sydney, and a visiting Professorial Fellow at the Sydney Jewish Museum. Michael worked in acute adult and community psychiatry for 20 years and coordinated a clinical service for survivors of psychological trauma. He has been Deputy Editor of *Australasian Psychiatry* for more than a decade and an assistant editor of the *Journal of Bioethical Inquiry*. He is a member of the Australian Institute for Holocaust and Genocide Studies and the International Association of Genocide Scholars.

Kirril Shields

Kirril Shields teaches in the School of Communication and Arts at the University of Queensland, and in the School of Arts and Communication at the University of Southern Queensland. He is an Auschwitz Jewish Center Fellow, and a Fellow of the Institute on the Holocaust and Jewish Civilisation, Royal Holloway. Kirril is a member of the Australian Institute for Holocaust and Genocide Studies.

Colin Tatz

Colin Tatz is Visiting Professor of Politics and International Relations at the Australian National University, Canberra. He writes and teaches about comparative race politics, Holocaust and genocide studies, Aboriginal affairs, migration, youth suicide, and sports history. Colin has edited seven books, co-authored five, and is sole author of 12. His most recent books are *The Magnitude of Genocide* (co-authored with Winton Higgins, 2016), and *Australia's Unthinkable Genocide* (2017).

Garry Walter

Garry Walter is a Professor of Psychiatry affiliated with the Northern Clinical School and Centre for Values, Ethics and the Law in Medicine (VELiM), University of Sydney, and Dalhousie University, Halifax, Canada. He is also Foundation Medical Director of the Doctors' Health Advisory Service (NSW and ACT), and a Visiting Professorial Fellow at the Sydney Jewish Museum. He was long-standing Editor of *Australasian Psychiatry*, published on behalf of the Royal Australian and New Zealand College of Psychiatrists, and is currently International Editor-at-Large of the *Journal of the American Academy of Child and Adolescent Psychiatry*.

George Weisz

George Weisz is a Professor at the School of Humanities, University of New England and Senior Lecturer at the University of NSW. George was the first to access and evaluate the personal open files of Australian Prisoners of War housed at the National Archives of Australia, publishing his findings in the Journal of Law and Medicine in 2015.

Index

A

Aarons, Mark 53–54, 65
Abbott, Tony 65, 106
Aboriginal / Aboriginal and Torres Strait Islander / Indigenous
    Artists 31, 33, 172
    Athletes / sport 13, 15–17, 17, 172
    Forced removal / adoption / assimilation / intervention 9; *see also* Stolen Generations
    Legal Aid Service 35, 40
    Racism 8, 15, 17, 38, 39, 241
    Rights activism 3, 13, 14, 34, 38, 40, 43–47, 172, 174
    Studies / education 7, 11, 13, 18, 248
    Suicide 9, 22, 172; *see also* Suicide
Aboriginal Tent Embassy 52, 58, 60
Activism 14–16, 32–42, 43, 174
Australian Aboriginal Progressive Association (AAPA) 47
Adelaide, South Australia 56
Afghanistan 216, 218, 220–221, 223–224, 240
Africa / African 5–14, 16, 23, 30, 39, 48, 76, 99, 224, 228, 232, 240, 241
    Rwanda 192–205; *see also* Rwanda
Agamben, Giorgio 85, 86
Akayesu, Jean-Paul 236
Alexander, Leo 80, 87
American Alliance / Western collusion 51, 207–228
Anthropology 22, 166, 231, 240
Antisemitism 8, 13, 20, 78, 79, 247
ANZAC / Gallipoli 105, 106
Apartheid 5, 8, 39
Arendt, Hannah 79, 223

Armenian genocide (eliticide, denial, deportations, massacres, women) 3, 6, 9, 16, 105–112, 113–129, 147; *see also* Children: Armenian, Eliticide / roundups
Assyrian genocide 232, 240
Auschwitz 22, 69, 92, 99, 173, 177, 188, 190, 193–195, 212, 236, 237, 245, 249
Auschwitz-Birkenau 69, 212
Australia
    Colonial genocide *see* Colonialism (settler colonialism, colonisation)
    Denial *see* Denialism
    Domestic law 26–41, 46–48, 51–66
    Record in prosecutions 51–65
    Redress *see* Reparations / restitution
    Stolen Generations *see* Stolen Generations
Australian Capital Territory (ACT) 51
Australian Institute for Holocaust and Genocide Studies 2, 5, 6, 7, 247, 248

B

Balakian, Peter 118–119, 126
Balint, Ruth 57
Barta, Tony 2, 3, 11, 12, 14, 33, 66, 161, 246
Barthes, Roland 37, 176, 182, 184, 185
Barwick, Garfield 53–55, 66
Bauer, Yehuda 11, 242, 244
Bauman, Zygmunt 77–80, 82
Bazambanza, Rupert 197
Belzec 69, 173
Beneficiaries 66, 164, 220, 235
Berezowsky, Mikolay 56
Berki, Robert 15

Bin Laden, Osama 220
Biopower 70, 82–88
Birch, Tony 27, 32
Bjelke-Petersen, Johannes 57
Bosnia, Bosnia-Herzegovina, Bosniak, Bosnian, Bosnian Croat, Bosnian Serb 51, 66, 110, 112, 213, 214, 233, 235, 240, 241
Brandt, Karl 87, 102
Bringing Them Home 2, 26–42, 44, 62
Budapest 197, 198
Buddhism / Buddhist 155–156, 166
Bureaucracy / Bureaucratic 20, 31, 37, 39–42, 69, 77, 79–85, 177, 230, 238, 242
Bush, George W 207, 211, 218, 221, 222
Bystanderism / bystanders 37, 66, 89, 164, 207, 212–213, 215, 234, 244

C

Cambodia 65, 66, 148, 149, 155, 166, 212, 213, 214, 233, 236, 240, 241
Canada 36, 54, 65, 146, 242
Canberra, ACT 32, 51, 58, 236, 250
Cham (Muslim Cham) 155, 241
Children
    Armenian 105, 109, 111, 113–130
    Disabled 75
    Forced removal, Stolen Generations 9, 16, 21, 26–42, 44, 48, 61, 62, 64, 169, 173, 233–234, 242–244
    Indonesian 133–144
    International rights of 210
    Jewish 56, 182, 193, 200
    Muslim in Bosnia 110
    North Korean 156, 157
    Rawandan 197, 201, 205, 206
    Turkish 110
    Vietnamese 234
Chile / Chilean 66, 219
China / Chinese 84, 88, 112, 151, 153, 154, 155, 239, 241
Christian 23, 45, 97, 102, 103, 105, 107, 112, 147, 155–157, 193, 241
Church (bystanderism, collaboration, faith) 50, 102, 105, 109, 111, 120–130, 196–205
Clendinnen, Inga 36, 165, 191
Coetzee, J.M. 169

Collective
    Amnesia, innocence 37, 230
    Guilt 164, 170, 171
    Histories / past 41, 67
    Memory 38, 117, 181, 183, 189
    Responsibility 170
Colonialism (settler colonialism, colonisation) 32–33, 41–42, 58, 147, 166, 171, 172, 240
    Australian colonisation 26–41, 43–50, 61, 63, 66, 161
Communism / Communist Party 47, 57, 131–141
Comparative Genocide 6, 7, 8, 9, 18, 23, 116, 248, 249, 250
Compensation 29–34, 49–50, 62, 77, 94
Concentration camps 8, 75–86, 92–103, 105, 115, 130, 177, 238
Convention on the Prevention and Punishment of the Crime of Genocide / Genocide Convention 28–30, 44, 52, 59–64, 107, 109, 131, 148, 154–155, 158, 168, 208–211, 233–234, 242, 244
Crane, Susan 182–186
Crete 90–104
Crimes against humanity 63, 65, 101, 146–158, 207, 209, 212, 234, 247
Crouch, Colin 209, 225–227

D

Demidenko (Darville, Dale), Helen 187
Democracy 20, 65, 79, 84, 102, 106, 146, 208, 215, 242, 243
Deogratias: A Tale of Rwanda 192, 197–206
Denialism 4, 28–31, 37, 66, 110, 186, 230, 233, 235, 243
Deportations 54, 106–111, 115, 118, 124, 128–130, 197, 232, 236–240
Disease 47, 71, 75–86, 93, 98–99, 131
Dispositif 83
Doctors' Trial (Nuremburg) 87, 101, 236
Don Dale Detention Centre 40
Dowling, Carol 40

E

Education / teachers / teaching 2, 4, 5–22,

97–104, 107, 113, 116, 123, 124, 133, 140, 164, 171, 183–184, 198, 201, 230–245, 246, 249, 250
Eichmann, Adolf 79, 107, 164
Einsatzgruppen 69, 236–237
Eliticide / roundups 114, 117, 123
Ethnic cleansing 45, 71, 138, 240
Eugenics / euthanasia / social Darwinism 70–75, 78–89, 92, 102, 242
Evans, Gareth 54

F

Family / families
   African and Carribean 241
   Armenian 114–130
   Australian Aboriginal / Indigenous 27–40, 48–50, 172; *see also* Aboriginal / Aboriginal and Torres Strait Islander / Indigenous
   Care, therapy 72, 76, 118
   German 97, 171, 177
   Indonesian 132–144
   Jewish 8, 11, 147, 161, 198–205, 230
   Photographs 177, 181, 185, 187
   Population control 84
   Revenge 108
   Tutsi 192, 197–206
   Ukrainian 187
Famine crimes / starvation 72, 75, 86, 105–108, 130, 135, 139–144, 154–155
Feminism *see* Gender
Film / movies 8, 151, 168–172, 181, 231, 235, 237
Final Solution (*Endlösung*) 69, 97, 243
First World War / World War One 20, 72–74, 77, 97, 113
Forced adoption 36, 39
Forced army recruitment 125
Forced assimilation 41
Forced labour 94, 101, 131, 140
Forced marriage 116
Forced sterilisation 92
Forcible removal of children / forced removal / child removal / transfer of children *see* Children
Forgetting (of Genocide) 26, 36–39, 52–53; *see also* Collective: Amnesia, innocence

Foucault, Michel 82, 82–85
Franzen, Jonathan 168
Freud, Sigmund 71, 76

G

Gaita, Raimond 11, 12, 30, 37, 168, 244
Gallipoli *see* ANZAC / Gallipoli
Gas chambers 69, 75, 105, 164, 165, 177, 213, 232, 236, 239
Gender 113–130, 136, 179, 185, 247, 249
Geneva Conventions 93, 103, 210; *see also* Convention on the Prevention and Punishment of the Crime of Genocide / Genocide Convention
Genocide
   Definitions 7–8, 19–22, 29–30, 33, 39, 47–48, 55, 61, 64, 85, 107–109, 114, 136, 146–159, 167, 214–215, 231–239
   Intent 19–22, 29–30, 38, 43–45, 50, 55, 59–67, 72, 78–80, 85, 88, 91–93, 97–98, 106, 107–111, 113, 123, 126, 129, 131, 136, 149, 154, 158–159, 164–165, 170–172, 174, 176–180, 183, 190, 197, 201–205, 213, 236, 239–244
   Punishment, prosecution 3, 23, 51–67, 79, 92, 101–102, 109, 110, 150, 153, 159, 194, 219, 230, 236; *see also* Convention on the Prevention and Punishment of the Crime of Genocide / Genocide Convention
   Studies, scholarship, research 2–4, 5–23, 111, 116–117, 127, 136, 161–174, 185–190, 215, 230–243; *see also* Australian Institute for Holocaust and Genocide Studies
Germany / Germans 20, 22, 37, 69–88, 90–104, 106–108, 120–122, 128, 147, 150, 161–171, 175–191, 197, 227, 232, 235, 236, 238, 242, 246, 247
Graphic novel 4, 192–206
Gutzeit, Kurt 98, 100
Göring, Hermann 76, 91–92, 97

H

Hanson, Pauline 59

Hawke, Robert 52, 54, 57
Haylen, Leslie 30
Hepatitis 90–102
Herero 241
Herzegovina *see* Bosnia, Bosnia-Herzegovina, Bosniak, Bosnian, Bosnian Croat, Bosnian Serb
Himmler, Heinrich 98, 99, 103, 164, 174, 177, 222
Hirsch, Marianne 176–190
Hitler, Adolf 57, 69, 75, 87, 94, 97, 102, 105, 171, 175, 191, 230, 238
Holocaust 2–4, 5–21, 30–31, 47, 51, 57, 69–89, 91, 115–122, 129, 147, 161, 164, 169–170, 175–191, 192–204, 212, 231–245, 246, 247, 247, 248, 248, 249, 249, 250
Howard, John 28–29, 31, 49, 58–59
Human Rights - Australian Human Rights Commission 3, 36, 44
Human rights / Human Rights Commission 2, 9, 17, 28, 32–33, 36, 40, 44, 50, 65, 70, 133, 146–156, 166, 209–211, 228, 240, 243, 247
Hussein, Saddam 213, 235
Hutu 197, 200, 201

I

Indigenous *see* Aboriginal / Aboriginal and Torres Strait Islander / Indigenous
Indonesia (1965 killings) 3, 65, 112, 131–141, 150, 219, 249
Interahamwe (Hutu militia) 200–203
International Court of Justice 109–110
International Criminal Court / Rome Statute 63, 107, 148, 211, 233
International Criminal Tribunal (Rwanda, former Yugoslavia) 51, 110, 236
International Military Tribunal 55, 101, 211
Iraq 66, 207, 208, 213–225, 235, 240

J

Jakarta 131
Japan / Japanese 52–53, 111, 137, 140, 155, 241
Jews *see also* Children: Jewish
Australia 9, 54, 161, 232
Crete 92
European 56, 69–89, 97–99, 102, 105, 107, 164–165, 175–186, 232, 234–243
Sydney Jewish Museum 14, 247, 248, 249, 250
Women 116, 118–128
Ukrainian 56
Theology 193, 199
South Africa 7–8
Sigmund Freud 71
Physicians, therapists, doctors 73, 76, 97
Jihadism / ISIS (crimes, Yazidi genocide) 66, 105, 106, 107, 112, 220, 224, 233, 244, 248
Johnson, Chalmers 207, 209, 217
Judaism 11, 24, 194, 205

K

Kaplan, Marion 113, 116, 118–120, 127
Katin, Miriam 192, 197–200, 204, 206
Keating, Paul 28, 36, 49, 57, 174
Khmer Rouge 65, 149, 213
Kim Jong-un 150
Korean War 217
Kraepelin, Emil 71–74
Krankenmorde 74, 81, 85
Kristallnacht 79, 120
Kurds / Kurdish 213, 235, 240

L

LaCapra, Dominik 188
Langer, Lawrence 115
Lanzmann, Claude 165, 170, 179, 230, 237
Lemkin, Raphael 14, 33, 108, 114, 147–148, 167, 170–174, 209, 232, 248
Lessing, Doris 5
Lithuania 8, 234

M

Mabo (Court decision) 58
Malan, D.F. 8
Marcus, David 154
Maus 195
Maynard, Fred 3, 43–50
Melbourne, Victoria, Australia 3, 35, 64, 93, 94, 113, 161, 162

Memorials / monuments / memory 7, 23, 31–32, 33, 74, 94, 169, 175–190, 233, 236; *see also* Collective: Memory, Postmemory, Yad Vashem
Mengele, Josef 177
Menzies, Andrew 54–55, 64
Menzies, Robert 53
Meythaler, Friedrich 91–104
Modernity 77, 78–85
Morgenthau, Henry 108, 212
Morton, Samuel 241
Moses, Dirk 49, 170
My Lai massacre (Vietnam) 22, 234
Myall Creek Massacre 236

N
National Sorry Day 27, 40, 42
Nationalism 20
Native Title / land rights 47, 58–59
NATO 106, 208, 213, 215
Nazi
   Concentration camps *see* Concentration camps
   Doctors, medical experiments 69–88, 91–103, 184, 239, 242; *see also* Eugenics / euthanasia / social Darwinism, Final Solution (*Endlösung*)
   Hat makers 7
   Ordinary 164–165
   Photographs *see* Photography / photographs
   Propaganda *see* Propaganda / language
   Regime, Party 69–88, 91–104, 148, 168, 175–190, 198–199, 234–244; *see also* Third Reich
   War crimes 51, 57, 66, 105, 108, 111, 148; *see also* Nuremberg (laws, trials)
Nemes, Irene 66
New South Wales (NSW), Australia 7, 13, 31, 47, 48, 50, 106, 236
New Zealand 90, 246
North Korea (Communism, famine crimes, Inquiry, non-cooperation) 3, 146–159, 239
Northern Territory (NT), Australia 35, 40–41
Nulyarimma, Wadjularbinna 58, 59
Nuremberg (laws, trials) 55, 79, 87, 101, 104, 148, 209–211, 216, 219, 236, 237, 238, 247

O
Ofer, Dalia 116, 117
Obama, Barack 106, 111, 223
O'Donaghue, Lowitja 31
Operation *Merkur* 90
Ottoman Empire / Ottoman 105–111, 113, 212, 232, 237

P
Pasha, Talaat 108
Peloponnesian War 146
Persecution 55, 65, 70, 80–83, 88, 102, 113, 117–119, 129, 132, 154, 179, 197
Photography / photographs 3, 175–191, 214, 221; *see also* Graphic novel
Pinker, Steven 146, 147, 208, 216, 224
Pogrom 120, 234
Poland 69, 75, 98, 101, 105, 234, 236
Political prisoners 122–127, 132–144, 154–157, 228
Polyukhovich, Ivan 56
Postmemory 176, 182
Power, Samantha 208, 212–215
Prisoners of war / POW 3, 52, 90–103, 111, 210, 250
Propaganda / language 8, 109, 122, 131, 171, 175, 181–190, 237
Psychiatry 3, 69–89, 92, 95, 99, 248, 249, 250
Pyongyang 150

Q
Queensland, Australia 27, 48, 57, 58, 243

R
Racism / racial / race
   Analyses 7–9, 14–21, 237, 240–242
   Australia 74; *see also* Aboriginal / Aboriginal and Torres Strait Islander / Indigenous: Racism
   Medicine 80, 85
   North Korea 154
   Rwanda 202

Rajapaska, Mahinda 65, 110
Rape / sexual abuse, violence 27, 41, 107, 115–130, 136, 202, 233, 249
Reconciliation 23, 27, 32, 63, 111, 172
Redfern Speech 36, 49, 174
Religion (faith, God, absence of) 105, 140, 157, 158, 192–205, 231, 240
Reparations / restitution 22, 28–31, 29, 62, 111, 133, 223, 230, 233
Rescue / rescuers 28, 57, 115, 122, 127, 233, 235
Riefenstahl, Leni 168
Roman Empire / Roman Republic 82, 105, 216, 222, 223
Rome Statute 148, 153
Roosevelt, Eleanor 210
Rudd, Kevin 32, 49, 62
Russia / Russians 12, 108, 109, 112, 147, 153, 171, 180, 200, 212, 241
Rwanda 4, 21, 52, 65, 66, 112, 148, 166, 192–206, 207, 212–214, 231, 233, 236, 240–242, 248
Rüdin, Ernst 71, 74

S

Sadlier, Richard 45
Schabas, William 156, 168
Schindler's List 170, 237
Second World War / World War Two 7, 47, 52–56, 90–104, 140, 155, 207, 209, 225, 235
Serbia 110, 150, 212–215, 236
Shoah 85
Shoah (film) 170, 230, 237
Singapore 84, 90
Slavery 101, 107, 147, 155, 178, 179, 234, 238, 242
Smile Through the Tears 192, 197, 200–206
Sobibor 69, 173
Solomon, Robert 161, 162
Son of Saul (film) 170, 237
Sontag, Susan 177, 180, 187, 189
Sorry Day *see* National Sorry Day
South Africa 5, 7–23, 39
South Korea 152, 155
Soviet Union (USSR) 53, 76, 88, 154, 217, 220, 223, 240

Spiegelman, Art 195
Sport 5, 13–21, 172, 246, 250
Srebrenica 109–111, 213
Sri Lanka 65, 110, 112, 233
Stalin, Josef 57, 154
Stanner, W.E.H. (Bill) 37, 43–44
Stassen, Jean-Philippe 204, 206
Stolen Generations 3, 9, 26–42, 49, 50, 236; *see also* Children: Forced removal, Stolen Generations
Sudan / South Sudan 112, 235
Suharto 132, 138
Suicide 5, 9, 12, 21, 22–24, 27, 92, 115, 129, 172, 250
Sukarno 138
Sumatra / West Sumatra 137, 140, 141
Survival / survivors 91–103, 115–130, 131–144, 147, 164, 168, 170, 172, 182, 192–199, 232, 235, 237, 245
 Testimony 27–28, 50, 60, 95–96, 115–130, 134–145, 164, 193
Sydney Morning Herald 46
Syria 105, 107, 219, 221, 223, 239, 240; *see also* Assyrian genocide

T

Tasmania, Australia 63
Tatz, Colin 2, 5–24, 30–31, 37, 39, 44, 51, 61, 66, 78, 116, 161, 164, 172–174, 216, 224, 228, 230, 250
Tent Embassy *see* Aboriginal Tent Embassy
Testimony 56, 151–158, 235; *see also* Survival / survivors: Testimony
The Hague 93, 110, 210
Third Punic War 146
Third Reich 8, 20, 92, 94, 102, 175, 180, 181, 190, 238
Tiergartenstraβe 4 (T4) 75
Tikkun Olam 24
Timor-Leste / East Timor 65, 233
Torres Strait 9, 17, 26–41
Torture 65, 114–115, 120, 123–130, 131, 139, 207, 210, 219–222, 249
Treblinka 69, 173

Trials *see* Doctors' Trial (Nuremburg), Nuremberg (laws, trials)
Triggs, Gillian 63
Turkey / Turkish Government 9, 16, 31, 105–111, 115–128, 147, 212, 232, 237, 239, 240, 241, 243
Tutsis (Rwandan Genocide) 112, 192–203, 212, 239, 241

U
Ukraine 56, 234, 239
United Nations Human Rights Council 146
United Nations (UN) 28, 34, 59, 65, 131, 148, 149, 173, 210, 233, 248
United Nations Security Council 152
United States of America (USA, United States, US) 4, 21, 36, 74, 85, 101, 106, 108, 111, 158, 166, 180, 181, 207–229, 236, 241–244

V
Victims / victimisation 7, 17, 19–22, 28, 36, 57, 66, 69, 75, 78–79, 85, 91, 93, 97, 103, 106–107, 111, 112, 113–129, 133, 141–142, 147–148, 154, 159, 164, 176–189, 190, 214, 221, 229, 230, 233–235, 239, 245

Vietnam / Vietnamese 22, 155, 212–213, 220, 234, 241
Voice of the North 49

W
Wagner, Heinrich 56
War crimes 23, 51–67, 91–93, 101, 110–111, 136, 234, 247
We Are On Our Own 192, 197–205
Weber, Max 78, 228
Wehrmacht 76, 90, 91, 98, 177, 184
Weitzman, Lenore 116
West Germany 73, 79
Western Australia 40
White Australia policy 52
Wiesel, Elie 12, 193, 245
Wilde Euthanasie 75
Wolfe, Patrick 32, 41

Y
Yad Vashem 7, 8, 11, 236
Young Turks 105–111, 239
Yugoslavia 51, 110, 148, 156, 171, 212, 240, 241

Z
Zentai, Károly 57

www.ingramcontent.com/pod-product-compliance
Lightning Source LLC
Chambersburg PA
CBHW071000160426
43193CB00012B/1861